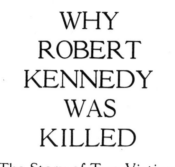

WHY
ROBERT
KENNEDY
WAS
KILLED

The Story of Two Victims

WHY
ROBERT
KENNEDY
WAS
KILLED

THE STORY OF TWO VICTIMS

by Godfrey Jansen

foreword by Abdeen Jabara
member of Sirhan's defense team

THE THIRD PRESS

Joseph Okpaku Publishing Company, Inc.
444 Central Park West, New York, New York 10025

Printed in the U.S.A.

Designed by Barbara Kohn Isaac

Contents

This picture - across two columns on page 3 - appeared in "The Independent" (Pasadena) on Monday, May 27, 1968, eight days before Senator Kennedy's assassination on June 5. "The Independent" was the local newspaper subscribed to by the Sirhan family. The caption read "BOBBY SAYS 'SHALOM'—Sen. Robert F. Kennedy, wearing a traditional Jewish yarmulke, addresses the Neveh Shalom congregation in Portland on his campaign tour of Oregon. He told the congregation the U.S. must support Israel against outside aggression." It was such publicity that convinced Sirhan Sirhan that Robert Kennedy was totally committed to the Israeli cause. (See page 190)

The greatest thing in the world are people,
and what you learn from people
you cannot even learn in school.

———— *Sirhan Sirhan as a young child.*

Well, sir, when you move—when you move a whole
country, sir, a whole people, bodily from their own
homes, from their own land, from their businesses,
sir, outside their country, and introduce an alien
people, sir, into Palestine—the Jews and the Zionists—
that is completely wrong, sir, and it is unjust and the
Palestinian Arabs didn't do a thing, sir, to justify the
way they were treated by the West.

It affected me, sir, very deeply. I didn't like it.
Where is the justice involved, sir? Where is the love,
sir, for fighting for the underdog? Israel is no
underdog in the Middle East, sir. It's those refugees
that are underdogs. And because they have no way of
fighting back, sir, the Jews, sir, the Zionists, just keep
beating away at them. That burned the hell out of
me.

Testimony of Sirhan B. Sirhan,
in People v. Sirhan, page 4926 and page 4928
of official transcript.

Foreword

I

In 1963, Sirhan Bechara Sirhan, a nineteen year old freshman at Pasadena City College, read the biography of Gandhi, *Gandhi,* by Lewis Fischer. The passages which Sirhan underlined in this book are, perhaps, as revealing about Sirhan's state of mind on June 4, 1968 as anything that has appeared concerning Sirhan until now. Next to the following passage, Sirhan wrote "profound":

The British were masters in somebody else's home. Their very presence was a humiliation. . . . Even if the British had converted India into a land flowing with milk and honey . . . they would have been disliked. . . . Subjection breeds a desire for liberation . . . and there can be no good colonizers.

The parallels between India and Palestine, Zionist and British, must have been obvious to Sirhan. Sirhan's acute awareness of the phenonemon and logic of colonialism is further indicated by his underlining of the following passage, beside which he wrote the word "vulgar":

It is this consciousness of the inherent superiority of the European which has won us India. However well-educated and clever a native may be and however brave he may have proved himself, I believe that no rank which we can bestow on him would cause him to be an equal by the British officer.

Another underlined passage beside which Sirhan wrote "most profound" reads:

"You are right," Gandhi replied. "I hate privilege and monopoly. Whatever cannot be shared with the masses is taboo to me. That is all."

It is no accident that this nineteen year old Palestinian, his communal life having been destroyed through the full force of Western colonial intrusion, should underline these words. Colonialism, with all of its doctrines of exclusivism and racial superiority, had pushed Sirhan and his fellow countrymen out of their ancestral home and, in so doing, destroyed what they cherished most: their social and biological mazeway.

Palestine, you might say, as did Martin Peretz writing in *Ramparts* magazine after the June, 1967 war, does not fit the "classical" mold of colonialism. You might say that Zionists did not go to Palestine to exploit the native population, as the French went to Algeria, or the English to Rhodesia, or the Dutch to South Africa. The Zionist desire for a pure Jewish state avoided the "classical" colonial situation where the native population was neither rejected nor assimilated. In Palestine, the native population was simply rejected, pushed across the borders, because the logic of a Jewish State would allow for nothing else.

The process of colonization and driving a people from its land has a psychology of its own. As the famous psychiatrist, Franz Fanon, points out in the chapter "Colonial War and Mental Disorders" in *The Wretched of the Earth,* the constant downgrading, discrimination, and persecution of the "native" can and does constitute a trauma which may easily produce a "psychically disturbed" person. Fanon has detailed this process:

Because it is the systematic negation of the other person and a furious determination to deny the other person all attributes of humanity, colonialism forces the people it dominates to ask themselves the question constantly: "In reality, who am I?"

The defensive attitudes created by the violent bringing together of the colonized man and the colonial system form themselves into a structure which then reveals the colonized personality. This "sensitivity" is easily understood if we simply study in our lives the number and depth of the injuries inflicted upon the native during a single day amidst the colonial regime.

This is no idle theorizing. One need only talk to those survivors of the proud and broken American Indian people, the Chicano farmhands in the Southwest, or listen to the black anger which daily resounds from America's crumbling tenements and concrete alleyways to discover this final bastion of the soul.

For Sirhan, as a child of four years of age in Palestine of 1947-48, the bombs, the blood and the hunger of those days between the announcement of the withdrawal of the British and the establishment of a Zionist State was only the beginning of what would reverberate in the kitchen of the Ambassador Hotel twenty years later. When Dr. Bernard Diamond, one of the chief defense witnesses in the Sirhan trial and an eminent professor at the University of California, placed Sirhan under hypnosis and asked Sirhan, "Remember the bombs, Sirhan? Remember the bombs?", Sirhan broke into a paroxysm of sobs until he was convulsed with crying. Waking, Sirhan was frightened, and when asked what had happened, he replied, "They . . . they killed him." Diamond had been able to retrieve from the depths of Sirhan's unconscious one of the violent atrocities that Sirhan had witnessed as a small child in Jerusalem.

But it was not just these conditions of warfare that played upon the mind of Sirhan. This would be too simple. It would not explain why those events in Palestine should find their way to Los Angeles and the death of Robert Kennedy. The answer can also be found in the enormity of the irony that was forced upon Sirhan by the United States. The United States, having lent decisive economic, political and military support to the Zionist takeover in Palestine and the destruction of Sirhan's cultural and communal habitat, told Sirhan in 1956 that he could come to America and construct a new life. Sirhan's family was one of 2,000 Palestinian families for whom Congress had provided special immigrant visas under the Eisenhower administration.

In the United States, Sirhan aspired to achieve all of those things he might have had in a society which had been destroyed. He loved to read textbooks in high school civics about the American system of government and its checks and balances. He desperately wanted to believe that in America, through perseverance and hard work, a young man might grow to influence the course of events. His interests were broad and he studied several different languages, but constantly dogging him was the fact that he was an Arab, a Palestinian Arab. He was told by the American mass media and American governmental policy that he and the rest of the Palestinians did not count, and that what had happened to him had not really happened. Sirhan learned that America's use of the words "justice" and "equality" were camouflages when it came to a consideration of Palestinian claims against Israel. Edward Said's essay, "The Arab Portrayed," describes the feeling most aptly:

If the Arab occupies space in the mind at all, it is of negative value. He is seen as a disrupter of Israel's continuing existence, or in a larger view, a surmountable obstacle to Israel's creation in 1948. This has been, of course, part of the Zionist attitude to the Arab, especially in the years before 1948 when Israel was being promulgated ideologically. Palestine was imagined as an empty desert waiting to burst into bloom, its inhabitants imagined as inconsequential nomads possessing no stable claim to the land and therefore no cultural permanence. At worst, the Arab is conceived as a shadow that dogs the Jews.

Likewise, the Palestinians were chastized for their failure to be "realistic." Palestine had been transformed into a Jewish state with Jewish institutions, Jewish nationality, and a mandate to ingather Jews residing outside Israel at the expense of the Palestinians; and it is precisely this fact which, so the argument runs, the Palestinians would not be realistic about. Of this, Said says: ". . . It is precisely the Arab sense of fact that is being denied in this argument, that sense which sees Israel, funded without limit from abroad, displacing a whole population into a limbo that now seems, factually, to be their fate without limit of time."

Before he is evaporated into an innocuous object of sympathy as an "Arab refugee," the Palestinian, along with his fellow Arabs, is somehow hyperbolized into a caricature of rhetoric and backwardness, incapable of being understood or understanding on any other level than brute Israeli force—in short, all of the racist stereotypes which avoid the real issues and which abound in the American mass media.

II

As one proceeds north on Broadway Street in Los Angeles, past a row of dying department stores, one notices the almost carnival atmosphere of the sprawling city. Mexican music blares out of the doorway of a record shop amidst stalls open onto the street, while people crowd onto the sidewalk. Across the Hollywood Freeway lies Los Angeles' Chinatown with studied pagoda structures and cheap Oriental wares. At night Chinatown seems to blossom with tourists and Los Angeleans seeking the diversions of a strange environment in their otherwise similar existences. Off to the right, up Temple Street, is Japanese town, and in the northeast corner of the area surrounding the intersection of the Hollywood-Pasadena freeways, is Olvera Street, a casual cobbled street for tourists, featuring Mexican-American architecture, food, and handicrafts. A certain vitality seems to exist in the diversity and movement of this area that is hard to find in any other part of Los Angeles or its not-so-glamorous suburbs. One can spend a warm afternoon here browsing in the stalls and shops and restaurants and listening to the sounds and enjoying the odors, forgetting for a moment that one is in Southern California.

Situated in the middle of this rectangular area is the Hall of Justice of the City of Los Angeles. A huge, gray, imposing building, it sits astride the south side of the Hollywood Freeway on a small hill that gives it, perhaps, some of its forbidding and authoritative airs. It is probably not atypical of most older criminal court houses in most larger American cities. It is but a block away from such other important places as the Los Angeles Times building, the Music Center complex, and the City Hall. It was in this building for four and a half months that Sirhan Sirhan was later to be tried and ultimately convicted of first degree murder for the death of Robert F. Kennedy.

My involvement in Sirhan's case began in September, 1968 when I received a telephone call from an Arab-American attorney in Long Beach, California, who had been approached by a member of the Sirhan family concerning the case. Being an attorney and an Arab-American who publicly supported the Palestinian Arab position, my immediate response was to accept the request for my services. George Shibley, the Long Beach attorney, had talked with Russell Parsons about the case and Parsons needed help. It was arranged that I would meet Russell Parsons, Mike McGowan, an investigator in the case, and George Shibley on September 20, 1968. I flew to Los Angeles on the 19th and the following day, a Friday, George Shibley and I went to Russell Parson's office. Over lunch, Parsons told me that he needed assistance developing Sirhan's defense with respect to how the Palestine-Zionist conflict had affected Sirhan. At this time I had not met Sirhan but Parsons assured me that not only was this the only defense that Sirhan had, but the only one that he wanted. Parsons gave me a letter on his letterhead dated September 20, 1968 in which he wrote: "This will confirm our meeting and discussion of today. I authorize you to make such efforts as seem necessary to carry out our plans for the defense of Sirhan B. Sirhan. I will appreciate your memorandum as early as possible as to your thoughts in connection with certain phases of our defense and the Arab-Israeli conflict and the names of qualified persons who could testify concerning this area."

During the return flight to Detroit that weekend, I began to ponder the connection between Palestine, Sirhan and Kennedy. From the few garbled press reports concerning Sirhan's statement to Jessie Unruh on the night of June 4, 1968 that "I did it for my country," the inflamatory statements made by Mayor Yorty concerning notebooks of Sirhan's which were found in Sirhan's bedroom, that Sirhan belonged to "Communist organizations," and the information that I gleaned from Parsons, I knew that in some as yet unexplained fashion a very real relationship existed between them. After receiving all of the investigative materials from Mike McGowan, including transcribed interviews of various members of the Sirhan family, witnesses to the shooting, and psychiatric reports and interviews of Sirhan in his cell, it became clear that the trauma Sirhan had experienced in his childhood in Palestine, the disruption of his family life, and his alienation in American held the key to who Sirhan was and why.

I spent much of my time for the next month contacting and visiting numerous people throughout the country who, in some way, were experts on the Palestine-Zionist conflict. Would they be ready to testify? Many of the answers were unqualified refusals because, I sensed, they were afraid. Some of them were equivocal.

Meanwhile, Parsons and I kept in telephone contact and, on one occasion, met in Chicago, to discuss the progress of the development of the defense. He told me that Grant Cooper would be entering the case, but that this would not change any of the plans that had been made. I sent Parsons considerable amounts of material dealing with the Palestine-Zionist conflict and prepared various memoranda concerning the development of Sirhan's defense around this data as well as on the facts of the case.

At the end of December, 1968, as the opening of the trial drew near, I flew to Los Angeles and found the situation completely different from what I had been led to believe existed. Grant Cooper, who had been involved in the Friar's Club case, was directing the defense team with the assistance of Emile Zola Berman. My first meeting with Cooper, after I had met with Sirhan and discussed his defense with him, indicated to me that Cooper did not intend to raise the Palestine-Zionist issue in the trial. "We," Cooper said, "are only interested in saving Sirhan's life. We'll only use Sirhan's background to the extent that it is helpful to that end. Expert testimony on the Palestine problem would not be admissible. Anything Sirhan knows about it, he can testify to from the stand."

My initial fears that an attempt would be made to suppress the real facts about the trauma which caused Sirhan to kill Robert Kennedy were reinforced when I received a copy of an article that appeared

December 27, 1968, in the East Coast newspaper, *Jewish Post and Opinion*. This was sent to me by Moshe Menuhin, father of Yehundi Menuhin and an ardent anti-Zionist Jew. The article was entitled, "Sirhan's New Lawyer, Active Jewish Leader," and was based on a telephone interview of Emile Zola Berman. When asked whether or not the trial might "not be used by Sirhan to express his anti-Israeli views," Berman responded that "this would be against the advice of his attorneys." Further, the article indicated that Berman had often addressed meetings of the United Jewish Appeal and B'nai Brith, both of which have acted as Zionist agencies in this country. Since Berman had been invited by Cooper to act as associate defense counsel while Cooper was attending an American Bar Association meeting in New York, my suspicion was further aroused as to Cooper's role.

The evening of the day before the trial started, Shibley and I had a conference at Cooper's office with Cooper, Parsons, and Berman, at which time we confronted Berman concerning his statement in the *Jewish Post and Opinion*. He stated that he had been misquoted and denied he would attempt to suppress the political issues in the case. Cooper, however, reiterated his position that "he was only interested in saving the life of Sirhan," suggesting that raising the political issues would not further this end. Thus, on the opening night of the trial, it seemed that everything Parsons had told me from September through December and much of what I had learned about the case would be irrelevant in the long trial that lay ahead.

My fears proved correct. In its opening statement at the trial some weeks later, the defense stated that it would show that Sirhan had been exposed to warfare as a child, and that this, together with his failure at Pasadena City College, his failure as a jockey, his fall from a horse, his being beaten by his father as a child, and the death of his sister Aida, had so affected his mind that he did not have the capacity to deliberate maturely his killing of Robert F. Kennedy. Here was a grab bag for the jury. Nevertheless, there was one missing link in this formula which Cooper and Berman could only deal with in a superficial way: "why Kennedy?" and "why Sirhan?"

As the trial of Sirhan Bechara Sirhan entered its fifth week, Douglas Kneeland, one of the correspondents for *The New York Times* at the trial, wrote a dispatch which appeared in the *Times* on Sunday, February 2, 1969. In probably one of the most trenchant commentaries on the trial, Kneeland worte that the trial:

has remained strangely remote from the realities to which it is bound. Heavy sheet steel blocks the windows of the stuffy eighth floor courtroom at the Hall of Justice, shutting out sun and sky and the street world of the city below. And for four plodding weeks, as attorneys have questioned prospective jurors or wrangled over motions, more than the sun and sky seemed to have shuttered from the room. . . . Also largely absent from the courtroom, but in some ways inextricably intertwined with Sirhan's defense is the continuing crisis in the Middle East."

Indeed it was. I had submitted to Berman, Parsons and Cooper a list of sixty questions which should have been posed in the examination of prospective jurors. I had prepared these after calling Charles Garry and obtaining the voir dire questions he had used to detect racism among prospective jurors in the Huey Newton case. Among these questions were the following:

1. Do you possess any prejudice or bias against Arab or other dark-skinned peoples?
2. Do you think that, basically, Arabs are illiterate, uneducated nomads without settled homes, towns, businesses or lands?
3. Do you believe that every people have the right of self-determination; that is to say, the right to keep and govern their own country without interference by outside nations or people?
4. Do you believe that it is anti-Semitic for a Christian Palestinian Arab to object to the killing of Arab Palestinians by Zionist Jews?
5. Would you be prejudiced against an Arab Palestinian because he believes the press, television, radio and other media of communication in the United States are dominated and controlled by pro-Zionists and pro-Israelis?
6. Would you be prejudiced against an Arab Palestinian because he believes that by force or fear or murder, almost one million of his countrymen were driven from their homes in Palestine in 1947 and 1948 by Zionist Jews?

7. Would you be prejudiced against an Arab Palestinian because he believes his countrymen have been murdered or expelled, and their land stolen with the support and help, financial, military, and moral, of the United States and of millions of citizens?

Cooper and Berman laughed when I gave them these questions and paid no attention to them at all. In selecting the jury, Cooper restricted his questioning on racism to the simple leading question, "The fact that this man is a Palestinian won't affect your consideration of this case, will it?" Parsons didn't do much better.

What followed after the selection of the jury was the opening of the case by the prosecution and weeks of tedious reconstructing of the shooting of Kennedy and Sirhan's activities prior to that night in the kitchen of the Ambassador Hotel. In an effort to shorten the trial, Cooper had offered to concede that Sirhan had killed Kennedy but the court would not permit this stipulation.

I could not help but think how the tedium and the priorities of the respective participants in the trial were exceedingly remote from the real issues in the case. The judge, stern and unyielding, saw this as a last big case before retirement. Defense attorneys emphasized that they were handling the case as a "public service" without fee because every man in the United States accused of committing a crime was entitled to legal representation. The publicity of the case was secondary.

After the prosecution rested, it was time for the presentation of the defense. It became readily apparent that, for Parsons and Berman, Sirhan was just a young man who had experienced the trauma of war and killing at an early age and one who had the further difficulty of assimilating into a new culture. The testimony of the defense witnesses began with an account of the lives of the members of the Sirhan family. Sirhan himself took the stand and gave a detailed account of the birth of Zionism and the take-over of Palestine under British and United States sponsorship. This testimony was probably the most moving and dramatic of the whole trial. A correspondent from the Associated Press, himself an ardent Zionist, left the courtroom saying, "I can't listen to this!" Berman, Sirhan's own Jewish defense attorney, threatened to withdraw from the case. Although Cooper later allowed Zial Hashimeh, a childhood friend and neighbour of Sirhan's, to testify about Sirhan as a young boy in the old city of Jerusalem and about the conditions of destitution and deprivation under which Palestinians lived, no further effort was made by the defense to relate Sirhan's personal tragedy in Palestine to the case.

After the introduction of testimony concerning Sirhan's life in Pasadena from friends, school administrators, and former employers, the weeks of psychiatric testimony started. The testimony of the Sirhan family was ultimately obfuscated in the seemingly endless days of confusing and confused psychiatric testimony that followed. Through the psychiatric testimony Sirhan was transformed into an abstraction, someone or something unreal. Of this, Sirhan said, "It doesn't seem that this trial is about me. It seems like they're talking about somebody else." A number of jurors were totally confused by the psychiatric testimony. After the trial, Benjamin Glick told Martin Kasindorf of *Newsweek* magazine that "not even the experts could get together among themselves." Another juror, Albert Frederico, stated emphatically, "All these psychiatrists! They really had us all stirred up. It was confusing. It stunk!" Kasindorf also reported: "As the prosecution had hoped, the jurors administered to themselves a Rorschach ink blot and other psychological tests that the defense experts used . . . the tests backfired on the defense when several of the jurors found some of their responses startlingly similar to Sirhan's "paranoid reactions."

Adding to the confusion of the jurors resulting from the barrage of psychiatric theories, it became apparent that the defense attorneys disagreed as to how the case should be handled. For example, during the closing arguments to the jury, before the jury retired to consider Sirhan's guilt or innocence, Parsons' statement spoke of Sirhan's life back in Jerusalem, of the warfare and how it affected him. Berman, on the other hand, in his closing statement maintained that Sirhan's problems started after he arrived in the United States.

Everyone had an opinion as to why the defense had failed. Cooper saw it as a backlash reaction of the jurors against the violence in the United States. Robert Kaiser, an author and member of the investigative staff for the defense team, thought political considerations in the trial had mitigated "the only real defense Sirhan ever had." No one however suggested that perhaps Sirhan had been forgotten in the trial, that Sirhan as an individual capable of thought and feeling, Sirhan as a sensitive young man had been rendered, in the larger sense, into a non-person by the conduct of his trial.

By refusing to offer testimony on the Palestine-Zionist conflict and the intense Arab nationalism it engendered, possibly out of their own political considerations, Sirhan's attorneys may have gambled away his only chance of avoiding a death sentence. The diminished capacity defense required a foundation of information making Sirhan's condition credible to some members of the jury who, like Sirhan, may have experienced discrimination and oppression. More importantly, Sirhan's own statements and diary entries tended to prove that the killing had been a deliberate and wilful act. What was called for, therefore, was evidence which could be the basis for judicial clemency or a recommendation of mercy by the jury. Such a strategy would have coincided with Sirhan's own wishes. Sirhan never denied his guilt and never expected complete acquittal. Sirhan wanted the world to understand his behavior as the undeniable protest of a fervently patriotic man whose country, homelife, and aspirations were crushed by imperialism and racism.

In the following pages of this book, Godfrey Jansen makes a detailed review of "the other Sirhan." His investigation and interviews with the people who knew Sirhan throughout his life, both in Palestine and in the United States, provide valuable information in answering the question of who Sirhan is and why. The book is the effort of one man, an Asian, to examine the actions of one man, another Asian, in the context of the totality of his life experience and a considerably different view of the world than is held by most Western men and women. I am convinced that without an understanding of this non-Western, non-colonial view of the world, any attempt to understand Sirhan will, at best, be fruitless and, at worst, self-serving. Perhaps this is what Dr. Diamond, the defense psychiatrist, meant when he said in an interview which appeared in *Psychology Today* that the result of the trial would have been different if the victim had not been Robert Kennedy, and the defendant, Sirhan.

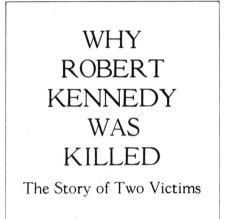

WHY
ROBERT
KENNEDY
WAS
KILLED

The Story of Two Victims

Introduction

I heard the news of the shooting of Robert F. Kennedy at about ten
o'clock in the morning of June 5th in the shop of my newsagent in
Beirut, when I went there to collect the daily batch of foreign
newspapers. I was talking with the newsagent about the one subject
that was uppermost in everyone's mind—how the Arab countries would
commemorate the first anniversary of the June war—when his young
female assistant who had been taking a moment off to listen to popular
music on a transistor radio, jumped up and exclaimed that an
announcement, cutting in on the music, had just been made that
Robert Kennedy had been shot and that he was in serious condition.
The first reaction of all three of us was shock and sadness. We hurriedly
surmised that the shooting was the work of the same people who had
killed his brother, President John F. Kennedy.

The eleven o'clock news bulletin on the World Service of the B.B.C.
gave further details: the assailant, a swarthy, dark-haired young man,
had been seized and, at the time of the shooting, had called out "I can

explain. I did it for my country. I love my country." We presumed that he was, most probably, Cuban.

I sent a despatch to my newspaper on how the June 5th anniversary had been marked in Beirut by silent processions. I decided to escape from the humid heat of Beirut's summer by spending the evening and night in the cool quiet of a small Lebanese village in the hills behind the city. It was there that we learnt, from radio bulletins, that the suspect was "a Palestinian Arab" and that his name was "Sirhan Sirhan." As is customary in multi-religious Lebanon there was immediately much discussion as to whether he was Muslim or Christian, for the name could be either. Later bulletins mentioned that he came originally from Jerusalem and that his name was Sirhan Bechara Sirhan, which made it clear that he was not only Christian but, most certainly, a member of the Greek Orthodox Church. "Thank God, he is not a Muslim," was the comment of my Lebanese neighbour, himself a wise and gentle Christian.

Thus it was only at the end of the day that we knew that the "country" about which Sirhan had cried out was Palestine and that the deed he had done for Palestine was only the latest act of violence in the tortured, bloodstained history of that tragic land.

Thus also it was that the case of Sirhan Bechara Sirhan became of direct concern to me as the Middle Eastern correspondent of my newspaper. The despatch I sent the following day was, naturally, on this latest incident in the unfolding of the Palestine Problem, that problem which every thinking person in this area (and that sometimes includes foreign correspondents) has to live, eat and breathe every day of the year, every year.

What is this problem? As an Indian, and also because I think they were correct in their analysis, I view this problem in the same terms used by Mahatma Gandhi and Jawaharlal Nehru: the Palestine Problem concerns the struggle of the Palestine people to regain their homeland from the Zionists who had succeeded in capturing it, partly through their own dedication, skill and courage and partly because of substantial help given to the Zionists by Western Powers, especially the United States of America.

The Palestine Problem is thus an integral part of the wide-ranging struggle for freedom waged by the peoples of Afro-Asia against the West for the past eighty-odd years.

It is against this large and turbulent background that the shooting in the kitchen of a hotel in Los Angeles has to be seen.

Against that sweeping backdrop it may seem a small, insignificant deed; and yet it is of unique significance, both in personal and in historic terms.

The chances that the life of an obscure and impoverished young Palestinian refugee from the ancient, walled city of Jerusalem should intersect with the life of a rich and world-famous Irish-American politician from Boston, and that this violent intersection should take place on the shores of the far-distant Pacific Ocean—the chances of such an incongruous encounter coming about are one in a billion.

Historically the act of Sirhan Sirhan was one of political protest carried out at extreme range, the projection of a liberation struggle across the width of a sea, an ocean and a continent. The depth of this penetration into the opposing camp is unprecedented in Afro-Asian history.

A review of the history of assassinations reveals that victim and assassin are normally citizens of the same country and that the deed usually takes place in their country. Such was the case with Abraham Lincoln, the Archduke Ferdinand, Mahatma Gandhi and President Kennedy. Seldom are the two protagonists from different countries and even in such cases, the crime has been committed either in the country that has produced the particular political problem or in a nearby one, invariably on the same continent.

The Jewish Problem with its off-spring, the Palestine Problem, seems especially productive of international assassinations. Such were the cases of the young German Jews, Schwarzbard and Frankfurter: the former assassinated the Ukranian anti-Semitic leader Petliura in Paris and the latter assassinated Gustloff, the Nazi gauleiter of Switzerland in that country. But these were all Europeans and the scene was Europe.

We approximate the Kennedy-Sirhan encounter in the assassination of the Englishman Lord Moyne, carried out by two young Zionists from Palestine in Cairo and of the Swedish Count Bernadotte, also by Palestinian Zionists, in Palestine itself.

In these two cases the violence was directed not against the direct antagonists of the Zionists, that is to say the Arabs, but against the representatives of a third party involved in the conflict, Britain and the United Nations.

Only in the case of Sirhan do we have a unique combination of all the unusual factors—the differences of nationality, the selection of a representative of the third party, and the locale in the country of that third party.

It is strange indeed that only in 1968 did this unique combination of factors come about. In the history of the Afro-Asian liberation struggle there are numerous instances of acts of violence directed against representatives of the metropolitan powers, even in India and despite the non-violence of Gandhi. But they all took place on the soil of the Afro-Asian territories. Britain faced nationalist uprisings, wholly or partially violent, in Palestine, Egypt and Iraq, in Ghana and Kenya, in India and Burma and Malaya; France had the same experience in Morocco, Algeria and Tunisia, in Syria, Madagascar and Indo-China; as did the Dutch in Indonesia. But no British, French or Dutch leaders were assassinated in Britain, France or Holland.

The only possible exception is Palestine, for Zionist terrorists attempted to kill or maim British leaders by sending them letter-bombs and, allegedly, by planting a bomb in the House of Commons.

It took the passions aroused by Palestine to produce the killing by an Asian of an American, deeply involved in the Palestine Problem, and on American soil.

At the longest possible range, the world-village struck back at the world-city, and in the heart of the city.

I know of at least one precedent for a book of this type dealing with the subject of assassination. It is a direct precedent because it deals with an assassination produced by the Palestine Problem. I refer to *"The Deed, the assassination of Lord Moyne"* by Gerold Frank.* In "A Note To The Reader," Frank describes his book thus: *"The Deed* is the story of two boys who gave their lives for an ideal. They killed a man—coldly, calmly, with premeditation. . . . Their cause was freedom, the freedom of Israel, but the means they chose was the assassin's gun, believing in

* Jonathan Cape, London, 1964.

the tradition of those who hold with political assassination, that by their act they could change the course of history. . . . The full measure of their role—the effect for example, of the attention it focused upon the sorry situation in Palestine—is a question for future historians."

Most, if not all of these words apply, *mutatis mutandis,* to Sirhan Sirhan. For Sirhan too, the "cause was freedom"—"I did it for my country"—and what he did has focused attention "upon the sorry situation in Palestine." But I hope that my approach to the subject will be rather different from that of Gerold Frank.

"The Deed" is a frankly laudatory work: Lord Moyne is the victim and the two boys are the heroes—young, gay, gifted, *sans peur* and *sans reproche.* Perhaps they were so, but I do not think that anything so simplistic can adequately explain the event of June 5, 1968.

In the incident at the Ambassador Hotel, there was not one victim and one hero: there were two victims—Sirhan Sirhan and Robert Kennedy. My objective is to show how and why the Palestinian came to kill the American, without condoning the crime and without trying to apportion praise or blame.

It is not that I disapprove of violence. Like a great many Indians, I admire and respect Mahatma Gandhi but never accepted his creed on non-violence. It is true, also, that international law recognises the difference between murder and political murder. Yet in the case of Sirhan, the primary need is not to excuse, but to understand him and his circumstances and his people.

I trust that what I write may be farily described in the words of Othello: "nothing extenuate, nor set aught down in malice."

PART I

THE FIRST VICTIM

1

The Why and How of this Book

I think there is need to explain why I, of all people, came to write this book, because I feel certain that several readers are going to be surprised at the fact of an Indian writing about an Arab; I also feel certain that there would be less surprise, or no surprise at all, if I were an Englishman, or an Italian, writing about Sirhan. Readers in the West still have not got used to the idea of Africans and Asians writing about fellow Africans and Asians or about African and Asian problems.

That this should be so came to me as a surprising discovery. In a bibliographical note to a book I wrote on Afro-Asia and Non-Alignment, I said, "From now on the history of Afro-Asia must not only be made but must also be written by Afro-Asians." When I wrote those words they seemed to me an obvious truism. And yet that one sentence more than anything else in the 400 page book aroused the wrath or irritation of Western reviewers: they made it abundantly clear that they considered me a Johnny-come-lately upstart. Their reaction reminded me that there are many kinds of colonial dominance—

political, economic, cultural, linguistic and academic; and that at least some Western writers were not prepared to willingly yield their academic hegemony over Asian studies. So far this monopoly has not really been seriously challenged by Asian writers across the length and breadth of Afro-Asia; only in certain countries has there been an assertion of Asian academic self-determination.

For instance, it is generally recognised that Indians and Pakistanis write, in English and in scholarly fashion, about themselves and their problems. A few Indians and Pakistanis have even written about East and West Asia. But for West Asia, and especially the Arab area, very few books have been written, for English readers, by Arabs, though a very large number of books have been produced by Jewish scholars, both in England and in North America. And no Arab has, to my knowledge, written about South or East Asia. So why a South Asian, like myself, should choose to write about a West Asian, like Sirhan, does perhaps call for some explanation.

Let me say at the outset that I did not undertake this task merely in order to make a politico-academic point. The killing in Los Angeles—and the nationality and nationalism of Sirhan—obviously was an event of major importance for an area which I cover as the West Asian correspondent of my newspaper. It was my professional duty to find out as much as possible about what happened, and why it happened, and to pass on this information to my readers.

But my interest was much more than just professional. I have lived and worked in the West Asian area, as a diplomat and as a foreign correspondent for fifteen years and I have concentrated on the Middle East because, after seeing many parts of the world, I decided that here was the most interesting and the most important section on the surface of the globe: here, where the three continents of Europe, Asia and Africa meet, is the navel of the world.

To this interest, individual but impersonal, was added a personal feeling. As I read the newspaper accounts (often incomplete and disjointed and contradictory) describing Sirhan and his family background, I could not but see numerous points of resemblance between him and myself. We are both Asian Christians which means that in Palestine and India we are members of small minorities; and members of minority groups, wherever they come from, have, willy-nilly, a basic fellow-feeling. There is a strange similarity in our family situations although, fortunately for me, this was not in the hardships that the Sirhans have had to endure. But I, too, came from a broken family and knew the effect of family feuds and what it was like to be brought up by only one parent instead of the usual two. At about the same stage in life—I was nine, he was eleven—our families moved from the countries where we were born to other lands. In my case, it was only a relatively short move from Burma to India, but it still involved some alienation. And by choice, not of necessity as with Sirhan, I have spent long years outside my homeland and know what it is to be an alien. Lebanon, which is my second home, is the most tolerant and friendly of countries, but, nevertheless, over a period of months, I spent much time and energy going from one government office to another, so as to acquire those two pieces of paper that are the bane of the alien's existence the world over, a work permit and a residence permit.

Even though Sirhan, like myself, did not see his country for many years, he called out, "I love my country," and so do I.

The most striking resemblance between our families was an intense, narrow religiosity that was a dominant factor in the family life, but which, at the same time, did not exclude a restless movement from one fundamentalist sect to another.

Therefore when I met Sirhan's father, Bechara Sirhan, it did not come as a surprise to me that he should bear a distinct physical resemblance to my father: both of them small, neat, precise, with rounded heads and strongboned faces. And after a very few minutes of conversation, Bechara Sirhan was revealing the same, all-too-familiar, intimate, obsessive knowledge of the Bible, especially of the Old Testament. Listening to him talk in his house in Taibeh, in occupied Jordan, I had only to close my eyes to imagine myself listening to my father on the verandah of our house in Bangalore, South India. Then both our fathers were conscientious servants of the British imperial Raj.

Far more than the professional interest, or the political factors involved, it was these personal similarities that made the prospect of my writing about Sirhan an immediate and fascinating challenge.

It turned out to be, by far, my most difficult assignment.

There were two reasons for this difficulty. The first was a Court Order, number 8233421—I prefer to call it a gag order—issued on June 7th, two days after the shooting, by Superior Judge Arthur Alarcon of Los Angeles which forbade all law-enforcement officers "or anyone subpoenaed to testify at the trial of this matter" to say anything about the case or about Sirhan. What in effect happened is that all sorts of people, reading the rather impressive description of the Court Order given in the local press, and even though they were not connected with law-enforcement and were not under subpoena, refused to talk: they, from fear or self-importance, assumed that they *might* be subpoenaed because of their connection with Sirhan. The result was an almost complete drying-up of sources of information, even of the most trivial and innocent variety.

The immediate cause for the issuance of this Court Order was a series of wildly tendentious statements on the alleged contents of Sirhan's diaries made by Mayor Samuel Yorty of Los Angeles. The origins of this ban go back a little further. To quote *The New York Times* of June 9th: "The police, exercising care for the rights of the defendant, confined themselves to making public a minimum of information. . . . This was the result of an order issued to all law enforcement officials. . . . The order was aimed at preventing the *official* release [my italics] of any information that could prejudice an impartial trial—particularly information that might be used as evidence against the 24-year-old defendant. Judge Alarcon's instruction— violation of which would constitute contempt of court—represented the first important application of new standards that have developed out of a series of court decisions, particularly since the Warren Commission's criticisms of official behavior after President Kennedy was assassinated in Dallas in 1963. The restrictions generally followed limits unsuccessfully sought by the American Civil Liberties Union in a landmark law suit brought last year against the Los Angeles police department and other law enforcement agencies. Law enforcement agencies that had opposed the A.C.L.U. today were adhering to the restrictions without protest. . . . In fact, a call to the county jail about Sirhan elicited from the officer in charge the response: 'who?' . . . Judge Alarcon's order was explicitly directed to public officials and persons specifically connected with the prosecution. His declaration referred only peripherally to other sources of information."

The task of journalists covering the Sirhan case would have been made a lot easier if everyone in Los Angeles and Pasadena had read this carefully-worded analysis; though, it should be noted, even *The Times* account omits to mention those subpoenaed as witnesses, which is the most restrictive injunction of the Court Order.

Since the Court Order was issued soon after Mayor Yorty's uncouth outburst against Sirhan, since it was favoured by the Civil Liberties Union, and since it was still fresh in the public memory how Oswald and Ruby were tried (and perhaps executed) by the American press and television, Judge Alarcon's Order was genuinely welcomed.

But until the general public is educated in its precise applicability, it will severely limit a far more important right than that of free trial—the public's right to know. Most of the American journalists I spoke to chafed under its restrictions and thought that it was being misunderstood and misused. At least one of my American colleagues said that the Order was merely a way for the conservative American Bar Association to get even with the probing and disrespectful American press. I give below some examples of how the Order got in the way of my finding out what sort of person Sirhan was, and I leave it to the reader to judge whether or not such a gag order is desirable. Happily for me, some very well-informed sources were ignorant of, or chose to ignore, the Order.

In my search for the real Sirhan, I would have preferred to follow the chronology of his life and so to visit Jerusalem first, where he spent his early years, and then go to Los Angeles—Pasadena, the scene of his adolescence and early manhood. This, however, was not possible and I had to make the visits in reverse order.

I arrived in Los Angeles on June 14th, nine days after the assassination and immediately, and during the following eight days, discovered that that city itself was the second major obstacle in my path. I had spent half a day in Los Angeles many years previously and promptly added it to the short list of cities—Calcutta and Baghdad—that I would willingly never see again. It had certainly not improved with the passage of time. Hot and humid and smog-ridden, the Los Angeles-Pasadena agglomeration is also tawdry and garish and vulgar. If there was ever a city that deserved the ugly epithet "conurbation," it is this. A vast urban sprawl yet singularly deficient in public transport where life, and work, is impossible without a car of one's own. Hence the ceaseless thunder of the automotive herds along the cement ribbons called "Freeways" that interlace the city and its suburbs. To try and reach someone on the telephone is a major operation, despite the help of a very efficient hotel switchboard. A great many people in Los Angeles (and this may be true of other American cities) have discovered that the telephone can be a monstrous invasion of one's privacy, with the result that the home telephone numbers, even of journalists, are unlisted: I seemed to spend half my time delivering messages into the recording machines of answering services. Also, Los Angeles is divided into a large number of telephone zones, communications between which count not as local calls but as toll calls. I did not discover the system on which the division was made and, as often as not, after dialling, would hear a recorded female voice, which I soon came to hate, inviting me to get in touch with the operator, so as to make a toll call. In Los Angeles, the telephone, as a means of communication, seems to have reached the final point of self-defeating absurdity.

I thought that the first place I ought to visit was the scene of the assassination in the passageway of the kitchen of the Ambassador Hotel. When I met the head of the hotel's security service—cold, blank blue eyes in a hard face—he began reciting the litany of the Court Order. He seemed disappointed that I had no questions for him and sought no information. "We're not supposed to do this but I'll show you around," he finally said and then gave me and my assistant, Mary Galle, a brisk tour of the Embassy Room, the passageway and the Colonial Room, where Robert Kennedy had been scheduled to meet the press.

The only other site of importance was, of course, the Sirhan home at 696 East Howard Street, Pasadena. It is a pleasant, tree-shaded street, quiet, and empty of people when we drove down it. The only thing marking the Sirhan house was a large, white police station-wagon parked in the driveway with a single policeman seated beside it, reading a newspaper.

Like every other newspaperman on this assignment, I would have given a great deal to be able to enter that house and talk awhile with its occupants, Sirhan's mother and brothers, for in an hour or even half an hour's conversation one could have discovered the clues to his personality; or so we felt. But it was not to be. I knew that it was pointless to try and gatecrash, apart from the total impropriety of breaking in on private grief, because really close friends of the family who had spoken to the Sirhans on the phone had been asked not to call—for their own sakes. Here we see the malign effects of the Court Order, which had, of course, been served on all members of the family. If they could not talk to their friends about the one subject that was uppermost in all their minds what, then, was the point of meeting? One got the impression that, following the Order, the Sirhans considered themselves as somewhat contaminated and infectious; and isolation in turn produced fear so that they would repeatedly warn friends on the telephone not to say too much. So they stayed, or cowered, immured in their small house in what seemed to me a thoroughly unpleasant and undesirable situation in which wholly innocent people should never have been placed.

After a day or so I wrote a letter to Mrs. Sirhan explaining that I was an Indian foreign correspondent who had come from Beirut and requested an interview. One copy was despatched by special delivery mail, the other we delivered to the policeman who handed it to one of the brothers who came to the screen door to accept it. The next day I phoned and spoke with Sharif who said that they had received the letters and would like to meet with me but that they could say nothing because of the Court Order. I said that I had some questions and that he was free to answer them or not. He did, in fact, answer some while others he received in silence. Before I left Los Angeles, I spoke, on the telephone, with another brother, Adel, to clarify some points, on the same take-it-or-leave-it basis. I believe I was lucky to make even these fleeting contacts, for other journalists who tried the telephone interview only received abuse.

One of the people who took no notice of the Court Order was the next-door neighbour of the Sirhans, Mrs. Olive Blakeslee, a dear old lady of great age, struggling with asthma and deafness, who was yet willing to give one as much information on Sirhan as she had.

Probably because the Sirhans were a religious family I found myself interviewing no less than three clergymen. The first was Father Paul Romney of the St. Nicholas Greek Orthodox Church for whom, on a Sunday morning, we waited in the vestry while he finished taking part in the morning service; while we waited, the church attendants sliced-up loaves of bread to be distributed to the congregation as a reminder of the miracle of the Loaves and Fishes. He was generous with his time and gave us valuable insights into the solidly respectable Arab-American community from which his flock is drawn. He was a sympathetic and understanding informant, which is more than can be said of his other two colleagues of the cloth. Doctors Charles Bell, of the First Baptist Church in Pasadena, told us all he knew, for which I was grateful but his relations with the Sirhans had been unhappy and something of that experience carried over into his tones of faint, detached disapproval. The Reverend Harry Eberts, of the Westminster Presbyterian Church, was positively evasive. I had not sought an interview with him but merely his permission to meet with the ladies who worked with Mrs. Sirhan in the nursery school attached to his Church. Because of the Court Order he felt that he had to block any such meeting and, very skillfully and politely, he did so, interposing himself instead. He said nothing, at some length, but revealed that he had advised the Sirhan family not to meet anyone, whereupon I could not refrain from telling him how wrong I thought his advice was.

The worst example of what I can only call evasiveness came at the Pasadena City College where a Doctor I.G. Lewis said he could tell the press only three things, and holding three fingers up in the air, he ticked them off: one, Sirhan Sirhan was no longer a student in the college; two, Sirhan had been a student in the college; three, anything else was private information and not to be divulged. Having decided on this approach of "that is all ye know on earth and all ye need to know" the college authorities had not even looked into Sirhan's college records—or so Dr. Lewis said.

In contrast to this bureaucratic reticence were four people who knew the Sirhan family well and who told all they knew. These were Miss Linda Massri and her mother Mrs. Kamakian, of Altadena, Mr. Jean Weidner of Pasadena, the owner of a health food store and Sirhan's last employer, and Mr. Lou Shelby of the Fez supper club in Hollywood where Adel Sirhan worked for many years. We had two interviews, covering several hours with Miss Massri and Mrs. Kamakian and though Mr. Weidner and Mr. Shelby are both busy men, they each talked with us for well over an hour.

I was able to meet with only one of the three other persons for whom Sirhan had worked in Pasadena. He was Mr. Jack Davies, a filling station proprietor; another filling station proprietor was away on vacation, and a retired gardner was not to be found at home. When we phoned a recorded voice informed us that "at the subscriber's request this number has been temporarily disconnected."

For me a disconnected phone conveys a suggestion of something sinister, a hint of menace. There was more than a hint of this feeling when I tried to contact the officers of the local chapters of the Organisation of Arab Students in the various universities located in the Los Angeles area. Time and time again we ran into the dead end of a disconnected phone. After a couple of days of fruitless endeavour, friends in New York, Boston, and Chicago tried to make contact, or provided yet other telephone numbers, but all to no avail—or almost so. Only within a few hours of my leaving Los Angeles was I finally able to run one of the O.A.S. officials down to earth. Not all of those disconnected phones were due to students going on vacation. After the assassination many Arabs in and around Los Angeles received abusive and threatening phone calls. The Sirhan family did: one of the few friends who visited them described how, during the visit, a caller on the phone told the Sirhans to "get out of town." Men forced their way into the apartment of the eldest Sirhan brother, Saadallah, and under threat of violence robbed him of photographs of the family. When I was in Los Angeles, there was an uneasy feeling abroad in the Arab community and the veil of silence which the Court Order brought down around the whole affair certainly did not help.

The local bureaus of the Associated Press and of the United Press were very helpful as were *The Los Angeles Times* and *The Pasadena Independent,* which only serves to make the following episode all the more strange.

In trying to understand Sirhan's motivations I thought it would be useful to study the coverage of the Arab-Israeli war of June, 1967, in the local newspapers and from the local television stations: we knew that the family took in both the Los Angeles and Pasadena papers and had a TV set. The events of that disasterous week were harrowing for any Arab, more especially for those far from home: the amount of time or space given to them, and the manner of presentation, would have had a direct bearing on the thoughts and feelings of a politically minded young Arab. We checked through the files of the newspapers from June 5th to 12th without let or hindrance. For television coverage, we chose the local station of the Columbia Broadcasting System, KNXT on Sunset Boulevard, because CBS, generally, has the best news coverage. We spoke to the news section of the station and asked whether we could see the logs in which are listed the programmes as they are telecast. (The printed programmes did not help much because during that week many scheduled programmes were hurriedly replaced with special war coverage). The news director of KNXT said there would be no objection but warned us that it might be an arduous task.

When we arrived at the KNXT studio we, as is normal, had to explain who we were and what our business was to the receptionist. It required a couple of telephone calls for her to find the right person for us to meet, and we were then asked to wait. After a brief pause, we met with Mr. Garth Hintz, Director of Community Relations, to whom I had to explain once more who I was, what I wanted and why I wanted this information: "Was I writing a thesis?" was one of his questions. Having satisfied himself of my *bona fides,* Mr. Hintz then told me that he would not show me the logs; that he had consulted the station's attorney on the matter and that the regulations of the Federal Communications Commission did not "oblige" the station to make this material available. I pointed out that I was not asking for anything confidential but merely for a listing of programmes that had been telecast and which had been seen by hundreds of thousands, perhaps millions, of people. After some discussion back and forth, the absurdity of his objections probably became apparent to Mr. Hintz and he finally went so far as to propose that while he still could not let me see the logs, he would get his office to try and make a listing of the programmes referring to the June events; but that it would be a very general listing. He was as good as his word and such a listing was forthcoming (for which I render thanks) and it was general indeed since it mentioned only two types of programmes—"U.N. meetings" and "Special Reports" with no further detail. It is obvious that a TV station's log cannot enumerate the items in a news bulletin but I would have thought that a station's log is of little value if it does not specify whether a "Special Report" was documentary material or news analysis or comment and on what aspect and by whom. I must say that I found this TV station's suspicions and reticence very strange indeed, but also not unusual in the general atmosphere prevailing in Los Angeles.

Naturally, we followed many false leads,—frustrating experiences except for one which was both amusing and illuminating. The editor of one of the two local Arab-American newspapers, Mr. Henry Awad of *The Hollywood Star,* who was disposed to be helpful, suggested that the proprietor of a shop called "Import City" on Hollywood Boulevard, knew the Sirhan family well. In the more-than-usually raffish surroundings of Hollywood (which may be the home of glamour but is singularly unglamorous itself), past that grotesque but world-famous night club called and shaped like "The Brown Derby," we found "Import City" and discovered that it was what might be called a hippy supply depot. It specialises in bells, beads and bangles, in talismans and incense sticks, in records of oriental music and Indian fabrics for the long-haired, bare-footed tribe of which one sees so many specimens on the streets of Los Angeles and Pasadena. In this incongruous setting, I pursued my enquiry into the motivations of a political assassination. I did not get very far because the proprietor did not know the Sirhans at all but, nonwithstanding this, and because they were in trouble, he had volunteered to take them into his home when the family, for its own safety, was moved out of 696 East Howard in the days immediately following June 5th. It was encouraging to find that Arab hospitality had not withered away even in the arid surroundings of Hollywood.

It was more than half a world away from hippiedom to the area where I next pursued my enquiries. This was Jerusalem and the Israeli-occupied West Bank of the Jordan. I went from Beirut to Nicosia to obtain my Israeli visa, on a separate passport, and then via Amman made the double crossing of the Jordan River into and out of

Israeli-controlled territory. In Amman, a Cabinet minister had to obtain a special dispensation for us from the Jordanian Army and Police because foreigners are normally not allowed to make the double crossing.

A car took us to the ruined Jordanian police station that stands next to the wrecked Allenby Bridge, its spans collapsed into the yellow-brown waters of the stream that is the River Jordan. Carrying our luggage, we walked up a dusty track to the temporary bridge and over it. In a sandbagged emplacement at its farther end, a blue-eyed blonde Israeli soldier glanced at our passports and waved us on. We trudged on for about half a mile through the thick undergrowth of cane and bullrushes that flanks the river until we came to the Israeli checkpoint. To walk across a frontier is itself a strange enough experience, but this is also a strange frontier. Here the frontier was busy with people going back and forth but just two hours earlier, just twenty miles north, the frontier had been busy with shells, mortar bombs and bullets flying back and forth between the Israeli and Jordanian armies. Despite a year-old "cease-fire" the Second Battle for Palestine still spluttered on.

The Jordan Valley is the lowest point on the surface of the globe and in the middle of the day, in July, the heat was ruthless. Under a sun that seemed to hammer the top of one's head, hundreds of people, and scores of trucks and cars were milling about a large dusty yard.

Here, in terms of living human beings, was the Palestine Problem. Most of the Palestinians standing in the long, sweaty queues, patiently clutching their all-important scraps of paper, were people from the West Bank paying visits to their relatives on the East Bank, a "concession" that the Israeli government had recently granted,-they were allowed a two-week visit and told not to return if they stayed longer. There were also some West Bankers and a larger number of persons from the Gaza Strip, a couple of hundred a month, who were leaving their homes for good, with the usual clutter of their domestic paraphenalia loaded into trucks. These were the "new" refugees and "old" expellees, about 300,000 in all, the by-products of Israel's military victory in the summer of 1967.

In short, the process of emptying the Palestinian people out of Palestine was going on. The Sirhan family had been part of the early stages of this process in 1948.

Recognising us for tourists, the Israeli border police were politely helpful and sped us through immigration and customs. Since there were no available taxis they even found transportation for us, in the ancient car of an Assyrian shoe-maker of Jerusalem who, he told us, had two sons in New Jersey. He was going only as far as Jericho, from where we caught a taxi for the Holy City.

On the outskirts of Jericho, beneath the slopes of the Mount of Temptation, the vast camps of the "old" Palestinian "refugees" lay empty. These were complete townships with schools and hospitals, all provided by the United Nations Relief and Works Agency—with the conscience money that the nations paid for their decision to carve up Palestine, the decision which led to 800,000 people leaving or being driven from their homes. Once again last June, the refugees in Jericho left or were driven from their camp homes by the Israeli Army. On the way to Jerusalem we passed the Inn of the Good Samaritan. Apart from impersonal international charity there have been few Good Samaritans to care for the wounded, spoilated Palestinian of today.

That evening I visited Sirhan's father, Bechara Salameh Sirhan, in his village of Taibeh. I drove across the lovely rolling countryside of Jordan and Samaria: bare, grey hilltops relieved by the green in the valleys of vine and fig and olive. We went through Bireh, where, by tradition, Mary and Joseph discovered that Jesus was not in the caravan for Nazareth and turned back to Jerusalem to find him disputing with the Elders in the Temple. We turned off another road that dropped down to Jericho and after rounding many curves, came to this small, clean village of Taibeh perched on a hilltop from which, in the clear morning hours, one gets a sweeping view of the Jordan Valley and the Dead Sea. Bechara Sirhan spoke to me for nearly two hours that evening.

The next day I located the house in the Musrara Quarter, outside the walled city in Jerusalem, were the Sirhans lived until Sirhan was four years old and from where they fled in 1948. I later visited the house, at the corner of Suq el Husroor and Al Malak Street, inside the walled city, where they lived in a room for the next seven years until they emigrated to the United States. I was lucky to meet someone who had been a neighbour of the Sirhans in that house for six of the seven years. And I also visited the school that Sirhan attended.

The following morning I visited Taibeh again, and had a further long talk with Bechara Sirhan. That afternoon we walked back across the Jordan bridge on the return journey to Beirut.

Perhaps I ought also to mention that on the way back from Los Angeles I paid brief visits to New York and to Boston, especially South Boston, from where the Kennedy family began their climb to fame and fortune.

That is how in California and Palestine, the material for this book came to be collected. Because of the lack of time, and because of the Court Order, I could not gather all the information I would have liked to have. Yet I have managed to visit the two cities and the four houses in which Sirhan lived. The trail of my enquiries led through churches and private homes, filling stations and a nightclub, shops and schools and newspaper offices. Some of the pieces of the jigsaw puzzle are missing but the main outline of the design is, I think, clear.

One last word about the Court Order. When reports appeared in the American press that Sirhan's father might visit Los Angeles, Mr. Wilbur F. Littlefield, who was then the Chief Trial Deputy appointed to defend Sirhan (he was later replaced) sent Bechara Sirhan in Taibeh a copy of Judge Alarcon's order with a letter in which Littlefield wrote: "I respectfully request that you make no statements to anyone concerning your son, his background or his case." The elder Sirhan treated this piece of impertinence with the contempt it deserved, and it is on the basis of what his father told me that it became possible to put together a picture of Sirhan's early life in Jerusalem and, especially, of certain violent incidents which had a determinant effect on his outlook and personality. This information was supplemented, very considerably, by evidence given during the trial by his mother and a friend from the troubled, unhappy years in the Holy City.

2

Without the City Wall

Bechara Sirhan spoke to me in the living room of his house at Taibeh. It was easy enough to find, not only because Taibeh is a small village, but also because, with the comings and goings of scores of journalists and cameramen, it has become Taibeh's best-known house. "Turn right just past the first church and go uphill and stop when you get to the second church," were the directions we received. Despite its small size, Taibeh has three churches—Greek Orthodox, Greek Catholic and Roman Catholic. This did not surprise me because the Arabs, both Christian and Muslim, are a devout people. Taibeh is wholly Christian.

Bechara Sirhan's house is built on a steep slope below the road and it turns its back on Taibeh. Only a narrow, stony path leads down to its front gate, which has two low strands of rusty barbed wire draped between the posts. These simple physical facts seemed to have a more than factual significance.

It is a solid two-storied building with about ten rooms. Bechara Sirhan is very proud of his home. "I designed it myself," he told me, "and you will see that everything in it is well finished. I used stone, because there is nothing like stone. I built partly with the money left me by my father and partly with what I saved. I worked very, very hard on this house and I love it very much."

It is something more than a piece of property for Bechara Sirhan. On a round plaque set high in the front wall is this inscription in beautiful, flowing Arabic script:

> "God Most High
> "I built this house for you on earth
> "May you grant me a house in heaven"

> *Bechara Salameh Sirhan*
> 1963

Yet it is a sad house because it has that air of loneliness that houses can acquire. Perhaps this is because it is much too large for Bechara Sirhan who lives there by himself. One gets the impression that he is camping in it because there are few pieces of furniture in the rooms and voices echo emptily off their walls.

I knocked on two doors before I discovered the real entrance leading in from a covered verandah. Mr. Sirhan greeted me politely in the entrance hall and then showed me into his living room. When I told him who I was, that I was a journalist, an Indian, and that I had been to Pasadena, his face broke into a smile and he said, "I'm very ready to talk to you, and to tell you all that I know." Then he excused himself and I heard the gushing sound of a primus stove come from the kitchen. I looked around me: the bare room contained two hard, narrow sofas and a wooden chair set round a table on which there were a packet of cigarettes, a large alarm clock, a thick copy of the Bible, a copy of the Koran and one of the New Testament, and some religious tracts and booklets—all in Arabic. There was a splendid view from the windows looking south-east: folds of olive-covered hills falling away to the Jordan. Yet I was able to see all this only when I opened the windows, so begrimed were they by the winter rain.

The only other piece of furniture was a small corner table on which was a pile of newspapers, *The Jerusalem Post*, the uppermost copy folded over to show the headline "Attempt on life of Sirhan's brother,"—a story on the shooting at Saadallah Sirhan while he was driving on the Pasadena Freeway.

When he came back into the room, Mr. Sirhan's first question to me was, "How is my family? Are they safe?" I told him of my telephone conversations and gave him such assurances as I could. He went out again to return with two cups of Arabic coffee, a sweet biscuit in each saucer.

This indispensible preliminary act of Arab hospitality having been duly performed, he lit a cigarette and asked me, "Now what is it you want to know?"

"Everything," I replied, "begin at the beginning."

I do not think Bechara Sirhan opened his heart completely to me and told me all he knew. I did not expect him to do this, for, after all, much of what I wanted from him concerned details of his family's life and about such things, among the Arabs, as among Indians, a decent reticence is observed. He did not tell me as much as he would have if he had been, for example, an American; and I probably did not get from him as much as if I had been a probing American journalist: there were reserves on both sides. Yet he told me a great deal, and this is his story.

The Sirhans are a family from Taibeh where his father owned some land, terraces of olive trees and some wheat fields which he has bought out of money saved during a period of years spent working as an immigrant in South America. He had also become a money lender which may, to some extent, account for the unpopularity of the family in Taibeh. The father is dead, but Bechara's mother, now 90 years old, is still alive. From the part she played in his later life, it is obvious that the mother and son are very close to each other, and yet she does not live with him, as might be expected at her age, but in another house in Taibeh. Bechara had two brothers and a sister; one brother is still alive.

Bechara's wife, Mary, also comes from Taibeh and they are blood relations.

"I have spent most of my life in Jerusalem," he said and it was there that he worked as an adult and married and raised his family.

Mary and Bechara Sirhan were married in 1930. They are said to be blood relations. She came from Jerusalem and has the typical pride of the Jerusalemite in that fact. When asked how long her family has lived in Jerusalem, Mary Sirhan replies, "For thousands of years. From generation to generation."

Bechara Sirhan is a mechanic by trade and by experience and with his intelligence he became, I would guess, something between a master mechanic and a rule-of-thumb engineer. "I don't have a lazy brain," he said. "I know a lot and can do many things. See how I built my house."

He was employed in the Public Works Department of the British Mandatory Government of Palestine. When this government came to an end in 1948, Bechara Sirhan ranked as a foreman. He had made his mark as a worker several years earlier. With quiet pride, typical of the class of government servants, he showed me a testimonial, signed by the British Director of the Public Works Department, commending him for his "zeal and courage" in the repair of water pipelines "in circumstances of danger" during the disturbances of 1936, for which the government wished to express its "appreciation." The water pipelines Bechara Sirhan repaired were, it should be noted, blown up by Palestinian nationalists who in 1936 began a three-year uprising against the British authorities.

Mr. Sirhan was not in the least embarrassed to produce this evidence that he had worked to undo the work of the nationalists; and it did not surprise me either. Before 1948, there were two kinds of Palestinians, those passionately dedicated to the liberation of their homeland and others dedicated, if not passionately at least whole-heartedly to the concept of duty and the qualities exemplified by the Mandatory Administration. All across the Arab world now, in the Palestinian Diaspora, one meets scores of these men, who all bear a certain physical resemblance even to Bechara Sirhan,—of medium height, neat and precise and soft-spoken. They are religious and good fathers of their families, frugal and abstemious. They fitted perfectly into the middle and lower middle ranks of the British regime like cogs into an efficiently functioning machine. This is not to say that they were hand-in-glove with the British or were their political lackeys. No, what they gave their loyalty to and what they had a special affinity with was the fairness and justice, the regularity and good order of the administration. "The daily round, the common task" did furnish all that they could ask. These qualities they carried over into the Jordanian administration of what came to be called the West Bank; which is why the towns and villages there were notably clean and orderly, like Taibeh today.

But alas! These very qualities made them singularly unable to cope with the storm of violence that broke over their devoted heads in 1947 and 1948. Still less were they able to adjust to the life of rootless refugees into which they were cast after 1948. This was certainly true of Bechara Sirhan, but that fate was still some years away.

In the 1930s and 1940s Bechara Sirhan was plodding up the rungs of the ladder of promotion and increment, while he and his wife, Mary were raising a family much larger than the world knows about now.

In Pasadena the Sirhan children were six in number: five boys and a girl—Sharif, Saadallah, Aida, the sister, Adel, Sirhan and Munir. But Mrs. Sirhan had once mentioned to a friend that she was the mother of twelve boys and a girl. Sharif denied to me that any of his brothers had died. Mr. Sirhan was extremely reluctant to talk about this matter when I brought it up but finally said that four boys had died before and after Sirhan's birth. "They were not children but just babies when they died," is how he tried to change the subject."It's so long ago that I don't remember the details." I would surmise that Mrs. Sirhan's memory is more reliable and that there were, in all, thirteen children, and not just eleven, of whom only seven survived infancy. Mrs. Sirhan sums up the sad family history in these words, "I had 13 children altogether. Now I have five sons, that is all." The parents were particularly unlucky with their daughters for only one, Aida, lived to adulthood although another survived for five years. Even Mrs. Sirhan is not absolutely certain about their numbers: there were either two or three before Aida and four after her. That the family has drawn a veil over these deaths is obviously because of a feeling that they reflect the adverse family circumstances. It is these deaths that account for the age gaps before and after Sirhan. In June, 1968, the ages of the Sirhan brothers were, approximately, Sharif 38, Saadallah 36 (Aida would have been 34), Adel 33, Sirhan 24 and Munir 19. Most newspaper accounts, with surprisingly precise inaccuracy, give Bechara Sirhan's age as 52. In which case he fathered his first son when he was 14 years old! I would say that he is about 60.

The Sirhans were, by any standards, a large family and one that it could not have been very easy to maintain on the salary even of a foreman in the Public Works Department. The Sirhans did not have a house of their own; they lived in three rooms on the ground floor of a three-storied house on what was St. Paul's Street in the Musrara quarter of Jerusalem. The house still stands, as Number 82, Rehov Shivtev Yisrael. The family lived in this ground floor apartment for seven years, up to 1948, and in retrospect and in contrast with what followed, these years appear as being more comfortable than they probably actually were. Mrs. Sirhan says that they had $4,000 in the bank after their marriage, which may be questioned, but one can accept her claim that the furniture was all paid for: "We don't take things and pay after," is Mrs. Sirhan's explanation, which accords with the thrifty pride of the Palestinians.

Some newspaper accounts describe Musrara as a "slum area." It has obviously come down in the world, but even now it is only slummy in parts. Before 1948, the area between St. Paul's Street, Prophet's Street and Suleiman Road must have been a pleasant middle-class residential quarter. What is now Number 82 is a good example of the traditional Arab house. Its roof of red tiles covers an internal courtyard and encloses rooms which even then were divided up into separate apartments. Elegant arched windows are set into thick stone walls. The quarter had electricity in 1948 but in Number 82 water was drawn from a cistern in the old Jerusalem fashion. The Sirhan apartment gave on to an open yard with a scattering of umbrella pines. Beyond a lower road, the quarter dips into a depression which rises again to form the north-western approach to the Damascus Gate.

Before 1948, the area, and Number 82, was mixed Arab and Jewish. Since then it has, of course, been wholly Jewish, and a blind Israeli war veteran now lives in what was the Sirhan apartment, the windows of which have been bricked up. The morning I visited the house, two small girls, about the ages of Adel and Sirhan in 1948, were playing in the yard where the Sirhan children must once have played. The girls were clambering over three tyres, painted green, red and blue, which the parents of Number 82 had, with remarkable practicality, embedded in a block of cement.

These were the immediate physical surroundings into which Sirhan Sirhan was born on March 19th, 1944. But what was the state of the ancient city and of the Holy Land that lay beyond the pine trees in his play yard?

Palestine in 1944 was in a period of temporary truce in a struggle for its possession between Palestinian and Jew that had begun over fifty years earlier. The larger issues of World War II had overlaid those of this local struggle; the world-wide violence had brought to an end, for the time being, the violence that had wracked the Holy Land throughout the 1920s and 1930s.

The violence in Palestine was the result of an extraordinary endeavour: an attempt by some European Jewish leaders to implant a large Jewish community in Palestine—which necessarily implied their taking all or part of this land away from the Palestinian Arab people who had been living there for centuries. This endeavour was called Zionism and its religious basis was to be found in certain prophecies of the Old Testament, that the Jewish people should "return" to Zion, that is to Jerusalem. Its prime slogan was the verse of the 137th Psalm which says, "If I forget thee O Jerusalem let my right hand forget her cunning . . ."

The main political text of Zionism was *The Jewish State* of Theodore Herzl, an Austro-Hungarian Jew, which was published in 1896. Herzl himself, at first, did not think that the Jewish State had to be in Zion or Palestine: he was prepared to consider alternative sites in South America and Africa. Having started the Zionist movement, he was more or less obliged by a group of Russian Jewish leaders within the movement to concentrate on Palestine as the only possible site for the Jewish State.

What the Russian Zionists wanted was simply a place of refuge for the Jews from the pogroms of Czarist Russia. Since they were, almost all of them, agnostics or atheists, they were not activated by any religious yearning for the Holy Land; yet they realised that only the deep religious feelings for Zion of the ordinary orthodox Russian Jew would provide a strong enough motive force to move large masses of them out of Russia and into a new home in Palestine.

Despite the pulling power of Zion, despite the propulsion of anti-Semitic persecution, despite the efforts of the Zionist movement from 1890 onward, very few Jews left Europe to settle in Palestine. In 1814, it was estimated that only 10,000 Jews lived there and a century later, in 1914, that modest figure had only risen to the still-modest figure of 35,000, out of a total world Jewish population figure of twelve million. No wonder that an embittered Herzl remarked, "Whenever the Return to Zion is spoken of the very opposite is to be read into it."

Even this small degree of European Jewish settlement aroused the fears and resentment of the native Palestinians, for Palestine is a small country. The first violent reaction to the Jewish settlers dates from 1886 and the first official Palestinian protest against Zionist immigration was made in 1891. From that date on the Palestinians repeatedly and with increasing vehemence expressed their opposition to Zionist settlement. Writing about the "Awakening of the Arab Nation" and of Zionism, the Christian Arab writer Nagib Azoury as far back as 1905 prophesied: "These two movements are destined to fight continually, till one defeats the other."

The Zionist movement was saved from failure by the outbreak of World War I and by the fact that Turkey was on the losing side. When the victors came to carve up the spoils of the Ottoman Empire, the Zionists took the opportunity to revive their claim to Palestine. The result was the Balfour Declaration issued by the British government in 1917 which pledged British support to the project for a "Jewish National Home" in Palestine which, at the same time, should not prejudice the interests of the "other non-Jewish communities." The 119 words of this Declaration probably constitute the most disastrous statement of policy issued by the British, or indeed any other government, for its provisions were patently self-contradictory and have been productive of nothing but violence and suffering from that day to this.

Behind the public words of the Declaration lay an informal but well-documented private agreement between the British government and the Zionist. One of the participants in the 1918 negotiations, Lord Seiff, has called this "the Compact of 1917 between Israel and Britain."

The terms of this "Compact" were: the British would support a Jewish National Home in Palestine which, once enough Jews had entered Palestine, would develop naturally into a Jewish State; in return, in the short term, the Zionists would use their influence to help secure for the British the Mandate for Palestine from the League of Nations rather than it going to the United States, France or any international regime; in the long term, the Jewish State would help protect British imperial interests in the Middle East, especially the Suez Canal.

With Zionist help, Britain did obtain the Mandate for Palestine and then she kept her side of the bargain: the doors of Palestine, guarded by British soldiers, were thrown wide open to Jewish immigration. But the Zionists were unable to fulfill this side of the Compact because Jews were notably reluctant to "return" to Zion. In 1922, the Jews in Palestine numbered 83,000 or eleven per cent of the population; after ten years of unfettered immigration, the figure had risen to no more than 174,000 or sixteen per cent of the population. Biblical prophecies and the words of the Psalmists were clearly not enough.

What they lacked, Hitler provided. After 1932, the number of Jewish immigrants fleeing from Nazi persecution rose rapidly; and they went to Palestine because Britain and America, who favoured the idea of a "Nation Home" would not accept Jewish refugees; though, if given the choice, the refugees would have preferred going to those countries rather than to inhospitable Palestine. Because of this deliberate channeling of the refugee flow away from Europe, the Jewish population in Palestine had increased dramatically by 1942 to 484,000 or thirty per cent of the population.

The Palestinians had already given violent expression to their rejection of the pro-Jewish policy of the Mandatory regime in 1920, in 1921 and 1929 in what were euphemistically called "disturbances."

Faced with the distinct possibility, after 1932, of eventually being outnumbered in their own land by a flood of foreigners from Europe, the deep-rooted fears of the Palestinians erupted in 1936 in what has been called "The Arab Rebellion." It lasted for three years and by the end, Britain had to put about 100,000 troops into Palestine. In one year alone, 1938, the official casualty figures, which err on the side of moderation, was 1600 Arabs killed. It was during the first year of the

Rebellion, in 1936, that Bechara Sirhan earned his commendation for repairing water pipes blown up by his compatriots.

Faced with this massive protest from within Palestine, under pressure from other Arab countries, and with World War II looming on the horizon, the British government changed its course. In 1939, it issued a White Paper which severely limited further Jewish immigration and the sale of land in Palestine to Jews. Jewish opposition to this new policy was stifled by the outbreak of war, with Jewry cooperating with Britain in the fight against the greater enemy, Hitler. The Arabs too changed from opposition to passive neutrality.

This uneasy lull continued until the end of 1945 and it was during this period that Sirhan Sirhan was born.

However, the Jewish terrorist groups, Irgun Zvai Leumi and the Stern gang, did not observe any truce during the war years. Nor did the official Zionist organization desist from trying to bring in Jewish immigrants in defiance of the 1939 White Paper. In November, 1940, the immigrants on one of the ships, "The Patria," when refused permission to land in Palestine, blew up the ship and themselves in Haifa harbour and 250 persons died. In October, 1944, two young members of the Stern gang killed Lord Moyne, the British Resident Minister in the Middle East, in Cairo.

After the end of the war in Europe, the newly elected Labour Party government in Britain announced that, despite its previous pro-Zionist stand, it would abide by the 1939 White Paper recommendations. The entire Zionist organisation in Palestine began a campaign of violent resistance in October, 1945, and this reached such paralysing dimensions that Britain referred the Palestine issue to the United Nations in February, 1947. In November of that year, the General Assembly, under intense pressure from President Truman, who was seeking re-election in the United States, and after various dubious manoeuvres, voted by 33 for, 13 against and 10 abstentions to partition Palestine into separate Arab and Jewish states. Not one of the Asian member states voted in favour of the creation of this new state in Asia.

1948 was a Presidential election year, so too, 1956 and 1968, all years of crisis in the Middle East: after the War, the domestic politics of America and the Palestine Problem were tightly intertwined.

When the British finally quit Palestine, they had fully carried out their side of the 1917 Compact because, thanks to their protection, the composition of the population of Palestine had been altered so drastically that a Jewish State was now possible. Under the British Mandate, the Jews had increased by 600,000 and of these, 484,000 were immigrants; of these foreign settlers, eighty per cent came into West Asia from Europe.

In the collection of Zionist myths, those of The Promise and of The Return are the most important. On a lower level, but of considerable practical value, has been the myth of The Venal Arab—that the Jews had a new right to Palestine based on the purchase of much of this land, at exorbitant prices, from venal, unpatriotic Palestinians; and that the funds for these purchases came from poor Jews the world over.* However, the unromantic land records of the British administration show that up to 1948, the Jews, despite large and tempting offers, could acquire only 5.6 per cent of Palestinian territory and of this area less than two per cent was bought by them from Palestinians. The Palestinian peasant proved that he could say, with Sirhan, "I love my country." The British could bring Jews into Palestine but both of them together could not get the Palestinian to move off the land to make way for the Jew. It took organised expulsions to do that.

The Jeruslaem into which Sirhan Sirhan was born in 1944 was then, as it is now, though much changed, the most marvellous city on earth. Its core is the Old City, surrounded by massive walls of golden-hued stone built in the 16th century by Suleiman the Magnificent. These are pierced by seven gates, the best known being the Damascus Gate to the north and the Jaffa Gate to the west. Within the walls the tempo and quality of life was and is much the same as it was in the time of the Crusaders, or even earlier.

"Without the City Wall" is the new city where the Palestinians lived in older areas more or less adjacent to the Old City to the west and south-west and the Jews in the more modern quarters to the north-west. The Musrara quarter was a mixed one of Arabs and Jews lying to the north-west of and close to the Damascus Gate.

* A particularly eloquent version of this myth is given by A. Koestler in his book, *Thieves In The Night.*

After 1932, the large influx of middle class Jews from Germany and Central Europe produced a veneer of cultural sophistication on the city's rather stolid provincialism. The war years greatly added to the cosmopolitan glamour of Jerusalem for soldiers from many nations served or vacationed in Palestine. They brought to it a quality of youthful gaity that heightened the atmosphere of harsh solemnity that normally broods over this city. But it was a discreet gaity, for things, like nightclubs and cabarets, were forbidden in the Holy City, and have been permitted only since the Israeli annexation in 1968.

But the social whirl of wartime Jerusalem had little relevance to the sober, simple life led by the Sirhan family dwelling side by side with their Jewish neighbours on St. Paul's Street in Musrara.

The slow, bloody tearing apart of Palestine, which is what partition meant, impinged with brutal directness on the life of the young Sirhan in December, 1947, when he was three years and ten months old.

The first shots in the preliminary phase of the First Battle for Palestine were fired in Jerusalem on November 30th, the day after the United Nations adopted its Partition Resolution; and violent incidents were recorded that day from Tel Aviv, Haifa and Lydda as well. According to the editorial writer of the Jewish-owned and edited *Palestine Post*, the Arabs in Jerusalem "went over to the offensive" on December 1st. In the issue of January 30th, 1948, he lists the following incidents: on December 1, Jewish houses near the Jaffa Gate were stoned; on December 2, Palestinians burned and looted the Jewish Commercial Centre; on December 3, three Jews were wounded when Palestinians fired on the Jewish Quarter in the Old City; on December 10, Jewish transport was fired on near the Jaffa Gate; and on December 11, Palestinians crossed roof-tops in the Old City to storm the Jewish Quarter. According to official figures, two Jews were killed and three injured in these four incidents.

In three "reprisal" bombing attacks on December 13th and 29th and January 7th, according to official figures, the Jews killed 35 Palestinian Arabs and wounded 123.

Sirhan Sirhan and his father narrowly escaped being killed in the bombing incident of December 29th.

These three attacks were made on the same sort of target and were all executed in the same way. The targets were crowds of Palestinian civilians standing at bus stations, the first two at the Damascus Gate and the third at the Jaffa Gate. The method was hit-and-run: to throw bombs, that is, sticks of dynamite or a barrel filled with dynamite, into the crowd from a passing vehicle,—taxis at the Damascus Gate and a stolen armoured car at the Jaffa Gate (after Jewish taxis had been forbidden to ply because of the earlier incidents).

The Palestine Post of December 14th gives this description of the first, December 13th, incident: "5 Arabs were killed and 47 were injured [the final figures were seven and 54, respectively] when two bombs thrown from two speeding cars exploded among crowds standing near the Damascus Gate bus station just after noon. Eye-witnesses claim the attackers were Jewish and that the two cars also opened fire with automatic weapons as they disappeared towards Herod's Gate. The entire area was thrown into a panic by the explosions and the street was littered with wounded who were rushed to Government and French hospitals. The explosions dug 20 centimetre holes into the road and the walls of nearby buildings were marked by flying shrapnel."

The Damascus Gate is by far the biggest and busiest, the most elaborate and the most beautiful of all of Jerusalem's gates. It is a minor masterpiece in its combination of solidity and grace, the solidity of its strongly-proportioned facade and of the arched portal itself and the grace of its fluted cornices and the airy crenelations of its battlements. The tourist is surprised to discover that it actually functions as a door to the city—it opens and shuts: the leaves of the nail-studded doors are so massive that one assumes they could never be shut but would stand perpetually ajar. But in times of trouble for Jerusalem, the Damascus Gate does shut its doors and those seeking admittance bang on it with their fists and shout and are then, perhaps, admitted through the low postern set into the main doors. Within the square structure of the Gate building, the roadway from outside turns sharp left and then sharp right into Suq Khan el Zeit (the Market of the Oil Inn) which is the Old City's main shopping centre. These two bends have always been lined with the booths of money changers, confectioners and haberdashers.

The outward aspect of the Damascus Gate loses something of its impressiveness because one approaches it down a short, sharp slope; and also because the slope and the wide road-junction above are busy, noisy places. In 1947, buses gathered there; now it is the gathering place for taxis. But today as yesterday, the same cries are raised—"two seats for Bethlehem, one seat for Jericho" and so on. Because of recent excavations along the front wall of the Gate a rather fussy arrangement of short flights of steps has now been constructed between the main road and the doorway. But in 1947, the curve of the slope was unbroken except for the waiting buses, with people going in and out along two long, shallow flights of steps that curved in from left and right. It was at this spot—a strange combination of bustling modernity and medieval dignity, that the Palestine Problem nearly cut short the life of one small Palestinian boy called Sirhan Sirhan.

Before giving Bechara Sirhan's account of what happened there on December 29th, it would, perhaps be useful to set down two descriptions of the incident as given by American, Jewish and Palestinian newspapers. The official figure for casualties was eleven Palestinians dead and 32 wounded.

The New York Times of December 30th has the headline "Irgun Bomb Kills 11 Arabs, 2 Britons" and the story reads: "A bomb thrown by the Jewish terrorist organization Irgun Zvai Leumi from a speeding taxi today killed eleven Arabs and two British policemen and wounded at least thirty-two Arabs by the Jerusalem Damascus Gate, the same place where a similar bombing took place sixteen days ago . . . Irgun's bombing of a crowd around Damascus Gate has dangerously aroused Arab feeling. A green taxi rolled past Damascus Gate at half past noon and a bomb was thrown into the crowd waiting at the Arab bus stop. The occupants also opened fire on the bystanders and both British policemen killed were victims of bullets rather than bomb fragments, according to the official report. A police car gave chase but the killers' taxi escaped."

The Jewish account, in *The Palestine Post* of December 30th says this: "A bomb attack at Damascus Gate at 12:40 yesterday morning resulted in the deaths of 15 Arabs and injuries to about 50 more . . . Riding in a green taxi, three Jews—two of them reportedly wearing tarbushes—dashed past the Arab National Guard at the New

Gate, continued down Suleiman's Way and tossed out a bomb near the bus station. The streets, crowded with Arabs waiting for buses to all parts of the country, were turned into shambles. Six Arabs were killed outright. Trucks, cars, Police vehicles and R.A.F. transport were used to rush the injured to the French and Government Hospitals, and an Arab girl and a British constable who were shot a few minutes later, were taken to the Hadassah Hospital. As the car sped away, Police, R.A.F. men and Arabs opened fire at it, and the gangsters replied. Their vehicle outpaced a pursuing Police car and was later found abandoned, its windowscreen smashed, near St. George's Cathedral . . . A few minutes after the attack, an anonymous call was received by Jerusalem newspaper offices from a person who claimed that the attack had been carried out by the I.Z.L. Indiscriminate firing continued near Damascus Gate for some time, and it was at this stage that the two British Policemen were fatally wounded. Armoured cars were in action against mobs of angry Arabs." Among the names of the dead listed by *The Post* are "Sua'al Amashe, 10 . . . Nawal Shama'a, 11, of Jerusalem, and "the bodies of a man and a child [were] still unidentified."

The Palestinian account is given in the two Arabic-language newspapers *Falastin* and *Al-Difa,* both of December 30th. The two papers carry much the same story with *Falastin* the more detailed. A new piece of information which they add is that at about 12:30 a Jewish taxi parked at a nearby crossing and three Jews got out of it and left. Because this seemed suspicious, the Police and Army stopped traffic and searched the taxi only to find it empty, "the Jews meaning this to be a trick so as to draw attention away from the surprise they were planning for the crowd at the Damascus Gate. There they opened fire with automatic weapons, and taking advantage of the panic this caused, they threw a large bomb from the car into the crowd. This rolled down the square which is built on a slope and exploded and was heard all over the city. Pieces of shrapnel from the bomb reached as far as the Musrara Quarter. The square was filled with the cries of women and children and the ground was splattered with their blood . . . An Arab driver followed the criminals' car and said that the terrorists left it near Mea Shearim and from there fled into the quarter. He brought the car to the Damascus Gate and set it on fire." The casualty figures quoted in

Falastin are 18 killed, including two children and three teen-agers and 27 wounded; *Al-Difa* says there were 14 killed and 30 wounded.

By some strange chance we have no less than two different photographs of the aftermath of this bombing incident. One is in *The New York Times* of January 4th, 1948; the other is in the selection of illustrations that precedes the test of *The Faithful City* by Dov Joseph, the first mayor of Jewish Jerusalem.* They both show, against the background of the Damascus Gate, the Jewish taxi burning, with Arabs and British security forces milling around it. The camera never lies, we are told, though it can quite often; but the captions to photographs definitely can. *The New York Times* caption reads, "British troops standing by last Monday to prevent further rioting as a taxi, set afire by the Arabs, burns in Jerusalem. This was immediately after raiders of the underground organization had rolled a large barrel filled with explosives down a slope where it detonated after reaching the crowded gate area. Thirteen were killed by the blast." The Dov Joseph caption reads, quite simply, "Arabs burning automobile in presence of British policeman." *Supressio veri.*

The Dov Joseph illustration could have perpetrated one of the minor curiosities of history: If at any time during the ten minutes it took for the taxi to burn, the photographer had swung his camera a little to the right, he might have captured an unusual fringe incident,—a small man leading by the hand a still smaller boy, blindfolded with a white handkerchief, hurrying up the right-hand steps leading from the gate. They were Bechara and Sirhan Sirhan going home to Musrara.

This is what Bechara Sirhan had to say of their involvement in the ghastly violence outside the Damascus Gate on that cold, sunny winter's morning. (We know it was sunny for the shadows in the photographs are clear and black overcoats against Jerusalem's biting cold are very much in evidence). "I was going to the suq to buy coffee and a few other things for the house and took Sirhan with me. We were just about to go into the Gate when I heard people shouting. I looked back and saw something black being thrown out of a car. It began to roll down the slope and then it exploded with a great bang. I picked up Sirhan and ran into the Gate and then to the left. He seemed to have fainted. I

* Simon and Schuster, New York, 1960.

was mad with anger. I laid Sirhan down on a shelf. He wasn't hurt anywhere but his eyes were shut. I rubbed his face and his hands. After a few minutes his eyes opened and I asked him, 'Sirhan do you feel any pain?' And he answered, 'No, Daddy.' I kept on rubbing his hands and his body. Then he got up and asked, 'Why do the Jews do this thing? Don't they believe in Christ?' You see, right from the beginning we taught all our children to love Christ and follow his wonderful teachings and to love everyone. I asked him if he could walk by himself or whether he wanted me to carry him. 'I can walk,' he answered. We also trained our children to manage on their own. But when we tried to walk in the suq Sirhan felt giddy so I carried him and decided to go home. Sometimes he walked, sometimes I carried him. When we went out of the Gate, there was a terrible sight. Though many cars and ambulances had taken away those killed and injured, there was still blood on the road and people with wounds and with broken limbs. I saw flesh and bones. Everybody was shouting and crying. Sirhan said, 'I don't want to see this, Daddy.' So I took my handkerchief and tied it round his eyes and took him home like that."

According to Mary Sirhan, father and son were on their way to the post office in the Old City. When they returned the young Sirhan said, "Mamma, the bomb came down and made the peoples' blood run down there at the Damascus Gate." She took a blanket and covered his face. He remained in bed for two days and for a further two weeks stayed close to home.

This was only the first of five other separate incidents of violence and death that Sirhan witnessed during the last few months of the family's stay in Musrara. Sirhan's physical reaction to the powerful explosion was a normal one of shock felt by a child. His first mental reaction may seem strange, coming from a boy just approaching four years of age. But not if we take into account his precosity, his strongly religious upbringing and the events of the preceding four weeks. The Sirhan house is, as the bullet flies, only a couple of hundred yards from the Damascus Gate. The boy could not have escaped hearing the earlier bombing, on the 13th, nor the shootings back and forth in the weeks before and after. From the talk of his family and his playmates, he would have known that this was Palestinian against Jew.

On December 5th, the British government had announced that it would not help implement the United Nations Partition Plan, and on the 11th, declared its intention of abandoning the Mandate and leaving Palestine by May 15th, 1948. That was the signal for Palestinians and Jews, all across the country, to begin a monstrous game of armed "grab," each side trying to seize as much territory or as many strategic points as it could to strengthen its position before the ultimate confrontation on May 15th. The events we have described in Jerusalem in December were only the open moves in this campaign.

All during the early months of 1948, the violence increased in intensity with daily accounts of bomb and mortar attacks, shootings and minings and kidnappings. And not least in Jerusalem which was the chief prize that the sides were determined to capture.

The Musrara quarter, because it was mixed Palestinian and Jew, was an especially sensitive area, and was the scene of many armed attacks and counter-attacks. "This was not a regular war," Mr. Sirhan explained, "it was a sort of gang warfare. We never knew when fighting would start and we would suddenly find bullets flying and bombs falling about us. This went on for weeks and weeks. We could only guess that the Jews were going to make a big attack when our Jewish neighbours, warned in advance, would start moving out."

The second tragic incident that Sirhan witnessed struck directly at the family because this was the violent death of his elder brother, "the first Munir, whom I never forget," to use the words of Mrs. Sirhan.

Because St. Paul's Street was an important road in a fringe area, the British had placed a barbed-wire barricade across it—"high as a man stands with his hands up"—at which vehicles and pedestrians could be stopped and checked. One day when Sirhan and Munir, who was about four years Sirhan's senior, were playing in the street, firing suddenly broke out and an Army truck, trying to get out of the line of fire, swerved hard around the barrier, hit Munir and killed him on the spot. It was Sirhan who ran home and told his mother "Munir is killed" and when his brother's body was lifted up, Sirhan, reliving the Damascus Gate incident, said, "It's the same bomb, Mamma." Even after twenty years Sirhan was able to recall the memory of himself walking round the burial casket of his brother. In later years, according to his mother,

Sirhan would ask, "Mamma, why is Munir taking so long to come back. Can't he come so I can play with him?" So she named her next son Munir: "Jesus took that one and he sent this to your Mamma," she told the boy. "I couldn't find any other way to comfort Sirhan."

The four other incidents did not bring personal suffering but were no less tragic and violent. It was, once again, the barbed-wire barrier on St. Paul's Street that was the scene of the event. By some unhappy mischance, it was Sirhan—of all the children in the family—who one morning saw the body of a neighbour, Abu Aziz, the grocer, lying near the wire. At first Sirhan thought he was merely asleep but then he saw the pool of blood and ran and told his mother, "It happened to him like what happened to my brother Munir, he is dead, he is dead." (The Sirhans do not mention the cause of this death: perhaps he was shot for breaking the night curfew that was frequently imposed on Musrara).

Mrs. Sirhan in her fluent but not always grammatical English, gives a particularly vivid account of a gruesome incident which the whole family witnessed. At this distance of time the precise details are not clear in Mrs. Sirhan's mind but she says that a group of Jewish gild soldiers entered the offices of a British Army unit which were on the two top floors of the building in which the Sirhan family lived. She believes their intention was either to dynamite those offices or to use them as a vantage point for an attack on the radio station that was (and still is) in a building lower down the steeply-sloping road. "We had our bathroom a little bit outside," asserts Mrs. Sirhan, "and I was bathing the children. When I took one to the house inside I saw the girl soldiers coming to take the view from our window. From the window they could see the street and whoever comes for help, they could stop it. Well, there was a soldier who had been on the top of the radio station watching; he was a watchman there, he saw them; they were going to put the dynamite in that building, so he came down himself and the dyna-mite exploded at the moment he was on the street. That man became . . . I don't know how many pieces you could count his body. His leg was hanging up on the tower of one church we had there for the Anglicans; his leg with his shoe was hanging up there on the bell. In the morning, after the curfew when everybody was allowed to move a little bit, we found a finger of that soldier right in our own back yard. Sirhan when he saw that thing got really pale. Everybody in the street and the children were looking up at that leg in the tower. I couldn't stop Sirhan from seeing it because he looked up too. He said, 'Is that from the bomb we heard yesterday? Look at the foot, because of the boot it will show that he is a soldier up there,"—Sirhan was obviously referring to the heavy, hobnailed "ammunition boots" then worn by British soldiers.

Not long after this the Zionists sent a truck loaded with dynamite rolling down the street, aimed, perhaps, at the radio station. "It went off with a hard explosion," according to Mary Sirhan. "And when he heard it Sirhan screamed, shaking and covering his face and eyes on my lap. Next morning we saw three houses destroyed just around the corner and for some weeks Sirhan did not pass in that street unless I carried him in my arms."

The last of the violent incidents witnessed by the Sirhans in Musrara was the aftermath of one of the most ghastly incidents of the Zionist-Arab for Palestine—the slaughter of the innocents at Deir Yassin. The small village of Deir Yassin—its very name tolls like a knell through this period of Palestinian history—lies just west of Jerusalem above the road to Tel Aviv, for the control of which hard battles were being fought at the near-by village of Castel. Many of the Palestinian fighters at Castel were villagers from Deir Yassin. On the 10th of April 1948 (Mrs. Sirhan still recalls that dreadful date without any prompting) the Irgun and Stern gang attacked Deir Yassin. They met little or no opposition for the men were away at Castel. The old men, women and children remaining in Deir Yassin, 254 in all, were massacred and their bodies were thrown down a well where the chief Red Cross representative discovered them despite obstacles put in his way by the local Zionist authorities.* Nor was this all. Perhaps an even worse fate awaited the young women and girls in Deir Yassin whom the Zionists did not kill. Mrs. Sirhan, and Sirhan too, saw them later that day in Jerusalem. In her words, "Passing along our street were open trucks and in them were the Palestinian girls from Deir Yassin. They were naked and they had their breasts cut. They were crying and ashamed to stand, and they were

---

* Jacques de Reynier: "A Jerusalem un drapeau flottait sur la ligne de feu." Geneva, 1950.

going on the street so everybody could see them. I saw the girls trying to hide themselves . . . They were naked and the Zionists were laughing and clapping hands. There was not only Haganah parties, there were two or three other parties (the reference is to the Irgun and Stern) and they were clapping hands and saying, 'See what will happen to your girls,' because they do know that we do care for our girls. Sirhan was with me and I tried to take my son and go, and I tried to hide his face so he couldn't see it, and I wasn't sure if he did. He must have, because of the noise, they were clapping hands, because he said, 'Mamma, look at the blood.' "

Sirhan both saw and remembered, but the perfervid imagination of the child heightened the horror because both then and much later he would talk of actually having seen a Jewish soldier cutting an Arab woman's breast.

(The Irgun and Stern at first claimed credit for this massacre, and then later said it was done on orders of the Jewish Agency. This Agency denounced this action but the Israeli High Court later ruled that the Jewish Agency was fully responsible for it. The leader of Irgun, Menachim Begin has been a cabinet minister in the Israeli government since June 1967. The Israelis have since converted Deir Yassin into a lunatic asylum).

And yet, during these months, normal life, of a sort, continued. "Sirhan," his father went on, "used to go to a small kindergarten which a lady organised in her house not far from ours. One day after school, Sirhan was just entering the front door when a mortar bomb fell in the street. Perhaps because of this bomb, or because of fright, the boy fell down the steps leading into the passage and bruised his face."

Mr. Sirhan continued. "One day Sirhan came running home from school; very excited and upset, he told us, 'I saw a Jewish man cutting an Arab woman.' "

"What exactly did he see," I asked. "Didn't you try to find out?"

His father replied, "No, his mother and I never encouraged the children to talk about violence or killing. If we had asked questions, it would have increased the child's fear. We always tried to make the incidents seem small. We kept telling them not to be afraid, not to hate anyone and that God would protect us."

This simple faith did not, unfortunately, stand up to the pressure of events. On Saturday, May 15th, the life that the Sirhan family had led in the area "without the City wall" drew to a close in violence, terror and flight.

As we have said, the Musrara quarter stands on high ground, overlooking a depression that leads to the Damascus Gate; it commands the north-western approaches to that strategic point and was therefore of considerable military value to both sides. If captured by the Jews, it could have been the rallying point for an attack on the Old City where the Jewish Quarter was already beleaguered by Palestinian partisans. If captured by the Palestinians, it could have frustrated any such attack and enabled them to advance into Jewish areas in the New City.

In particular, the small open space, with the pine trees, behind the Sirhan house, was a desirable military objective because, in this built-up area, it provided a clear field of fire. It became the focal point for some of the local fighting.

On the morning of May 14th when the last British forces left, the Jews began what they called "Operation Pitchfork," a three-pronged assault from the west on the Palestinian-held areas. The Jewish forces met with some resistance on the southern sector, but none at all in the central salient because the British, by pre-arrangement with the Jews, and taking the Palestinians by surprise, handed over the complex of principal government buildings to the Jews without a shot being fired. Things were very different in the area of the northern Jewish prong which was aimed through Musrara at the Damascus Gate, and through Mea Shearim at Sheikh Jarrah and the Hebrew University on Mount Scopus.

Dov Joseph* describes the general battle situation:

"For the sixty hours from Friday morning [the 14th] until Sunday night [the 16th] the entire city was like a single front, with firing throughout the area, fighting being fiercer at one point, then at another, and shells bursting throughout the night." A vivid detailed description of the fighting in the immediate vicinity of the Sirhan house is given by Harry Levin in *Jerusalem Embattled*:†

* *Op. Cit.*, p. 132.
† Gollancz, London. 1950. pp. 159–60.

"Through peepholes and between sandbags we saw the battle area. St. Paul's Road and the Street of the Prophets where we were, is a kind of cross-roads for mortar shells and bullets . . . Hardly a minute of quiet. We seemed to be in the centre of a circle of fire, one semi-circle Jewish, the other Arab. A couple of score of yards to our right a battle was going on across St. Paul's Road."

The Sirhan house, on St. Paul's Road and about a hundred yards from its junction with Prophets' Street, must have been almost in the dead centre of that "circle of fire." This was the night of May 15th. Later, Levin goes on, "a loudspeaker burst out in Arabic. Haganah broadcasting to civilian Arabs, urging them to leave the district before 5:15 am: 'Take pity on your wives and children and get out of this blood bath,' it said. 'Surrender to us with your arms. No harm will come to you. Or get out by the Jericho road, that is still open to you.' "

And how did the Sirhan family fare in the middle of this prolonged and hard-fought battle? "For two days and nights, without any stopping, the Jews used bombs and mortars and shot machineguns all around the house," Bechara Sirhan said. "When there was very much firing, we told the children to stand in the corners, because the British had told us that corners were safe places. But for how long can a child keep standing? We made them sleep on the floor in the corners. It was unbearable. Once when the firing was less, a woman who lived above us looked out on to the street and saw an officer and she called on him to arrange for the fighting to stop so that we could get away." The Haganah announcement may have been the result of some such appeal or a psychological move to get the Palestinians out. "When we left, we went as we were," Mr. Sirhan continued. "I was in my nightsuit and my slippers. I didn't even have time to put my shoes on. We just ran from the house. I held a child in either hand. Everything we had we left behind." Mrs. Sirhan remembers that it was 4 a.m. when they left, "I had a baby in my arms. Part of the way we crawled on hands and feet." And Sirhan's recollection: "I remember that it was in a hurry, it was in a rush, it was in a state of panic that we moved. I was naked at the time." This was how the Sirhans, stumbling through the night, went through the City walls and into a new, uncertain life as refugees. They left more than their material possessions behind them.

During Sirhan's trial this exchange took place between Mrs. Sirhan and her son's lawyer:

Now, when you left that house did you expect to go back to it?

We tried to. But how can we? We didn't have it. We didn't have . . .

Well, did you expect to go back to it?

Yes, my husband thought it would be only two days. We had locked very good. We took the keys.

You never returned to it?

Never.

Why didn't you return?

How can we? We have no . . . They drove us out from our homes. They drove us out from our land which we call home. We didn't have anything, where to go or what to do, where to eat, where to sleep.

Thus the Sirhans, like many thousands of Palestinians, careful to the last, meticulously locked up everything in their homes and took the keys with them in the vain hope of a quick return.

Should and could, the Sirhans have stuck it out in their Musrara home and thus avoided becoming refugees? Hardly. A family with young children, they had already endured two days of noisy danger and if they had stayed, they would have had to endure it for a further three days, because the fighting in Musrara went on till the 18th, and, until the end, the area remained divided between the combatants. When the armistice lines were finally drawn one of them ran at the foot of the slope on which their house stood; the opposite slope, up to the Damascus Gate was designated as "No Man's Land." It may be mentioned that, according to Dov Joseph,* the Jewish authorities, as early as April, "withdrew part of the Jewish population from mixed quarters."

In any case, the Israelis have not permitted any Palestinians to live so near the Armistice Line in Jerusalem, so the Sirhans would have had to move eventually.

They fled directly eastward because they had no place to go. Westward lay Jewish areas and there was fighting going on to the north and south. And if the Sirhans went into the Old City rather than down the

* *Op. Cit.*, p. 73.

road to Jericho, as so helpfully suggested by the Haganah broadcast, it was because, for a Jerusalemite, the Old City is the real Jerusalem and its splendidly solid walls are the ultimate symbol of strength and protection. There was a Palestinian fighting force inside the Old City, and, also, some of the Sirhan family's relatives.

In Pasadena some friends of the Sirhans repeated to me a story they had been told by the eldest brothers of their part in the events of May, 1948. It is an account curiously full of circumstantial detail. According to it, Sharif and Saadallah actually took part in the fighting and at least one of them, Sharif, was wounded. He showed people the scars of wounds on his legs. According to them, their father told them, "Don't kill the Israeli boys; shoot at their legs; they are the same people as us; someone has incited them." This advice sounds authentic because it accords with the pacifist sentiments of the Sirhan parents. I asked Sharif to confirm this story when I spoke to him on the phone, but this was one of the questions that were met with silence. Mr. Sirhan clearly denied that his sons had fought at all, but said that they could very well have been wounded because during the final two days of their life in Musrara, there were lots of ricochetting bullets, pieces of shrapnel and splinters of stone from the building flying around. This particular point remains a minor mystery for the time being.

These incidents from December, 1947 to May, 1948, have been described at some length because through them Sirhan Sirhan and his family became involved personally and directly in the tragic history of their country. It has been said by some that it is not possible for a child who was between three years and ten months and four years and two months in age to recall in later years what he witnessed or experienced as so young a child. This is not correct, for many children do recall certain things that happen to them after their third year, especially if these are frightening or unusual experiences. I, for instance, can recall in vivid detail my first day in school when I was three and a half years old, mainly, I think, because it was for me a thoroughly searing experience. But it was not remotely comparable in intensity with what Sirhan went through—the panic of the flight from the house, the knifing of the woman, the incident of the mortar bomb and that of the explosion at the Damascus Gate.

I asked the father if Sirhan remembered these happenings and he replied "As you know, we never encouraged the children to talk about or remember violent things, but Sirhan never forgot what happened. Over and over again months later, he would ask me, "Daddy, why did the Jews do that to us? I had to leave my toys. The Jews are now playing with my toys.' Or he would say, 'What kind of people are the Jews who throw bombs at other people? Don't they know anything about God and Christ?' Sirhan's question was always, 'Why did it happen? Why? Why?' "

The depth of the impression made on Sirhan by these events and the continuing fear that their memory aroused is indicated by this recollection of his father: "The day after we arrived in Pasadena, and Sirhan was nearly thirteen then, he asked me, 'Do you think there will be any bombs here, Daddy? I hope not.' " He recalled the stabbing of the woman to several persons, as, for instance, in 1967, to the wife of his last employer.

One of the prosecuting lawyers during Sirhan's trial suggested that Sirhan "was just a frightened little boy back there in Jerusalem." On which remark Dr. Bernard Diamond, one of the innumerable psychiatrists involved in the trial, made this comment, "It's my opinion that he was much more than a frightened little boy. War does more than frighten little boys. It psychologically damages them . . . It psychologically damaged all the other four year olds in Jerusalem to some degree."

But almost certainly not to the same degree as Sirhan, who, by mischance, witnessed so much bloodshed.

History is full of ironies and among them will certainly be accounted the numerous, and uncanny resemblances between Sirhan Sirhan and the two young Jews of the Stern Gang who killed Lord Moyne in 1944.

The most striking of these resemblances concerns the younger of the two, Eliyahu Hakim of Haifa: "When the passengers aboard the "S. S. Patria" blew themselves up in Haifa Harbour on the morning of November 25, 1940 [Hakim was then fourteen years old], he stood on the terrace of his home on Panorama Road, high above the bay, watching the terrible scene through binoculars . . . He saw the wreckage: he saw the headless bodies of men, women and children fished from the water with fishhooks . . . If he would never forget the sight, he would never forget the name MacMichael"* (the British High Commissioner in Palestine at the time). Arthur Koestler affirms that "according to a statement of the members of his [Hakim's] family to this writer, [he] had never recovered mentally from the consequence of the shock."†

There would seem to be complete parallelism between Eliyahu Hakim seeing Jews die in Haifa harbour and Sirhan Sirhan seeing, and then shutting his eyes to, the blood and wounds of Palestinians at the Damascus Gate. But the comparison would be more accurate if Hakim had been younger and more impressionable; if the Jews had not blown themselves up but had been blown up by a Palestinian bomb; and if Hakim did not witness the event from a distance through binoculars but had been present on the wharfside and narrowly escaped death from the bomb.

Despite these crucial points of difference, the similarity between the incidents is striking enough.

An epitaph on the life that the Sirhans led in Musrara, reasonably happy and settled as far as we know, is provided by a group photograph of the family taken in 1947. It shows the parents with their six young children, Munir still an infant held in his mother's arms. It is the usual stiff and ritualistic picture taken on such occasions with everyone in their Sunday best staring straight into the eye of the camera; the one thing that lightens it is a wide, mischevious grin on the face of the daughter, Aida. Sirhan, still with the puppy-fat of childhood, sits especially solemn in a zipped-up snow suit next to his father. It is a group of small, dark people. The one strong impression the picture gives is that there is a solidly respectable family. The Sirhans, after 1948, were never to be quite that ever again.

In May, 1948, Robert Kennedy, 23 years old and a senior at

* *The Deed*, pp. 171–72.
† *Promise and Fullfilment*, p. 94.

Harvard, was in Palestine reporting for the *Boston Post* on the country's violent disintegration.

But we must now turn to following the fortunes of the Sirhan family as, amid the continuing clangour of battle without and within the City walls, they began a very different sort of life in very different surroundings.

3

The Expellees

The Old City of Jerusalem, within the walls, is, in its physical fabric, still a perfect example of a medieval Middle Eastern town. It is a city of stone. Its tightly packed houses are built of stone, and its narrow, winding streets are cobbled with stone. Since Jerusalem is "a city set on a hill," these streets are often long, muscle-stretching flights of steps. In 1948, it was divided into a Muslim quarter, a Christian quarter, a Jewish quarter and an Armenian quarter, which huddled around the great shrines of these faiths—the Dome of the Rock, the Church of the Holy Sepulchre and the Hurva Synagogue.

With pilgrims thronging here from the four corners of the globe one, perforce, has to rub shoulders in the crowded suqs with people of every race and colour, wearing a fascinating variety of clothes, and speaking a bewildering variety of tongues.

If despite this motley throng, Old Jerusalem has always been a Palestinian rather than an international city it is because it has retained its own essential character, many-coloured and overpoweringly strong.

Jerusalem lives off the foreigner, but it has for them the same lofty disdain that Venice has for the tourist, only more so.

Motor vehicles cannot be used in its narrow streets so the means of haulage are women's heads, the back of porters and the panniers of donkeys. Every so often one has to dodge into a shopfront or flatten oneself against a wall to avoid the donkeys which the Jerusalemites drive through the crowds with unheeding speed. The Jerusalem fire brigade had to evolve a special hand-drawn water pump to cope with the Old City.

In the early hours of May 15th, the streets were empty of people except for those fleeing or fighting, and the fire fighters were very much in evidence because a particularly stubborn and ferocious battle was being fought out within the Old City. Showing great courage, the 1,200 Jews in the Jewish Quarter were holding out against all attempts by the Arabs to capture the area, whilst Jewish forces outside made repeated assaults on the walls in attempts to break through and link up. All these attacks were beaten back but it was only on May 28th that the Jewish quarter surrendered, after the synagogue and much of the area had been destroyed.

As soon as the fighting ended, Jerusalem was formally split into two cities—Arab and Jewish—with miles of barbed wire bordering a meandering stretch of No Man's Land. It became the world's first divided city. Fourteen years before the Berlin Wall, a high, solid stone wall cut across roads and back gardens. The left hand curve of steps up from the Damascus Gate which the Sirhans had used on December 29th, disappeared beneath this wall. Sirhan was never again able to visit his childhood home.

For these first two or three weeks, perhaps a month, when fighting continued within the old city, the Sirhans lived, helter skelter fashion, in the Greek Orthodox Convent of St. Nicholas, which had hurriedly been converted into a reception centre. Mrs. Sirhan describes the conditions: "There were thousands and thousands of people living in that building, all refugees ... It was used as a school and part of it as a hospital, but the hospital moved away and it was empty; there was a big hole in it from the shooting ... Each family had a small space on the floor ... We have nothing then. We have only our children. Some of us brought a coat and some did not. We didn't even have a blanket to put on my baby."

Thereafter they were allotted one room in a house that still stands, derelict now, on the corner of Suq al Husroor and Al Malak Street. A few doors away are houses ruined in the 1948 fighting.

Having lost everything, they had to begin life again at the beginning. "Everything was changed for us," Mr. Sirhan said. "In Musrara we had a home, with furniture and other things. Now we had nothing but an empty room. Of course Sirhan noticed the difference, how could he not? We all did."

I found Bechara Sirhan reluctant to talk about the nine years that followed, perhaps because they were years of privation and unhappiness for the family. With the withdrawal of the Mandatory regime, the elder Sirhan had, after 22 years service, lost his job, and with it the security and minor prestige of government service. Hundreds of ex-government employees like him were out of work and only a few could be absorbed into the attenuated services of the Jordan government that took over Jerusalem and the area called the West Bank. Mr. Sirhan said that soon after the flight, he went to Amman and obtained employment there in the Public Works Department but that job did not last for very long; nor did any of the other jobs he managed to find; in fact, for most of this nine-year period, the head of the Sirhan family was unemployed, which was particularly galling for someone who had been a conscientious worker.

It was from one of the Sirhans' neighbours, a Mr. Hashimeh, that I learned something of their life during these years. I had been trying to locate where the Sirhans lived, and it is characteristic of Jerusalem's indifference to the passing world that though the whole world had by then been informed that Sirhan Sirhan once lived on that particular street, English-speaking shopkeepers a hundred yards down the Suq Al Hasroor did not know where the Sirhan home had been.

My query to yet another shopkeeper, a one-eyed man, was answered by a man, neatly dressed in a suit and tie, sitting on a petrol can beside the door in the narrow street. "That's where the Sirhans lived," he said, pointing up to the first floor of a house ten feet away. "I was their neighbour for six years. I knew them well—as well as one could know them."

For over an hour, standing on the corner (there was no where else to go) at the crossing of the narrow suq and the still narrower Al Malak Street, Mr. Hashimeh spoke to me in the same correct but careful English that Bechara Sirhan used, a residual result of the former British presence.

Since newspaper accounts had alternated in saying that the Sirhans had lived in the Jewish and the Armenian quarters, I asked Mr. Hashimeh to clear up this confusion first. "This road was in the Jewish quarter," he said, "and Jews lived in these houses before we came. But it is on the border of the Armenian quarter and this house we lived in is owned by an Armenian convent. In fact, almost all the property in the Jewish quarter was not owned by Jews but belongs either to the Armenians or to Muslim waqfs [charitable endowments]. The house was in very bad condition even when we came. There were no shutters in the windows; the Sirhans put up wooden shutters but in our room we only had a blanket to cover the window during the first winter. The convent didn't care to repair the house and now, as you can see, it has fallen down inside." Through a gaping window, I could see a hole in the roof of the room next to the one in which the Sirhans had lived; it was almost impossible to go up to the first floor because the stairway had collapsed; only the more adventurous children managed to squeeze through. "The Armenians didn't care because they got very little rent from us; sometimes for several months we didn't pay because we had no money; when we had money, from time to time, we paid." He continued, "The house did not have electric light for many years; we had it put in when we had enough money. We got our water from a cistern in the house but it was not good for drinking; we had to bring drinking water from there, down the street." He pointed down Suq Al Husroor, away from the City's centre.

According to Ziad Hashimeh, the son of my interlocutor, who immigrated to America and testified at Sirhan's trial, nine families, a total of 50 people, lived in that single small two-storied house. Sirhan himself mentioned seven or eight families. For all of them there was one small toilet on a landing of the stairway which the municipality would come and clean when it became too evil-smelling and overflowed into the streets. Mrs. Sirhan recalls, incorrectly, that their room had only three walls—she was probably referring to the gaping windows. "We had to renovate the building," her son says, "cement it, whitewash it and clean it up." Just how tightly packed the Sirhan family was in their single room is clear from this description by Sirhan: "Munir and I slept on one bed. My head at his feet, his feet at my head. We didn't have enough beds or enough room." The "beds" that Sirhan speaks of were in fact matresses with a stuffing of old clothes. The only heating they had during Jerusalem's cruelly-cold, wet winters was from an occasionally lit charcoal brazier.*

"I lived across the landing from the Sirhans, seven people in their family, ten in ours" and Mr. Hashimeh gave a shy, depreciating smile. "We lived that way for six years but we had little to do with each other. They kept to themselves—very much. They were good people; honest, correct, polite and quiet. And we would say, 'Good morning, good evening, how are you?' but we very seldom talked. This is very strange," he went on, "because when people are poor, like us refugees, we have to help each other. When one person has food and the other hasn't, we must share. When one family has illness but no medicine, if we have medicine we should give it to them. Then when we haven't food or medicines, they will try to help us in return. That's the way we lived with the other neighbours, but not with the Sirhans. When they left some Armenians took their room. They were nice and friendly. We talked and shared with them. But not with the Sirhans. They weren't unfriendly, but they were different. They came home and locked the door and stayed by themselves inside."

As he talked I could see that Mr. Hashimeh was still puzzled by what

---

* The necessity, in the United States, to balance off Arab against Jew is evident in this wildly inaccurate description of the Sirhans' new surroundings given by the senior police officer investigating the Sirhan case: "When the British left Jerusalem on May 15 Bechara and his family fled from the New City to the Old, just as so many Jews, whose homes were in the Old City, fled for their lives to the New. Soon the Sirhans had settled down in a much larger home than the one they had left, a home vacated by some Jewish family driven from it in May by the Arab Legion." Robert A. Houghton, *Special Unit Senator,* New York, 1970, p. 242. One can only hope that Mr. Houghton's professional investigations were more precise. Other versions speak of the Sirhans occupying a Jewish school and even a Jewish temple!—all giving the impression that the former Jewish occupants had, somehow, been wronged more than the Sirhans.

seemed to him this strange characteristic of the Sirhans. He still could not quite find the words to describe it—"nice people, not too proud, not unfriendly, but not wanting to mix."

I asked him why he thought the Sirhans behaved this way. His perplexity continued because he could supply no definite answer. "It may have been that they were Christians and we were all Muslims; but I don't think they felt that way." He said, "Perhaps Bechara Sirhan was angry with the whole world. Perhaps they felt ashamed. I don't know why but they locked the door."

This description of the Sirhans holding themselves apart was very familiar to me from many accounts given to me in Pasadena. They were especially aloof, people said, when they were in difficulties; and during these years in Jerusalem they were in difficulties almost all the time.

It seemed a sufficiently distinctive family characteristic for me to discuss the matter with Mr. Sirhan when I met him for the second time. I told him what his neighbours had said, in Jerusalem and Pasadena. He was slightly nettled, that something so obvious should have been made the subject of comment. "Yes it is true," he admitted. "We don't mix with other people. This is what my father taught me and what I taught my children: when people are in trouble and you can help them, then go to them and mix with them and do something. But if they do not need help, we should leave other people alone; it is not good to interfere in other people's affairs. Let them lead their lives and you lead your life." I suggested that perhaps the difference in religion played a part during the Jerusalem years. He did not accept the idea: "It is true that our religion was different and that in Palestine we Christians are only ten per cent. But that is not important. You see I have the Koran here with the Bible and I read it a lot. I behave the same way here in Taibeh. This is my village. Everyone is Christian. I was born here. But if you ask the people, 'How many people does Sirhan visit?' They will tell you, 'Very few.' I like everyone. I try and help. But I do not interfere with others."

This family characteristic of a friendly aloofness towards others is, I believe, one of the keys to the understanding of the personality of Sirhan Sirhan. It is a distinctly unusual trait in the Arab countries, as it would be in India, or the United States. It is not that in Asian countries any great value is set on positive "togetherness" as in America, but at the same time "keeping oneself to oneself" is not considered a desirable, or necessary, social quality as it is in England.

From what we know, three generations of Sirhans, at least, have exhibited this characteristic. How this one particular Palestinian family came to acquire this quite unusual quality cannot be stated with any certainty. It may have been due to a quirk in personality of the Sirhan grandfather or of some earlier Sirhan; or they may have done something of which their village of Taibeh disapproved and they then made a virtue of non-interference, out of the necessity of ostracism. To a certain extent it is my feeling that this is what Bechara Sirhan is doing in Taibeh today.

In the years after 1948, in the Old City, I do not think that the aloofness shown by the Sirhans was only due to a family tradition. There was some anger with a world that had served them so ill, some shame at the drastic change in the family fortunes, some little feeling for the difference in religious community, and much pride.

Whatever the origin, there can be no doubt that the aloofness was one of the main causes of the difficulties that the Sirhan family encountered in America, where aloofness is positively discouraged.

Incidentally, or perhaps not so incidentally, the meaning of the family name "Sirhan," was especially appropriate. One Los Angeles newspaper at first said it meant "good news" but there was, later, general agreement on saying that it meant "wanderer." That would be a fitting description of this Sirhan family, but it is not a wholly correct translation. "Sirhan" actually means "one whose attention is wandering," or, better still, "one who is abstracted, lost in thought."

The years in the Old City were, in a way, one long expression of family pride. Because of Bechara Sirhan's almost continuous unemployment, the family was very poor during this period. Many persons who knew them have affirmed this, and the family would not have lived huddled in a single room if they could possibly have afforded anything better. Yet the grandfather in Taibeh, with his land holdings, was a man of modest affluence. "Did he in any way help his son's family," I asked Mr. Hashimeh. "Not in any way that we could see," replied Mr. Hashimeh. "Why not?" I asked. He continued, "It would probably have meant that he would have had to sell some land to raise ready cash, and people who own land in our country will never sell it; they hold on to it till the end."

I questioned Mr. Sirhan on this point and he seemed surprised at my question. "Why should I ask my father for help?" he asked. "I was a grown man with a family and I alone was responsible for them. We had to meet our difficulties in our own way." This independent pride does not, however, explain why the grandfather did not volunteer assistance. In fact, there seems to have been surprising little contact between the branches of the family in Jerusalem and in Taibeh. According to his father Sirhan visited Taibeh only once during the entire Jerusalem period—a very strange isolation indeed.

According to Mr. Hashimeh, it was the mother, Mary Sirhan, who carried the family aloofness to unnecessary lengths. He mentioned two incidents. His daughter was friendly with Aida and one day the two girls helped each other have a bath—one poured water from a pottery jar while the other scrubbed herself; a perfectly familiar routine, but Mrs. Sirhan got very angry with Aida when she came home, and forbade her ever to do it again. On another occasion, Bechara Sirhan asked Mr. Hashimeh for empty bottles with the intention of giving them back filled with olive oil (the oil probably came from the farm at Taibeh). But Mrs. Sirhan stopped him making the gift of oil. Small incidents in themselves; but when families, large families, live cheek-by-jowl such happenings loom large—which is why they were remembered. They certainly indicated that the Sirhans wanted to have as little as possible to do with their immediate neighbours.

With Bechara Sirhan no longer the family breadwinner how did the Sirhans manage to live? Mr. Hashimeh suggested three possible sources of income and support: odd jobs that the two elder boys did in churches and church schools, the assistance provided by the United Nations Relief and Works Agency for Palestine Refugees (UNRWA, for short), and the help in cash and kind given by the Lutheran Church to Mrs. Sirhan in return for her running a sort of crèche.

Having resolved to partition Palestine, a decision which the Zionists implemented in a way that made three-quarters of a million Palestinians homeless and destitute, the United Nations set up UNRWA in 1951 to look after them. Most of these unfortunates lived in camps which, like the ones we saw at Jericho, became separate townships. UNRWA helped with some building material for their make-shift huts, with rations and with medical services and free education. On modest annual budgets of about $40 million, UNRWA has been doing a splendid job, even though it has been able to spend only seven U.S. cents a day on the up-keep of each person in its charge.

The most important of its services was the ration card which gave each person a diet of about 1500 calories a day. This consisted of 11.7 ounces of flour, 0.7 ounces of pulses, 0.7 ounces of sugar, 0.5 ounces of rice, 0.04 ounces of oils and fats, daily. One piece of soap was provided per month and some kerosene, for heating, in the winter months.

Bechara Sirhan confirmed that he and his family were registered as refugees with UNRWA and that they drew rations from the Agency. In fact, these rations would have provided the bulk of their food. These rations kept the refugees alive, but the rations kept them alive to resent the fact that having once been breadwinners, like Bechara Sirhan, they were reduced to eating the bitter bread of charity. Outside observers have frequently commented on the bitterness of the refugees and have deplored their "ingratitude." The Palestinians see the rations and UNRWA's other services as a repayment in small installments of the collective wealth and property of which they were robbed.

Mrs. Sirhan says that the UNRWA rations filled their stomachs but did not provide much nourishment, and she gives this as one possible reason why the children were so lightly-built when they arrived in America. Sirhan is more explicit: "I don't remember any starvation pangs. We always cleaned up whatever was put before us. We could have eaten more had there been any more. We were lucky to have ration cards. Some people did not have them and these were the more miserable ones than us in the Old City. That's why we always tried to share what little we had with these people." And Munir remembers that the family ate meat very seldom, as a treat on some special Sunday.

For a refugee, Mr. Sirhan was being exceptionally mild when he remarked to me, "I never like the U.N. They should have left us alone from the beginning,"—the familiar cry of people from many a small country, who are not going to be left alone by world politics.

According to Mr. Hashimeh what Mrs. Sirhan did was to run a combination of crèche and Sunday school. Evidently she took small children off their parents' hands for a couple of hours a day and to hold their attention, she told them Bible stories. She did this in a disused shop, a single room abutting on the street, a little way down Suq Al Husroor. The project was sponsored by the Lutherans but the parents paid Mrs. Sirhan directly. That his wife should become a wage-earner, when he was not, was not at all to the liking of Bechara Sirhan. This would be an understandable reaction in any husband, but more so in an Arab, or an Asian country where the husband is very definitely expected to be the head of the family, in name and in fact.

Mrs. Sirhan's work in this nursery is the first direct evidence we have of the tendency of the family to be connected with one or other Protestant sect, even though the Sirhans were members of the Greek Orthodox Church and never formally left it. This moving away from the ancestral church was partly a matter of conviction and partly the product of mundane necessity.

Both mother and father are deeply devout, with their Christian faith founded on a direct and intimate knowledge of the Bible. The copy of the Bible on Sirhan's table was well-worn and numerous passages in it were underlined in coloured pencil. This continuing personal link with the Word of God itself, the essence of Protestantism, would naturally alienate them somewhat from the older churches, more ceremonious in their forms of worship and more insistent on hierarchical authority. It was this same insistence on the unimpeded approach to God, through knowledge of the Bible itself, that moved my father away from formal Anglicanism to the less formal non-conformist sects. And if the Sirhans, like my own parents, then moved from sect to sect, it was because they were in search of ever greater simplicity, directness and intensity of God-contact. It is ironic that Christians of this sort, who reject the dogmas of an organised church, usually end up with another sort of dogmatic rigidity based on the narrow, intolerant certainty that they and they alone have won through to Salvation and that the overwhelming mass of humanity is utterly damned.

I asked Mr. Sirhan why the children had not gone to an UNRWA school. "No, I didn't want them to," was all he would say. He was

prepared to accept UNRWA's food but not its education—most probably because it was secular.

Instead the Sirhan children went to the Martin Luther School
attached to the Lutheran Church of the Savior, which stands facing the
door leading to the courtyard of the Church of the Holy Sepulchre.
"Why a Lutheran school and not a Greek Orthodox school?" I pursued.
"There were no Greek Orthodox schools in the Old City," Mr. Sirhan
replied and then after a pause, "They don't care about their people;
they are more interested in what the people can give to the Church
instead of what the Church can give the people."

I took his words to apply equally to spiritual as well as material
giving-and-taking, but after 1948, it was the material giving of the
Church that mattered to the Sirhans. The Lutherans did much for the
Sirhans. The children went tuition-free to school, they passed on
second-hand clothes and they provided occasional employment for Mrs.
Sirhan and the elder sons. Yet in 1956, the Sirhans withdrew from the
Lutheran Church, never to return, for other quite practical reasons.

As an Asian Christian this behavior does not appear to me as oppor-
tunistic as it might be to other people. There has always been a strong
element of the *quid pro quo* in the work of the proselytising Protestant
sects in Asia. Having totally failed to make converts, in any numbers,
from Islam, Hinduism or Buddhism these sects could gain adherents
only by guerilla raids on the flocks of older churches, or of each other.
The Roman Catholics were impenetrable but in the Middle East the
more tolerant and easy-going Greek Orthodox and Armenian churches
provided fruitful ground for Protestant missionaries. Much of the non-
spiritual work of the Protestant groups has been in the true spirit of
Christian charity, to succour the ill and the poor. Many missionaries, in
many Asian countries, have lived lives of great self-sacrifice. But some
of their charitable work, wittingly or unwittingly, had the appearance
of inducement to conversion. The pejorative epithet "rice Christian"
that is applied to Christian converts in India is not wholly unfair.

If Protestant groups, in Jerusalem and Pasadena, provided badly-
needed material assistance to the Sirhan family it is no reproach to
either side to surmise that this was done in the hope that the Sirhans

would eventually change from their adherence to the Greek Orthodox Church.

As we know, the Sirhans never did this but they did keep their side of this spiritual-material understanding. For as long as they were receiving aid from a particular sect they gave it their loyalty and were regular in attendance at its place of worship. So it was with them and the Lutheran Church of the Savior in Jerusalem, and other groups in Pasadena. The pastors of some of these churches in Pasadena have accused Mrs. Sirhan of being "narrow" in her belief. So she may have been, but that they, members of "narrow" sects themselves, should use this reproach reflects, I believe, their disappointment that, despite everything, the Sirhans remained affiliated to their original church.

As Sirhan's elder brothers grew into manhood, it was inevitable that the circumstances in which they lived—crowded together, with little work and less money—should have put a great strain on family feeling. In the end it resulted in a major crisis between the father and the two elder boys, Saadallah and Sharif. According to Mr. Hashimeh, these boys displayed earlier on in Jerusalem the fecklessness of which they gave later evidence in Pasadena.

Specifically, the complaint against them was that they would take money to buy things for the house and then spend it on themselves; and also that they would borrow money in their father's name and spend it in the same way. According to Mr. Hashimeh, Bechara Sirhan would always repay these "bad" debts but he finally became exasperated and enraged with his sons. "In the end, he expelled them from the house, said that they must never return, and told the rest of the family not to have anything to do with them. But you know what a mother's heart is," he went on. "They lived in a room just near here and Mrs. Sirhan would quietly send them food and give them money." After many years the break was healed between Mr. Sirhan and his sons, at least to the extent that Saadallah writes to him, but from that time to this Mr. Sirhan has never again lived under the same roof as his two eldest boys.

This episode clearly indicates that there is a hard, unforgiving streak in Bechara Sirhan's character but this does not necessarily mean that he was cruel to his children. This is the charge that has been made against him by several persons who claimed to have known the family in the Old City. It has been reported, in many newspapers' accounts, that he fought frequently with his wife, smashed the family furniture, beat his children with his fists and with sticks and once, pressed a hot iron to Sirhan's naked heel. From these reports Bechara Sirhan appears to be a bully and a sadist. I, for one, cannot accept the accuracy of these charges. Having talked to him at some length, I found he conveyed the opposite impression. Furthermore, the accounts of these acquaintances are so full of factual inaccuracies (to which I shall refer later) on many other matters as to throw doubt on everything they said.

Above all, there is the testimony of Mr. Hashimeh, who was, literally, the Sirhans' next-door neighbour. He presented a fair but by no means flattering picture of the Sirhan family. But when, on the basis of earlier accounts, I questioned him about fights or violence between the Sirhans, he said that he knew of no such thing. And if Bechara Sirhan had smashed furniture and thrashed his children, it could not but have been heard by people living across the landing.

Finally, I asked Mr. Hashimeh what recollections he had of Sirhan. "What does one remember of a 12-year old boy after 12 years?" he replied, with a smile. And I contrasted his honest answer with detailed, almost psychoanalytical accounts of Sirhan's personality given by others who seemed to have no difficulty in spanning the 12-year gap, even though they did not live in the same house. "He was a quiet, well-behaved boy who, one could notice even then, was cleverer and more studious than his brothers. There was nothing unusual about him. We saw him coming and going from school with his books; and he ran errands to the shops for the family like any other boy."

Farther up Al Malak Street, a noisy game of football was in progress while we talked on the corner. The children of Old Jerusalem (who have a type of cocky independence that is all their own) are the only football players I know of who can carry on a game uninterruptedly in an alley six feet wide, along which scores of adults and donkeys are passing. "Did Sirhan ever play in the street like that with other children," I asked.

"No, very seldom, and probably not at all," was Mr. Hashimeh's answer. This does not seem to be a wholly correct recollection for

Sirhan's brothers and friends recall playing the Arab game "Aseer," a form of tag using a ball, also the special Jerusalem variety of football and the universal "hop-scotch." Like any boys being boys, they amused themselves chasing cats among the ruined houses that were everywhere in the area. A treat for them was to be able to hire a tricycle or bicycle, but, as Munir puts it, "It would take us a hell of a long time to earn an hour's worth of riding."

Mr. Hashimeh went on, "When Sirhan came home from school he sat in their room doing his homework or reading books: I think they were religious books."

This unusual quietude was confirmed by the father: "He was a quiet, gentle boy who always preferred reading to playing outside. Even at home there were never rough games with toy guns or things like that. He preferred books."

I pressed this point further, for such signal-minded bookishness did not seem true to life: "If Sirhan had wanted to play in the street would you have let him?" I asked.

"No, we would not let him play in the street," was the reply, "though he never asked to."

"Should he not have mixed with children of his own age," I queried.

"He did that at school, but when he came home we liked to keep him with us, and he seemed to want that too," Mr. Sirhan answered.

Here was one more example of the Sirhans' aloofness in operation.

"Of course, Sirhan had friends who came to the house and they had tea and cakes together. But I remember," his father went on, "that once, after two boys had left, that he said one boy should be invited again but not the other, because he used bad language."

The boyhood friend, Ziad Hashimeh, provides further evidence on Sirhan's strictly moral views. Having confided to Sirhan a plan to steal a cone from an icecream man he was promptly lectured on not stealing, especially because, "That man makes very few piastres (the Jordanian coin) and he has to feed a family." On another occasion Sirhan delivered this homily to his young friend: "If you lie to people, people are clever enough to lie back to you. The greatest thing in the world are people, and what you learn from people you cannot even learn in school." Sirhan also tried to persuade Ziad, a Muslim, to attend his mother's religious classes saying that they were not specifically Christian.

This rather priggish purity, not at all normally boyish, was of course the outcome of Sirhan's strictly moralistic religious upbringing and his own evident devotion, genuine or induced, for things religious. His after-school reading was confined to the Bible and religious tracts; he said his own prayers regularly at home; and he was regular in attendance at church and Sunday school. Naturally enough, Scripture was his best subject in school: in his five years at the Lutheran school his average marks in it were over eighty per cent.

This being the degree of Sirhan's religious devotion, a statement of Bechara Sirhan that he told his sons "to keep away from communism and other dangerous ideas" would surely not seem to apply to Sirhan, though perhaps to his elder brothers. And it is against this personal background that we must set the ludicrous tale that Sirhan was put under police surveillance at the age of eleven because he was politically potentially dangerous!

But political ideas that were dangerous to some people were abroad in Jerusalem and on the West Bank, where the Palestinians chafed under the rule of the Hashimite monarchy from the East Bank. In 1951, a group of Palestinians assissinated King Abdullah as he was entering the Aksa Mosque. The King was accused of being too subservient to the British and too accommodating with the Israelis, and the accusations were known to everyone.

Mr. Sirhan has said that Sirhan was much interested in this event: it would have been extraordinary if he had not been. The Aksa Mosque is ten minutes walk from where the Sirhans lived, and the Old City was in such a turmoil that Friday afternoon that the great gates were closed and the Jerusalemites found themselves locked in like naughty children. The obvious moral of the King's assassination was this: that the Palestinians felt themselves so put-upon that they were prepared to strike back violently. This plain, brutal fact could not have been lost, even on a seven year old boy.

Sirhan, though technically a citizen of the Kingdom of Jordan, has repeatedly said that he has never considered himself anything but a Palestinian; and during his trial when his people were referred to as "Arabs" he frequently interjected the correction "Palestinian Arabs."

In Jerusalem there was no lack of adults willing to guide the feet of the young on the paths of Palestinian Arab patriotism. Sirhan recalls a teacher in his school, a certain Suheil, who bitterly compared the present-day Arabs, who had let themselves be beaten by and expelled by their enemy, with the great Arab warrior Saladin who had expelled the foreign Crusaders from Jerusalem. Suheil, dramatically, would tell his pupils that from his grave Saladin was putting to them the reproachful question, "Do you want me to come back from the grave to do for you what you ought to be doing for yourselves?"

Sirhan also describes how, with his friends, he once climbed up to the nearby sentry post of the Arab Legion above the Zion Gate and persuaded the soldier on duty to let him look through his binoculars at the Israeli-held sector of Jerusalem. While he was doing so the sentry said, "That is our land out there, our country." Sirhan goes on, "At that time I couldn't really understand actually, but now I do understand what he meant and I understand the import of what he said, the impact of what he said."

The principle facts available about Sirhan during this period relate, of course, to his record at school. He was a diligent, industrious student whose performance was above average. During the five years he was consistently in the upper half of his class. In the first year, he stood fifth out of 26 but had slipped to seventh out of 16 in 1956. His marks were always high in Arabic, English and singing; and also for "conduct" for which they varied between 75 and 80. In sports he was usually marked around 65,—not too satisfactory but enough to show that he was not just a book-worm. He was not particularly good in history; and was persistently weak in arithmetic and drawing. The "general remarks" about Sirhan were usually complimentary such as "satisfactory" or "good character." His report for 1955—1956, his last year in Jerusalem, when he was 12 years old, reads: "Religion, very good; Arabic, very good; English, good; Arithmetic, very satisfactory; Geometry, good; History, satisfactory; Geography, satisfactory; Science, good; Natural History, satisfactory; Drawing, satisfactory; Singing, good; Conduct, good; Diligence, good; Cleanliness, good; General Comment, satisfactory."

One of the reasons given for the Sirhan children attending the Lutheran school rather than any other was that it was nearby, which is true, for it is not much more than five minutes walk away. Without any excessive use of the imagination we can follow the road the young Sirhan took on his way to and from school. From a contemporary photograph we know that he was small for his years, and dark, with his wiry hair well plastered down,—it gleams in the picture, to give him a left-hand parting. He would have walked down the slope of Suq Al Husroor and then turned left into King David Street. He would have had to elbow his way through the throngs in this busy bazaar redolent with the smells of meat and fish, fruit and spices, and loud with the noise of bargaining; all the merchandise is open to display to be fingered and prodded and smelt; nothing is packaged. In the street he would have brushed past monks and nuns and priests of every Christian denomination as also turbaned Muslim ulema; the shopkeepers in Western suits of long, striped caftans; bedouins in flowing burnous; and the women of Palestine in their long black dresses with the bodices embroidered in elaborate cross-stitch with varying designs and colours indicative of their town or region.

Under an arch and through a tall iron gate, Sirhan would have turned into the comparative quiet of Muristan Street, the whole right-hand side of which was taken up by his school and the Lutheran Church with its tall belfry. At the end of this street, over on the left, the slender minaret of a mosque and the grey cupola of the Church of the Holy Sepulchre faced each other. It was in this setting of immemorial holiness combined with a vivid humanity that Sirhan spent his school years in Jerusalem. Nothing in all the world could be more different from what he was to find in Pasadena.

What impelled the Sirhans to uproot themselves from Palestine and make the long move to the United States? Undoubtedly, economic need. After 22 years of steady work in government service, Bechara Sirhan found any continuation of his last eight years of very occasional employment something not to be endured. And the future held no promise of improvement for himself or for his growing sons. He preferred to give me his reasons in positive terms: "I had heard a lot about America," he said, "that it was a wonderful country where one could always find work and make money." Nor was emigration to America anything unusual for Christian Palestinians. For several decades there had been a westward flow of families from the Christian centers of

Ramalah, Jerusalem and Bethlehem. Christians found it easier than
Muslim to obtain immigrant visas presumably on the calculation that
they would fit more easily into a Christian society.

The way in which the opportunity to emigrate presented itself was
completely fortuitous. Bechara Sirhan described how, "One day I saw
one of my friends talking to a foreigner. I stopped to greet him and he
introduced me to the person he was talking to. From his accent I knew
he was an American so I said to him directly, 'You are an American; I
want to go to your country; will you sponsor my family?' And the
American said that he would try to help and later he did arrange to
sponsor us."

When I remarked that this was a lucky accident, Mr. Sirhan replied,
"Nothing in life is an accident. If God wants to open a door, He can
always find a way."

On the more practical level, the door to America was opened by two
families belonging to the First Nazarene Church in Pasadena, which is
why the family went all the way across the continent. Who paid their
travelling expenses is not precisely known: it was either the Nazarene
Church or UNRWA or part payment by both. UNRWA has assisted
some Palestinians to emigrate, a surprisingly small number of not more
than a couple thousand. If they possibly can help it, Palestinians do
not like to leave their country.

In 1956, Bechara Sirhan was not yet reconciled with his two elder
sons, so he took the strangely unpaternal decision not to include them
in his plans for emigration. Accordingly, Saadallah and Sharif remained
behind in Palestine when Bechara and Mary left Jerusalem with the
other members of their family for the United States at the close of
1956, where they arrived in January, 1957. Sirhan was then two
months short of his thirteenth birthday.

The Sirhans entered America under a special decree of President
Eisenhower by which 2,000 Palestinian "refugee" families were allowed
to immigrate. Bechara Sirhan would have liked to have followed his
father's example and have gone alone to the New World to make his
fortune there; but he was not allowed to do so under this special plan
which applied only to families. But he tried to keep the family's departure secret and, when it became known, he attempted to dissuade the

neighbours from giving them a modest farewell party, a further example of Sirhan aloofness which the neighbours found puzzling and, in this particular case, rather hurtful.

One may surmise that Bechara Sirhan's secretiveness was the expression of embarassment and pride because to emigrate in such circumstances was clear proof that he, as the family head, had failed to re-establish himself in his own city.

One other member of the family was positively opposed to the idea of leaving Jerusalem in order to go to the United States. This was Sirhan Sirhan who, describing his feelings at the time, says, "I was very hesitant; I didn't want to leave; I wanted to stay in my own country with my own people. I knew that the U.S. was against the Arabs and was friendly with Israel, and a friend of my enemy is my enemy. I knew about U.S. policy because I did a lot of listening on the radio to the Voice of America." As to the troubled conditions in which he was then living in Jerusalem he adds, "I thought they would subside eventually"—another vain hope shared by many Palestinians. Because of his doubts Sirhan ran away from home the day before the family was due to leave and went to the town of Ramallah, about 15 miles north of Jerusalem, where he spent the whole day in the public park. Loneliness and the onset of darkness drove the boy home. His angry, and worried, father wanted to beat him but the elder brother Adel dissuaded Bechara with the plea, "Let's leave here in peace."

The Sirhans went by road from Jerusalem through Amman to Beirut and then by ship, via Naples, to New York. Sirhan does not recall seeing the Statue of Liberty at the entrance to New York Harbour. The splendidly declamatory words on the base of the statue with their references to "the huddled masses," "the poor," "the refuse" were particularly applicable to the incoming Palestinians sailing through "the Golden Door." The Sirhans made the long journey across the American continent by train, which the children found a particularly thrilling experience.

In January, 1957, Robert Kennedy, then 32 years old, was appointed chief counsel of the Senate Select Committee on Improper Activities in the Labour or Management Field. He had already served four years as counsel to the Senate Permanent Committee on Investigations.

When the Sirhans left the Arab world in December, 1956, the Arabs, from Marrakesh to Muscat, were in a mood of triumphant elation because by then it was clear that Egypt, led by President Nasser and backed by all the Arabs and many friends, was going to come out on top of the power struggle known as the Suez Crisis. All through the summer and autumn months of 1956, during which the Sirhans were going through the formalities of emigration, tension tightened between Egypt and the Western Powers over Egypt's nationalization of the Suez Canal. Taking advantage of this situation, Ben Gurion, the then Israeli Prime Minister, proposed to Britain and France that they overthrow their common adversary, Nasser, by attacking Egypt and inflicting on him a humiliating defeat. In collusion, and with the French providing direct military assistance to Israel, the three countries attacked Egypt at the end of October, 1956.

Through this second act of collusion, the Zionists in Palestine, at long last, thirty-eight years later, carried out their part of the bargain which they made with Britain in the first act of collusion, the Balfour Declaration. In the "Compact of 1917" the Jews promised to help protect British interests in the Suez Canal and in 1956 they went to war to do so, incidentally.

Whatever military success may have been achieved by the tripartite aggression, it was in political and diplomatic terms, a social failure for its originators. Russia and America joined in halting the attack and then in ordering Britain, France and Israel out of Egyptian territory. The whole of the Afro-Asian world rallied behind Egypt.

Above all, it was within the Arab world that the aggression had its biggest boomerang effect. By rejecting the Anglo-French ultimatism, President Nasser, almost overnight, came to be considered the greatest Arab hero since Saladin. No Arab government did anything very much to aid Egypt but, as some of these governments soon discovered to their dismay, the Arab masses followed the leadership of Nasser. And especially was this true of the younger generation.

Sirhan in Jerusalem could not have escaped, even if he wanted to, the surging thrust of this wave of Arab nationalism. What has been called the "Transistor Revolution," the widespread use of transistor radios, carried Nasser's words and all the details of Arab politics into almost every home and shop and cafe and restaurant. At times of crisis, like that of Suez, the problem was not how to hear the radio news but how to escape from its omnipresent echoes.

In many another country, it could safely be said that a twelve-year old schoolboy, like Sirhan, would not have a political idea in his head; and would be regarded as a precocious freak if he had. NOT in the Middle East, and especially not in Palestine where politics enveloped life.

Jerusalem was not only a divided city, it was also a frontier city, a front-line city particularly sensitive to international and national politics. Shooting across the City walls between the Israelis and the Jordanians happened every now and again, so that the Palestinians could never forget that, quite literally, the enemy was at their gates. In December, 1955, when the Jordan government almost agreed to join the Western-sponsored Baghdad Pact, rioting in Jerusalem, where the gates were shut again, and in other West Bank towns was so serious that the government fell and the idea of Jordan joining the Pact was abandoned: an incident which showed that direct action could effect policy and also that the Western Powers were still trying to exercise control in the area, though now by indirect means. In October, 1956, Jerusalem was on the qui vive because, as part of their deception plan, the Israelis threatened to attack Jordan, including troop movements, before suddenly launching themselves against Egypt.

However much Bechara Sirhan may have wanted to keep "dangerous ideas" away from his sons, an alert and intelligent boy like Sirhan could not but have known of the turbulence the Arab world was passing through.

In their evidence at his trial the friends and relatives of Sirhan tended to give an over-dramatized picture of the political-security conditions prevailing in Jerusalem after 1948, which, in truth, were bad enough. Fighting and violence were not part of normal daily life there, but only occured sporadically. What was constant, however, was the fearful expectation that shooting could start at any time and without warning. When it did happen Mrs. Sirhan would plug her children's ears with cotton wool and rush them down to the basement. Within the city walls Sirhan Sirhan, once again, had direct experience and knowledge of the violence produced both by turbulent Arab nationalism and by the Arab-Israeli conflict which fuelled that nationalism. When the French consulate in Jerusalem was sacked in 1956 during the riots that followed the Suez Aggression (in which, of course, France participated alongside Israel and Britain) his class teacher at school expressed angry disapproval and told his pupils that this was the wrong method to use: "Difficulties and problems," he said, "should be solved through peaceful means by discussion and negotiation." Sirhan says that he agreed with these ideas then and that he still does so.

During a particularly bad "shoot-up" across the armistice line in Jerusalem an Israeli bomb scored a direct hit on a grocery shop in the Suq al-Husroor, a score of yards from the Sirhan house. The owner was blown to bits or, in Mrs. Sirhan's picturesque language, "He was all out and every part of his body was in" (in other words, he was turned inside out). "Sirhan," she says, "nearly fainted when he saw this bloody mess that was once a human being."

Ziad Hashimeh recalls Sirhan's horrified yells at something that happened when Sirhan was nine or ten years old. One of the daily chores of the children was to draw water from the cistern in improvised rubber buckets. One day a human hand "severed at the wrist" came up in Sirhan's bucket. How this gruesome object could have got into the cistern is not clear but perhaps it was all that remained of another human being, disintegrated like the unhappy grocer by an Israeli bomb.

Nor were they altogether free of the memories of past violence. One of their neighbours was a widow called Umm Wadia. Before 1948, her son who was a resistance fighter had been captured by the Jews, strung up by his heels in front of his mother and whipped, "for days and days;" he did not survive and the ordeal drove his mother mad. As Mrs. Sirhan describes it, "She would scream in the middle of the night, 'They killed my son'; her hair used to stand up like this, her hair had become as white as coffee cream, and her eyes opened and she stared and she screams and screams." This used to frighten all the children of the neighbourhood.

Not all the memories that the Sirhans had of their lost life in the Musrara quarter were so horrific. Some were simply nostalgic. Sirhan recalls, "Many times I remember my mother saying this, that we had a lemon tree in the yard where we had lived and every time she needs a lemon for the cooking she'd say, 'Oh, I wish we had that lemon tree. Do you remember that lemon tree? Its lemons were big and juicy,' and her whole mood would change because there was no lemon tree." *
And Sirhan's fondest personal memories of the Musrara house was of a large stuffed toy tiger that could be ridden like a horse.

But the basic substrata of Sirhan's memory of the years in Jerusalem, of horror and violence piled on horror and violence, were not wistfully nostalgic. What it was came to the surface when the psychiatrist Dr. Bernard Diamond questioned Sirhan after having put him under hypnosis. To use the Doctor's words, "The supercilious, arrogant, remorseless assassin suddenly crumpled in agony like a child, sobbing and shivering in terror. The tears poured down his face. This happened first when I asked about Jerusalem and the bombing, but I later found that any question about helping his people, the Arabs, would trigger the same kind of response."

Thus did Sirhan, the deep-down Sirhan, weep for himself, for his people, and their joint sufferings. What, then, could his reaction be when, in 1968, he heard electoral promises being made by an American politician to send yet more bombers to Israel that would bring yet more suffering and destruction on his people?

"Expellees" versus "refugees"

This section has been entitled "The Expellees" and the reference is, of course, to the Sirhan family. Yet they, and all the other Palestinians who lost their homes in 1948, and again in 1967, well over a million persons, have been officially designated as "refugees." This, surely, is a loose and inaccurate use of that word. The Sirhans sought refuge in the

---

* Page 4855 of the reporter's transcript of Sirhan's trial. To be referred to hereafter as "Transcript."

Old City, it is true, but that was because they were expelled from their former home because of a military attack on eastern Jerusalem mounted by the Jews. Likewise, the 1,200 Jews within the Old City were expelled by Arab military action and should not be called "refugees," if they ever were.

So, too, the millions of persons who crossed over between India and Pakistan following the partition of 1947 were, almost entirely, expellees and not refugees. And the same holds true of those who have suffered because of violence in Tibet or the Congo.

A distinction surely should be made between those seeking refuge from the cruel whims of Nature and those compelled to leave their homes because of man's inhumanity to man. And here too a further distinction must be made between the "displaced person," who is moved from his home to another place, and the "expellee" who is just forced out of his home. The word "refugee" seems to lay emphasis, in indiscriminate and anodyne fashion, on the human results of a tragedy whereas "expellee" refers back in accusation, to the particular human cause. So cruel has our world become that perhaps it is now necessary to use the precise and condemnatory word "expellee" rather than the vague and exculpatory "refugee."

In the case of Palestine, especially, the use of the word "refugee" has, perhaps unwittingly, become part of the attempt to cover-up a major human tragedy caused to human beings by other human beings,— the forcible emptying out of a land of its original inhabitants and their replacement by foreign immigrants. As part of this attempt we come across yet another Zionist myth: that most of the dispossessed Palestinians are voluntary refugees because they, of their own free will, sought refuge in neighbouring Arab countries on orders broadcast to them from Arab radio stations. It took British and Arab historians twelve years to discover that there are no records of any such broadcasts ever having been made, while there are texts available—as well as recordings—of numerous Arab broadcasts asking the Palestinians not to move. Perhaps through constant repetition Israeli leaders themselves evidently believe this story. When I met the then Israeli Foreign Minister, Mrs. Golda Meir, that formidible ex-school mistress from

Milwaukee, in Jerusalem in 1961, she referred to this matter and seemed irritated when I told her that the voluntary refugee story had no factual foundation. She promised me that her Ministry would provide me with the proof. But after two days of prodding all that the Israeli Foreign Ministry could produce, rather shamefacedly, were the same third-hand rumours of someone told by someone who had heard about such broadcasts.

There is one group of people whom this Zionist myth has never misled and that, naturally, is the expellees themselves. The Palestinians know what happened to them, and because they know they are, for the most part, angry people—"angry against the world" was the phrase used by Mr. Hashimeh when talking of Bechara Sirhan. But, Mr. Hishimeh is an angry man himself. Towards the end of our long conversation, he became more personal and began to express his own opinions: "I say to hell with America and Russia. And the U.N.?—they are all crooks. When I think of how I have to live, I want to blow up the whole world"—and his hands jerked upwards in an explosive gesture.

From what we know of him, what sort of boy was Sirhan Sirhan in 1956 when he had to leave his country?

He was serious-minded and intelligent and bookish; a quiet, obedient youth.

From his family he had acquired two characteristics—an aloofness, and a deep devotion to religion. What neither he nor his parents knew was that they, as Christians, were taking to Christian America a type of upbringing and a code of moral behavior that had ceased to be common in America a generation or more before.

That sense of security within the family circle that children want and need had been destroyed for the Sirhans, for good, in May, 1948. A wary suspiciousness of what further blows the world might have in store for them is evident in Sirhan's question on the likelihood of bombing in Pasadena. Nor was Sirhan a member of a united or happy family: with his two elder brothers expelled from the house and then left behind when they emigrated, this could hardly be so.

The principal fact that all the Sirhans would have known and would have had to accept was this: that they were leaving this homeland not really because of a free choice but because they had to. So far the story of the boyhood of Sirhan has been an account not so much of what he was or what he did, but of what had been done to him and to his family. They could not choose or initiate; they had to accept and endure. And this remained true of their life in Pasadena.

4

Amid The Alien Corn

There are many good things and good people in America. But there are also many bad things and bad people. Life is difficult there for older people and especially religious people. It is very different from here, very, very different.

Thus, with much shaking of the head, did Bechara Sirhan sum up his experience of life in the United States. He spoke the words more in sorrow than in anger.

To judge by what happened to the Sirhans in Pasadena, he was speaking for the whole family.

The famous American architect, Frank Lloyd Wright, once said that if the United States were placed on a tray and the tray tilted, the loose bits and pieces would tumble into a corner and that would be Los Angeles.

Flying into this Southern California city, one is signalled of its presence, in frightening fashion, from many miles away. Coming in over the Sierra studded with parks and swimming pools, I noticed grey ectoplasmic tentacles reaching up the valley. They were the fringes of the blanket of smog that lies over Los Angeles for much of the year. Because of this smog, the circle of hills that rings the city is quite invisible—the vast city runs on and merges into the haze. The more prosperous residential suburb of Altadena, above Pasadena, lies on the lower slopes of the Sierra but not until one is within a mile of the hills does one see them, suddenly, looming through the smog. The oppressive feeling of being enclosed in a foul mist is just one of the many unlikeable aspects of Los Angeles-Pasadena.

Thanks to Hollywood, and tourist pictures of the towering complex at the lower end of Manhattan, many people around the world think that most American cities are cities of skyscrapers. This is not true of Manhattan, and even less of Los Angeles. What comes as a disappointing surprise is the discovery that, apart from a dozen recently-erected high blocks and some handsome and substantial commercial and civic buildings downtown, the rest of Los Angeles consists of grubby-looking single-storey structures. They look so insubstantial and temporary that they recall the film sets of a frontier town in a third-rate cowboy movie. In fact, if one took such a movie set, added thousands of cars in the streets, hundreds of ugly public utility poles along the pavements and liberally garnished the rooftops with neon signs, one would have a fair replica of Los Angeles-Pasadena. Hollywood and Sunset Boulevards and the glamour streets of the dream factory are no better. Of course, there are very pleasant residential areas in these cities and even the Sirhans eventually came to live in one; but it is not these parts that give the cities their distinctive flavour or colour. And in the residential areas, their pleasantness is also a monotonous pleasantness, probably because of the grid pattern of the streets—one of the most inhuman arrangements to be imposed on a living, human organism. The final impression given by Los Angeles is that here is something trashy and garish.

One aspect of life in Los Angeles-Pasadena may have appealed to the Sirhans and that is the multiplicity of its religious sects, though many of these too are garish and trashy. Driving around Pasadena and noting only the places of worship of the older denominations, there seemed to be more churches there than in the Holy City itself. Southern California is a strange combination of the blatantly material and the equally blatantly spiritual.

Indeed, if one had to choose the one city in the Western world into which the Sirhans would fit only with the maximum of difficulty, one would, after careful search, have to choose Los Angeles. In the United States they would have been happiest in any one of its thousands of quiet, respectable small towns. On the West Coast itself, San Francisco would have been a better choice; or Boston; or even New York. It was an extraordinary piece of bad luck that, because of their sponsors being in Pasadena, the family went farther and fared worst of all.

After their arrival the Sirhans stayed for two or three weeks in the home of their sponsor, Haldor Lillinas, who has since died. They seemed to have maintained contact with their sponsoring organisation, the First Nazarene Church, for only a little more than a year after their arrival in Pasadena. In 1958, they were in contact with the local First Baptist Church and the pastor, Doctor Charles Bell, recalls visiting them in their first home, east of Lake Avenue, which is the central north-south dividing line of Pasadena. In his words: "It was a modest apartment because they were a poor family. Yet, they were poor."

By this time Bechara Sirhan had already left his family to move to New York. This departure of the head of family is one of the two family occurences that the Sirhans do not talk about, probably because they feel that it is so unusual as to be rather shameful. What seems to have happened is that about six to eight months after their arrival in Pasadena, Bechara Sirhan and Adel were cementing the yard of their house and Sirhan kept interrupting and spoiling their work by trampling in the mud and then jumping on the new cement. After frequent warnings the father grabbed the garden hose to give him a beating. Once again, as on the eve of their departure from Jerusalem, Adel stepped between them to protect his younger brother and Bechara Sirhan then went inside the house to seek the aid of his wife in this second challenge to his parental authority. It was not forthcoming. He told Mary Sirhan that she would have to choose between him and the children: she chose the children. Bechara Sirhan promptly packed up, took all the family savings, amounting to $500 at the time, and left his family for good.

For Mary Sirhan and her children this sudden departure of the head of the family must have been a desolating experience. In Arab society the father is very much the *pater familias* with unquestioned prestige and authority which can be extinguished only by death. For them the loss of the head of the household would not only have had emotional and economic implications, it also would have set up deep societal reverberations because it set them apart as an unusual, even a peculiar, family. It is probably because of this feeling that the Sirhans, down to the present, do not discuss the matter and do not utter a word of criticism of the elder Sirhan. We know that for years afterwards, Sirhan questioned his elder brothers on the reason for their father's departure because it clearly was something he could not understand.

Yet, to a certain extent, the Sirhan family's experience of the loss of the father is an experience shared by the larger part of the Palestinian expellees although for them this has not necessarily meant the actual physical dissappearance of the father—as it did for the Sirhans—but rather the loss of the breadwinner and of the head of the household. Most adult Palestinian men have remained unemployed for years and have had to resign themselves to sitting at home in impotent idleness while the women continued with their usual work around the house. The mother's business and fruitful employment and making-do meant that gradually she began to be considered the centre, if not the titular head, of the family. Apart from all the other ill-effects, the dispersal of 1947-48 wreaked sociological havoc among the Palestinians.

Bechara Sirhan was equally reticent when I discussed this episode with him. He told me that he stayed about six months in Pasadena. I asked him why he left, and his answer was: "I couldn't find the sort of work that I knew I could do. I like to work well but if one is given a job one doesn't know how to do, then no one is happy—the boss isn't happy and you aren't happy and the work isn't done properly." I queried further why, with his considerable experience, he could not find suitable employment. A pained expression flitted across his face: "They always wanted me to be an American citizen," was his answer, and in those words he summed up one of the main reasons for his family's maladjustment in America.

The Sirhans entered the United States on "permanent resident status", which is accorded to people who apply for permission to live in the United States permanently while remaining a citizen of their country of origin.

In short, this Palestinian family from the start had decided that they wanted to remain Palestinians, and despite all of the difficulties this led to in later years, they insisted on remaining Palestinians, holding Jordanian passports. Only one member of the family, Saadallah, applied for citizenship after many years. He was to be interviewed about his application on June 5th, 1968.

I asked Bechara Sirhan why, having decided to settle in America, he did not complete the process by becoming an American citizen. "I was never sure that I liked America enough to want to become an American; and because I wasn't sure I kept putting it off", he replied.

What was there about America that he did not like, I questioned, and Bechara Sirhan described his experiences in New York, which are recounted here because, at this point, the Sirhan father moved out of the family picture; after he left Pasadena, Bechara Sirhan had no further direct contact with his wife and children.

The question naturally arises why the Sirhan marriage broke up. According to some accounts, the quarrels that were supposed to have taken place in Jerusalem continued in Pasadena and the break came because of what may be called a temperamental incompatibility. This could be part of the answer. The economic reason advanced by Bechara Sirhan was probably also partly responsible. Mr. Hashimeh in Jerusalem had heard of yet another reason. In Pasadena the father discovered that his wife was in correspondence with the two sons left behind in Palestine and was so angry that she had not obeyed his ban on any contact with them that he left the house. It sounds very much in character, but was doubtless only the final contributing cause.

His motivations were probably a combination of all three. The final break was, in effect, a repudiation of his wife and four children at a time when they were badly in need of his support. Bechara Sirhan, whatever his reasons, had clearly decided that he wanted no more of married life. For a man of serious cast of mind, such a decision could only have been the product of unhappy desperation, which his wife and children probably felt even more than he did.

"I found work quite easily in New York", he said. "Things were different there from Pasadena. They wanted workers and they did not care who you were: I was never asked about my citizenship. Most of the time I worked as a maintenance mechanic. The work was alright. After some time my old mother fell ill so I came back to Taibeh to be with her. Then I went back to New York. I returned to Taibeh a second time and then went to New York again for the third time. Whenever I went back I was able to find work. I lived there for five years in all, and I was thinking of going once more last year but I didn't because of the war in June".

We know that Bechara Sirhan worked part of the time for the Welbuilt Corporation, a manufacturer of heating equipment in Queens; and also as a fitter for Orlin Laboratories, a cosmetics factory in Brooklyn. He lived in an apartment on Allen Street, near the Manhattan end of Williamsburg Bridge, sharing it with another Palestinian.

"It was other things—beside the work—which I didn't like in America", he went on. "Write what I tell you because it is the truth. I always tell the truth. I don't lie. [He repeated this affirmation several times during our conversations.] So I said America is a good country but there is also much drunkenness, much immorality, much violence. I was held up four times in the streets and three of those times they took my money. But what is worse is that they don't help one another. One day I saw a man, he was a Negro, lying on the pavement. I went over to him and tried to see whether he was ill or perhaps just drunk; maybe he needed some sort of help. When I began to lift him, a man came out of a shop and told me not to interfere and that I might get into trouble with the police. I told him I only wanted to help but he said it was better to leave things to the police. So I went and stood on the corner and waited to see what happened. A police ambulance came after some time and they took him away. I never knew what was wrong with the man, but if he was ill, it may have helped if we had tried to do something for him before the ambulance came. But one is not supposed to do that in America". The impersonal atomisation of city life was too much even for the aloof Bechara Sirhan.

He then told me the strange story of his fourth hold-up, the time when he was not robbed. "You see this paper", he said, and he held up a copy of "Muhammad Speaks", the organ of the Hon. Elijah Muhammad, the leader of the Black Muslims. There was a large picture of the Hon. Elijah on the back page. "I used to read this when I was in

New York and found it interesting. I liked that man's religious ideas. One day I cut out a picture like this and kept it in my coat pocket. As I said, I think that this man has some good ideas. Then one night four black guys held me up and asked me to give them my money. I gave them what I had and they also took my watch. Then they began to search me and they found the picture of Elijah Muhammad. They asked me who I was and I said I was an Arab and a Christian, but that I kept the picture because I liked that man. One of the black guys said, 'Negroes and Arabs are brothers', and he made the others give everything back to me and they took me to a bar and gave me a drink". Bechara Sirhan smiled at the recollection of this unusual incident.

The fact that Bechara Sirhan travelled to the United States no less than three times showed that, economically, at least, he was able to make a go of things in that country. Likewise, from what he said, he did not strike roots there or take out citizenship because he could not adjust to the tempo and quality of American life. In particular, his puritanical moral standards were affronted by the laxity of American social life. He was economically integrated but was a socio-cultural misfit.

We have seen how Bechara Sirhan, during his five-year stay in New York, was faced with the fundamental challenge that confronts all immigrants to America—the problem of assimilation. He did not feel the full demands of the challenge because his stay was comparatively brief and was broken by two visits to his former home. Even so, the pressures of assimilation were enough to evoke sufficient resistance within him so as to prevent him from settling down or becoming an American citizen.

The pressures and the resistance were far stronger and insistent in the case of the younger members of the Sirhan family who, at least in theory, were supposed to be settling down in America. For them the mere process of daily living constantly produced the questions: "Should I stop considering myself a Palestinian and become an American? Should I discontinue this particular Palestinian social custom and adopt that particular one from American society? Should I deliberately try and make English my mother tongue and push Arabic into the background? If I let go of my Palestinian background, in which

I am rooted, and merge with America where I am rootless, will I lose myself as a person, as a human being with a distinctive character and outlook? Will America swallow me up?"

All the Sirhan brothers are, in their various ways, the products of a Toynbean situation of Challenge-and-Response. And their responses have been varied: Sharif has described himself as "a man without a country"; the more adaptable and gregarious Adel claimed that he "had the best of both worlds"; while the youngest brother, Munir, once confessed that "the two worlds are tearing me apart."

The problem of what to retain from the former life and what to acquire from the new life has, of course, faced millions and scores of millions of people in the United States. The more educated and sensitive the person the more acute the problem is; and it is more acute in America than it would be, say, in Britain and France. Though it is "a nation of immigrants or perhaps because it is a nation of immigrants, America demands a great deal from the immigrant, just as it has a great deal to offer him. Precisely because it is an agglomeration of various groups, America has, quite rightly, to insist that the groups eventually accept the American stamp, that they agree to be pushed or persuaded into a single American mould. If this reshaping process were not applied with the unrelenting firmness with which it has been applied, there would today be no such thing as the American people or the American nation, and probably no United States.

Hence it is that in the United States there is something called "Americanism", a quality that is believed to exist, that is considered desirable and is consciously promoted. For America, "Americanism" is a necessity; in any other country it would be an absurdity. What, for instance, would "Britishness", or "Indianism", or "Brazilianism" represent? And in the United States, on one day a year, there are perhaps, millions of people who solemnly avow, "Thank God, I Am An American".

Because it is still going through the self-generative process of creating an America, the United States cannot afford the luxury of excessive tolerance for the non-conformist or the alien. Woe betide the person who is both!

The task of taking in half a hundred nationalities at one end and producing "the American", pure and simple, at the other is a primary, perhaps the sole, objective of the American school system. Apart from the American bias in the curriculum, there is in most schools every single morning (at least until recently) the salute to the flag and the Pledge of Allegiance which every single child has to take whether he is America-born, or a complete foreigner, or has "permanent resident status", like the Sirhans. In no other country, to my knowledge, is the national flag so omnipresent, not even in the new countries of Afro-Asia which the American press so often describe as "touchily xenophobic". In which other country is the flag flown, as a matter of course, over many a filling station or petrol pump? And the flag-flying habit in America seems to be on the increase: most of the public buses in New York now display flag-stickers. Much of this flag-flying is chauvinistic jingoism, but, at base, it is nothing but an attempt, which must be made, to beat into the brains of the American individual that however disparate Americans may have been they are now in fact, or should be, one.

There are two obvious elements in "Americanism": Socio-cultural conformity and political loyalty. Conformity is enforced through such behavior-patterns as "togetherness" or "good neighbourliness" and, in practical form, through the absence of any dividing hedge, or fence, or wall between the houses in the residential areas. There are the multiplicity of neighbourhood organisations, religious and secular, that one is expected to join. American writers themselves have been among the first to decry the stultifying deadliness of social conformity, as witness that great American novel "Main Street" by Sinclair Lewis. But for all the anguished protests of novelists and artists, the force of conformity continues to sweep across American social life like an irresistable juggernaut.

The Sirhans in Pasadena, as we shall see, achieved some sort of compromise with the demands of social conformity. But it was almost impossible for them to come to terms with the demand for political loyalty because of the American government's policy towards Palestine since World War II.

The Palestinians are unique among all the many peoples who have immigrated to America: they are homeless immigrants going to

America because of the breaking up of their Palestinian homeland in which breaking up America itself played a large part. Without President Truman's backing, the Partition Resolution would never have been rammed through the United Nations and Israel would probably never have come into existence. Israel has remained the active antagonist of the Arab countries, including Jordan which absorbed what was left of Palestine and gave citizenship to the Palestinians who fell under its rule. But Israel's best friend and staunchest supporter has remained the United States government. The Jewish community in America is the richest and most influential in the world and the massive financial contributions it has made to Israel were essential to the continued existence of the Jewish State. Immigrants from many countries send contributions back home to their relatives but only in the case of Israel are these contributions made tax deductible by the U.S. government.

The United States has been and is, of course, antagonistic towards many of the countries from which immigrants have come, for instance, the pre-Communist and Communist regimes of Eastern Europe. This clash produces no emotional conflict within the hearts of these immigrants for they themselves are antagonistic to the regimes in their homelands, which they have voluntarily abandoned. The antagonism is not towards the countries as such but towards the regimes that are now in power, and the immigrants take the lead in advocating an activist American policy to "liberate" their former countries. The case is quite different with the Palestinians: they may grumble against the Hashemite monarchy but they certainly do not want to see King Hussein overthrown or Jordan defeated and least of all by an Israel that is armed and financed by America, their second homeland.

Considering what America did and continues to do in support of Zionism and Israel, and what these three forces have done to the Palestinians and Palestine, it is surprising that any Palestinians could bring themselves to go to America. Not many did go to America or any other non-Arab country. Of a world population today of 2.5 million Palestinians only 50,000 are to be found outside the Arab countries of the Middle East. The Palestinians have, quite simply, not wanted to move far away from home.

What reason was there in 1956 for a Palestinian to consider America favourably as a possible future home? After the tripartite aggression, President Eisenhower, showing great courage in an election year with himself as a candidate, resisted Zionist pressure and Zionist control of the American publicity media, and ordered Israel back across its frontiers. But this was a short-lived deviation in America's consistent policy of sustaining Israel and guaranteeing its continued existence, and, therefore, taking its side in its continued conflict with the Arabs.

This policy has put the Palestinian immigrants at odds not only with their adopted country but also with the other Arab-American immigrants who have no quarrel with America. Many Americans found the Sirhans strange and aloof, but it was perhaps the Arab-Americans who found them most strange and aloof because of their initial assumption that the Sirhans were going to be like them; which they were not.

In the United States today there are, perhaps, about 500,000 Arab-Americans. Most of them, around 300,000 are from what is now Lebanon, and the rest are from present-day Syria and what was Mandatory Palestine. The Jordanians, that is, those persons, like the Sirhans, who lived in the part of Palestine that came under Jordanian sovereignty after 1948 and emigrated to America at some later date, form a very small minority within the Arab-American community. There are about 25,000 Arab-Americans in the whole Los Angeles area but there are not more than 600 or 700 Jordanians among them; in Pasadena there are said to be fifty Jordanian-Palestinian families.

According to a standard work on the subject, *The Syrians in America* by Dr. Philip Hitti,* the first "Syrian landed in America in 1854, but "Syrian" immigration in substantial numbers did not start until the latter part of the 1870's. (Dr. Hitti uses "Syrian" in the pre-World War I sense to include what is now Syria, Lebanon, Jordan and Israel). By 1920, according to Dr. Hitti, they numbered 200,000. The bulk of the Arab-Americans are now third generation Americans.

The definition that Dr. Hitti gives of the "Syrians" is extremely revealing of the national feelings and motivations of the earlier settlers and also, of course, of Dr. Hitti himself. (Dr. Hitti, a distinguished historian, was born in Lebanon and has been an American citizen for

* New York, 1924.

many years.) The Syrian, he says, is not a Turk and not an Arab. To say, today, that a Syrian is not an Arab would seem a contradiction in terms, but it was obviously not a contradiction as comparatively recently as 1924.

The fact is that until 1924, and probably later, the Syrian immigrants did not want to be thought of as Arabs because they had come to America to get away from the Arab area and the Arab environment. The late President Kennedy in his book "A Nation of Immigrants"† gives three reasons for people coming to America: "religious persecution, political oppression and economic hardship". In analysing the Syrians' motivations Dr. Hitti reverses the order; according to him the reasons were econimic then political and then religious. But he conceded that most of the Syrian migrants themselves gave political oppression as their main motive followed by religious discrimination.

Arab-American attitudes have since changed with the changing status of the Arab Middle East. The first generation of immigrants had turned their backs on "Syria" and resolutely began the process of assimilation, though for many there was still the barrier of the English language. With the second generation, assimilation was carried forward and virtually completed. The links with the old country were reduced to two things, *tabouli,* an unnecessary complicated salad, and the *dabke,* a thumping sort of square dance. With the third and present generation, there has been some turning back to the Middle East. For them the problem of loyalties and belonging has been settled: they are Americans and, having that solid base, they can afford to take an intelligent, sympathetic but not overly emotional interest in what is happening in the Arab countries. On Palestine it is probably true to say that there are many of the younger third-generation Arab-Americans who are genuinely and actively concerned but not to the extent of participating commitment.

For many Arab-Americans the troubles of the Arabs in the Middle East have always been an unmitigated nuisance. They have had to call themselves Arab-Americans since Syria became the name of a definite

† New York, 1964, Introduction by Robert Kennedy.

national entity, but that is almost the limit of their identification with the Middle East. Their attitude is: "We came here to get away from the Middle East; if the Arabs are in trouble what has that to do with us? We are Americans".

There are other Arab-Americans who retain an interest in their homelands but not in their politics. When the occasion arises, as it did after the fighting in June, 1967, they donated generously to relief funds for the Palestinian homeless; but they will not go beyond a humanitarian interest to any criticism of American Middle East policy.

There are yet others who are interested in what is happening, politically, in the Middle East and who deplore America's pro-Israel policy. They may even try to do something about it like attending public meetings, or writing letters to the newspapers, or to their Congressman. But their attitude, and they expressed it to me more than once during my visit to Los Angeles, is: "When it comes to influencing American policy, we cannot compete with the Jews and Zionists. They are much stronger and richer than we are. What can we really do? We are helpless."

Only a very few Arab-Americans think that it is still worthwhile trying to battle on to get the Arab case presented to the great American public. Only with this restricted group would a Palestinian family find any rapport.

The Arab-Americans are, as a group, solid American citizens. From small beginnings as peddlers, confectioners and haberdashers they have risen in the world through sheer hard work. There are now quite a few very rich people among them and many others, perhaps most, are comfortably middle class. They have accepted the material standards of America and they are not much moved by abstract ideal or political enthusiasms. In most of these communities the centre of the community life is the church, around which revolves their cozy self-enclosed social existence.

A report in *The New York Times* on the Arab-Americans in the Los Angeles area has this to say of them: "The second and third generations of these immigrants are, in the words of Professor Gustave von Grunebaum, an Arab affairs specialist at the University of California, 'well-civilized, with a high percentage of the men in the professions'.

They are 'well-groomed, prosperous and not organized'. They are also passionately pro-American and English-speaking (even their monthly magazine 'Pyramid' is not in Arabic, except for one page). There are no Arab-American neighborhoods, few organizations outside the Syrian Orthodox Cathedral, no congregation places, except for that Church, and only a few broadly Mediterranean restaurants—with approximately 50 per cent Jewish patronage . . . The rest of the community (except for the Jordanians) is glad to be Americanized and—'grateful that we are here, where there is opportunity, and not back in the Middle East, where there is nothing but trouble', in the words of Philip Zogaib, a Syrian-American who edits 'The Pyramid' ".

It was into this sort of community—respectable, settled, conservative, and very American—that those newcomers, the Sirhans, were projected in 1957.

In their anxiety to acquire a local colouration, the Arab-American was quite prepared to change his name or accept American mispronunciation. [This would be understandable if Arab names were long and difficult, but they are not.] Thus Dabbaghi becomes, in the case of the world-famous heart surgeon, De Bakey, and Awad, the correct pronunciation of which is Ah-wud becomes Aye-wad. To a proud Arab, this unnecessary practice could be considered not assimilation but a surrender of identity. It was, therefore, significant that almost the first thing Sirhan Sirhan did in court, when he was arraigned, was to correct the judge's pronunciation of his quite simple name, which Americans mispronounce by dropping the "h" sound, so that it approximates to a popular brand name of a type of plastic wrap used in American kitchens. Here was a small but definite act of revolt on Sirhan's part and by making it on this issue of pronunciation, Sirhan indicated that he, for one, had not accepted the disposition to total assimilation of most Arab-Americans. He had made the same point, much earlier on, when, as a schoolboy, he had signed his name in his class year-books in Arabic: a deliberate show of "differentness".

These simple acts summed up the difficulties the Sirhans had with America at large and with their own Arab-American community.

Soon after their arrival the newness and the difficulties of the

American way of life seemed merely amusing. Mrs. Sirhan recounts: "When we came to this country we were happy to see the water. We went one time, my daughter, went into the bathroom and she flushed, flushed, flushed and then she went and sprinkled the water and said 'God bless America' and I said, 'We are lucky in this country', after standing sometimes half a day for a drink of water in Jerusalem". Munir suffered a day of minor anguish when he first went to school because with his inadequate English he kept on asking for the "laboratory" instead of the "lavatory" and the picture he drew to explain his need was of the traditional Arab hole-in-the-floor latrine. And the younger boys, starved of the use of bicycles in Jerusalem, received reprimands till they discovered that the bicycles, left around in such careless abundance, were not common property. However, in the years immediately after the departure of Bechara Sirhan, in 1958 and 1959, the troubles of the Sirhan family were primarily economic. The two elder sons arrived in 1960, so for the intervening two years the only possible wage-earners were the mother, Aida and Adel. Sirhan and Munir were both in school. Bechara Sirhan does not seem to have sent the family any money from New York.

Mrs. Sirhan obtained employment as a helper in the nursery school run by the Westminster Presbyterian Church on Lake Avenue. Her work was that of a housekeeper which she did five mornings a week for a salary of somewhere between $200 and $250. Aida obtained secretarial work and Adel probably earned occasionally as a carpenter, and an odd-job man. To make ends meet for a family of five on these earnings must have been anything but easy.

The listings relating to the Sirhans in the Pasadena City Directory, though incomplete and not always accurate, give an adequate picture of their marginal and fluctuating economic status. For 1961, when the family was living at 647 North Lake Avenue, there are listed Adel, wood carpenter; Aida, shipping clerk; Mary, helper, Westminster Nursery School; Saadallah, painter. For 1962, Adel drops out and Sharif is added as "accountant, Breakfast (sic.) Convention". In 1963, there is no mention of Sharif or Saadallah but Adel reappears as "musician", and in this year the family residence shifts to 696 East Howard Street. The combined Directory for the years 1964-65 mentions: Adel, musician; Aida, bookkeeper; Mary, mechanic (Mrs. Sirhan must have given her husband's profession) and Sirhan, student. The listing for the next year, 1966, is Adel, Aida, Mary, Saadallah, living on North Lake, no profession given, and Sirhan and Munir, students. In 1967, there are mentioned: Adel, Mary, Saadallah, no profession, and Sirhan and Munir, still students. In 1961, the Sirhans had four wage-earners in the family: five years later there were two. They began purchasing the house on Howard Street from the earnings of Aida and Mary Sirhan.

Things however were not quite all that grim although the Sirhans' economic position was not as good as it could have been with five young men in the family. From 1957 to 1966, when Aida left to work, and marry, in Palm Springs, there were only two regular wage-earners in the family, the two women, the mother and Aida. Adel was the next most consistent earner, whether as a carpenter or as a musician. Adel sometimes described himself as a professor of oriental music but he was, in fact, a performer on the *oud*, a Middle Eastern instrument resembling a guitar, and he worked off-and-on in several Arab restaurants and supper-clubs providing the musical accompaniment for singers and belly-dancers. Saadallah and Sharif were completely erratic in their employment and were sometimes out of work for long periods, a couple of years at a time. From 1965 on Sirhan began to work; and it is surprising that he should be listed as a student until 1967; in that year Munir also began to work.

With the family income as erratic and inadequte as it undoubtedly was, the Sirhans took something of a risk when in 1963, they moved in and began the process of buying the house at 696 East Howard. Its value is estimated at $15,000 and though there were times when they were almost not able to keep up on their payments, they somehow finally contrived to do so. As has been said, East Howard is a pleasant neighbourhood with many trees and well-kept houses and gardens. Father east of number 696 it becomes racially mixed and then wholly coloured, but around 696 it is almost wholly white; all the Sirhans' neighbours are white people.

The Sirhans are definitely a brown-skinned family, the colour of their skin accentuated by their black hair; they are, in fact, more brunette than most West Bank Palestinians. Nevertheless and despite the clear difference in colour, the Sirhan family got on well with their white neighbours.

But the socio-political implications of the colour difference struck the young Sirhan quite early because Mrs. Sirhan remembers that one day he asked, "Mama, are we Americans now?" and she replied, "Not yet, but we will be", and his counter question was, "Mama, if we are Americans are we going to be blonde very soon?"

Before attempting to give a picture of the Sirhans' family life, it would be appropriate to see how the family, except for the father, finally came together in Pasadena and what some of them were like at that time. According to Dr. Bell of the Baptist Church, Mrs. Sirhan and some of the children began attending the church and its Sunday school in about 1958. It was known that the family was in financial straits and in 1960 Mrs. Sirhan asked the church to assist in bringing the two older sons, Saadallah and Sharif, from Jerusalem. The Baptist Church provided the necessary sponsorship and funds; and the Sirhans later repaid this money to the church. Having made this repayment, the Sirhans were under no further material obligation to the Baptists. (The family also repaid to their sponsoring organisation the cost of their journey from Jerusalem).

Sharif had finished school in Jerusalem and had worked for a year as an accountant with Mobil Oil in Amman. When he came to Pasadena, the church helped him find a clerical post in the office of the Southern California Baptist Convention (the "Breakfast Convention" of the City Directory). Sharif, Dr. Bell said, was a modest young man, clean, always "neat as a pin", and normally quiet and retiring. The only members of the family to attend the church regularly were Mrs. Sirhan and Munir. Mrs. Sirhan struck Dr. Bell as being a modest and humble woman, and a hard-working and self-sacrificing mother; very loyal to her family and much affected by the ups-and-downs in the family fortunes. Munir, Dr. Bell described in fond terms as a well-liked and happy-go-lucky youngster; "he was a sweet, happy kid"; because he was small in size, he was pushed around but being full of life he managed to hold his own; everyone thought him "cute" and that he conducted himself well.

Dr. Bell said that he found it difficult to pin-point Aida, who attended the church from time to time: a serious young woman who asked to be put into the adult Bible study classes rather than with people of her own age.

From friends and neighbours, we get random glimpses of the home life of Sirhan and the rest of the family on East Howard Street. But putting them together one gets a picture of a reasonably cheerful group of people, who had a lot of troubles and who faced them united. In economic terms, at least, they own their survival to the Arab system of the joint family under which everyone's earnings go into a common pool. As Munir puts it, "My brother's money is mine and the money in my pocket is my brother's".

Father Paul Romney of the Syrian Orthodox Cathedral said that the Palestinians were usually aloof from the rest of his parish, but that the Sirhans were more than usually aloof. Nevertheless, they maintained their formal connection with their native church. Mrs. Sirhan borrowed religious books from the church library and would have liked to have attended services regularly but could not do so; the cathedral is in downtown Los Angeles, 20 miles from Pasadena and none of the sons were prepared to drive her that distance on a Sunday morning. Prior to 1968, Father Paul used to perform the annual ceremony of blessing the family home. When he visited them, he found the Sirhans hospitable but formal and protoclaire in their behavior: "for instance, they would always serve one with Arabic coffee and when they offered the glass of water that goes with the coffee, they wouldn't just hand it to one, but offer it on a plate". I suggested that this could have been out of deference for his position but he replied that he felt this correctness was part of the family style.

It was from Miss Linda Massri and from her mother, Mrs. Kamakian, that I learnt most about the Sirhans, for the two ladies were good friends of the family. From the start the Arab-Americans in Pasadena felt that the Sirhans were different and "superior." One gets the impression, that they were overimpressed, to the point of exaggerating some of the family's qualitites. What particularly seemed to impress was their dark, good looks, their polite manners and their command of English. It was more than just this that impressed Miss Massri: "They were serious minded; they all read a lot; and they were all concerned with the problems of the world. When one was with them, they didn't just gossip about this and that; they discussed things; we would have tremendous arguments about politics or religion or any number of things and we would end up shouting at each other. I learnt a great deal from them. One had the feeling that they were not just ordinary people, that this family had a destiny".

What also impressed the Arab-Americans of Pasadena was the fact that the Sirhans were unashamedly Arabs and did not seem to be greatly concerned with becoming Americans. The family spoke better-than-average English (or at least by American standards), yet they spoke nothing but Arabic between themselves, which very few Arab-American families wished to do or were able to do. Mrs. Sirhan's English was conversationally adequate but it was understandable if, like the first generation Arab-Americans, she preferred to switch to Arabic. But the young Sirhans preferred to do this too and without any feeling of self-consciousness or inferiority. Since assimilation to American society obviously depends on the immigrant's grasp of English, it is interesting to note that Sirhan claims, doubtless truthfully, that he thinks in English, which would indicate a high degree of assimilation. But this linguistic penetration does not seem to have been very deep for from his notebooks we know that when he wanted to recall the deeper levels of emotion that are expressed through poetry Sirhan turned to Arabic verse and even jotted down some verses of his own in Arabic. Further there are two ultimate tests of what is one's mother tongue—it is the language in which one dreams and in which one counts. From the notes he scribbled in the margins of the books he read we observe that even when the notations themselves are in English, Sirhan numbered them off with the so-called Arabic numerals (actually of Indian origin). Therefore one can say, with considerable certitude, that despite his many years in America and despite his all-English education, Sirhan's mother-tongue remained Arabic.

The Sirhans always served Arabic coffee, that symbol of Arab hospitality, and they tried to keep their food as near as possible to what they were used to in Jerusalem. Mrs. Sirhan used to receive gift parcels from her relatives with the spices and other materials she needed for Arabic dishes.

The Sirhans retained their family links—which Mrs. Sirhan did through a regular correspondence—and looked back home without regret or bitterness. Mrs. Sirhan often reminisced about the happy times they had in Palestine and never brooded over the misfortunes they had undergone, which, as we know, were considerable.

Though it was a close-knit family, the house on East Howard clearly did not have room for all of them. Mrs. Sirhan encouraged the two older sons to move out for this reason and also because they were trying to dominate the younger ones, which she did not like. After one particularly serious fight between Saadallah and Sirhan, the latter left the house for a couple of weeks. Mrs. Sirhan also felt that it would be better for the young men to be out in the world to grow by experience and learn to cope with their own problems.

Yet it was not always "plain living and high thinking" in the Sirhan household, for the older brothers were not adverse to the simpler delights of "wine, women and song." Both Saadallah and Adel were gregarious, cheerful types, especially the latter who with his *oud* was often the life and soul of any party. As the neighbours have testified, the Sirhans did not go in for many parties. But visitors were frequent, and they themselves were frequent callers; nor was their talk always on the Palestine problem. On one thing the friends are agreed: in company Sirhan held his end of the conversation and enjoyed a joke as much as anyone. But he always gave the impression of being the most serious and quiet of the five brothers. He was no shy recluse, but neither was he what may be called a good party man.

Whether or not because of Adel's musical profession, the Sirhan family as a whole seems to have been extremely fond of music—Arabic music. "There was always music playing in their house", Miss Massri said. They had a tape recorder. "They had lots of tapes and friends from Jordan sent them more". Like many an Arab-American family Miss Massri and her mother have quite a collection of Arabic music records which the young Sirhans enjoyed listening to when they visited. What is more, they insisted that Miss Massri listen to them seriously too. Which could be quite a trial when it came to the songs, two or three hours long, of Umm Kulthum, the most famous woman singer of the Arab world. Perhaps a few words about this singer will point out why Sirhan's interest in her music would seem odd.

I was somewhat surprised to learn that Sirhan was a passionate admirer of Umm Kulthum, for I did not expect that a young, serious-minded Arab would be as succeptible as he evidently was to her seductive langours.

Though her art is only now, and very hesitantly, becoming known outside the Arab countries, she has been for well over a generation, one of the most important socio-cultural-artistic phenomena of the Arab world. When she gives one of her Friday night recitals from Cairo radio, it has been estimated that one out of every two or three Arab listeners in the vast area from Morocco to Muscat is listening to her and, what is more, hanging on her every note.

Umm Kulthum, who must now be in her 70's, is a very well-preserved and rather generously-proportioned lady. She has a commanding stage presence and she plays on the emotions of her audience as skilfully as she uses her voice. This is a throbbing alto, very smooth and heavy, which drips and clings to the sliding semi-tones of Arabic music.

Each of her "songs" lasts for a couple of hours during which she improvises variations on a short poem, usually no more than a dozen lines, that forms the lyric.

What is extraordinary is that though Umm Kulthum sings religious songs, and in times of crisis, songs on patriotic themes, the main body of her repetoire, the songs that are really popular, relate to one single subject—the pangs of unrequited or lost love.

At a performance that Umm Kulthum gave at the Baalbeck Festival in Lebanon, I saw these songs moving society ladies in furs and diamonds and taxi drivers in shirtsleeves to tears and to shouts of ecstacy: an orgy of emotional self-indulgence. And this is standard practice at all her public concerts.

Why the sobbing accents of heartbreak and tender melancholy should have this profound effect on every sort and condition of Arab in every Arab country has never been explained, and when the Arab psychologists do provide us with the answer we may learn something very important about the Arab psyche.

Arab admirers of Umm Kulthum say that it is not the maudlin words of her songs that matter but the beauty of the music. The point is that apart from its undoubted subtlety, the emotional quality of her music is, invariably, melancholy and slow moving and plangent; it has "a dying fall", and is one long succession of dying falls.

What is clear is that the emotional effect that Umm Kulthum has is thoroughly enervating and debilitating as would be an undiluted diet of the music of Tchiakovsky for a Western audience. The Arabs say they need a national regeneration to face the threat of Israel; in this context Umm Kulthum is worth half a dozen divisions to the Israeli General Staff. Ironically her music is becoming popular with sections of young Israelis.

It is perhaps because of her marshmallow softness that Umm Kulthum is treated with some disdain by the younger generation of Arabs. Which is why I was surprised to find that Sirhan admired her greatly. Miss Massri described how, when he was still a schoolboy of 16, she saw him listening to an Umm Kalthum recording while he was having dinner and so rapt was he in the music that he not only stopped eating, but he forgot about his food altogether. This musical preference which for Sirhan was an old-fashioned one, shows that at some deep emotional level he retained a link with an "oceanic" Arab feeling, though what this consists of precisely, apart from a self-flagellating melancholy, no one seems to know, except, perhaps, Umm Kalthum herself. In his cell on Death Row, in San Quentin prison, her songs are still the music Sirhan listens to with the greatest pleasure.

One adaptation to the American way of life that Sirhan made, perforce, was that he learnt to be useful around the house, in a way in which few Arab boys are in their own homes. Neighbours have described him as the family handyman who mowed the front lawn, tended the garden, repaired the shed in the back yard and so on. On one occasion, when Linda Massri dropped in unannounced and Sirhan was alone in the house, he insisted on her staying for a meal. He then prepared a dish of meatballs, served it and later washed the dishes and cleaned the kitchen floor.

Like any other young man, but especially like any other young American, Sirhan was delighted when he acquired his first car, a venerable 1958 De Soto. The $400 he paid for it was carefully saved from the money he earned doing odd-jobs while at school and working throughout his summer vacations. He was much teased about it because its colour scheme was incongrously feminine—pink and white outside with pink and white imitation silk upholstery inside. Miss Massri even offered to exchange her car for his but Sirhan, who laughed at all the jokes about his car, insisted on keeping it even though its performance was unreliable. Unlike the average non-mechanical Arab he learnt to tinker with it and was even able to repair a bent axle.

On most days when Mrs. Sirhan finished work at the nursery school, her sons would be there to drive her home. It is a distance of only about six blocks, but in motorised Southern California one does not walk six blocks if one can ride.

In one other way Sirhan was like all young persons—he very much wanted to anticipate the future and to know, beforehand, what was going to happen to him. Here, however, an Arab touch was added because the fortune telling was done by "reading" the dregs at the bottom of cups of Arabic coffee. Mrs. Sirhan read the cups but it was Linda Massri who was Sirhan's favourite fortune-teller. "He enjoyed being told what was supposed to happen", he said, "but it was something more than that: it was almost as if he wanted to be figured out and told what he was".

Everybody who knew them agreed that the Sirhans gave the impression of being a very close-knit family and that the children were more than usually devoted to their mother. The family unity was especially noticeable when there was trouble: they then drew together and drew away from their friends, and made it clear that they positively did not want outside sympathy or pity, or help.

Considering the general aloofness of the family, Sirhan still managed to make a definite impression and favourable one on the neighbours. There was Mrs. Olive Blakeslee, their next-door neighbour, with whom Sirhan played the game of Chinese checkers. She taught him the game and he picked it up quickly and would invite himself over when he was at a loose-end. It is she who has commented on Sirhan's thoughtfulness: "He would even carry cups of coffee out to the trash man", she said, "and in hot weather he would take them cool, soft drinks". For her he was an exceptionally nice boy. She did, however, show some regret that she could not interest him in religion. She lent him religious books but when he returned them it was without comment.

Miss Massri recounts one unusual incident involving Sirhan. At a party in her house, Sirhan got into conversation with an Armenian guest who was much travelled and a good linguist. He put questions in several languages to Sirhan, who answered, correctly, in that language. From this test, so it seems, Sirhan emerged with some knowledge of no less than seven languages—English, Arabic, Hebrew, Russian, French, Italian and Greek.

One other impression that the Sirhan family gave to its friends—and it is by far the most important of all— is that they all hoped, someday to return home to Palestine and to Jerusalem. Saadallah, for example, held out against becoming an American citizen for a long time and this made it difficult for him to get certain jobs as a mechanic, or in the construction industry. Finally he decided to take out naturalization papers, and he asked Miss Massri to help him because he was not sure that he would understand all the intricacies of the document since he did not have a thorough grasp of English. He spoke the language well enough, but since he did not finish school, he did not know it as well as his other brothers, which in itself could have contributed to his employment difficulties. He has stated, ironically enough, that he used to listen to Robert Kennedy's speeches on television in order to improve his English to qualify him for naturalization.

If Saadallah had decided to cease being a Palestinian and to learn English a few years earlier, life would have been a great deal easier for him and for his family.

Saadallah's problems were not only politico-economic: he had been booked by the police a couple of times for driving while under the influence of drink. When the hearing on his application for naturalization, scheduled for the fateful morning of June 5th, was cancelled, it was these traffic violations, as well as his brother's case, that were given as reasons.

Sharif's problem was essentially personal but its origins were the socio-cultural difficulties of an immigrant. When we last mentioned him he was a neat, well-behaved young man working as a clerk for the Baptist Convention. He began going out with an American girl who was at that time a student in Pasadena City College. It was, for him, at least, something serious. After some time, the young woman broke it off because she felt that the Sirhan boys were too different in their attitudes towards the relation of the sexes: Sharif resented the fact that she, like any ordinary American girl, had a will of her own; she could not accept the fact that he, like any Arab man, expected to be the dominant partner in the relationship. The fact that it was the girl who took the first step toward breaking off hit Sharif particularly hard: it was a rejection that hurt him in his male pride. The fact that such "rejections" are a commonplace in many societies made no difference, because it was something utterly new in his experience. Certainly in Jerusalem any such step, if ever taken, would usually have come from the part of the man.

In an attempt to prevent a final break, Sharif enlisted the help of Miss Massri who lectured him on just how different the American way of life is, in this particular field, from what he was used to. And she tried to persuade the young woman to give Sharif time to make the transition from his old ways to the new American way of things. To no avail.

Sharif was so unable to accept what had happened to him that he began to act in a way that was a combination of foolishness and desperation. When threatening phone calls to the girl's home produced no results, he made two attempts to cut the fuel lines of her car. He next tried to sabotage its brake system. At this point, the girl's family informed the police who put Sharif under surveillance, so that it was under the eyes of the police that he made his third and most desperate attempt. On December 18th, 1963, a little after midday and on the open street, Sharif set about cutting open bullets so as to sprinkle gunpowder on the car's engine. He was caught red-handed with bullets, gunpowder and a hacksaw and charged with attempted murder. His exploit was described in detail on the front page of the Pasadena paper the next morning.

That he seemed to have no clear idea of what he was up to is indicated by the fact that a few days later he burst in on Miss Massri waving the newspapers and declaring that they had no right to describe him as an attempted murderer, which he certainly was.

When the case came for trial, the prosecution seems to have taken the view that this was a crime passionelle by an emotionally disturbed young man. Whatever the reason, the District Attorney declined to issue the attempted murder charge and Sharif was sentenced to be placed on probation for one year.

Unfortunately, Sharif's employers were not quite so understanding and he was dismissed from his job with the Baptist Convention. Mrs. Sirhan and Sharif let it be known that they considered the local pastor, Dr. Bell, responsible for this action and they forthwith ceased attending his church. Dr. Bell visited the Sirhan home to discuss the matter with the family but all that Mrs. Sirhan would say was that she definitely thought he was responsible and did not wish to discuss the matter further.

At one point in my talk with Dr. Bell I asked him whether he thought Mrs. Sirhan was a devout person and whether she had been a good church member. His reply was that he was not prepared to go that far, because though she had been regular in her attendance they could not get Mrs. Sirhan to become a full member of the Baptist Church "which is what we want".

One can only wish that the Baptists had been more forgiving, because for several years following this episode Sharif could not find a job; in fact it seems he never found steady employment thereafter. He kept himself afloat by gambling at the race track, sometimes with borrowed money.

This incident had an adverse impact on at least one other member of the family. Sirhan was "ragged" by his friends because of what Sharif did and some of the other Arabs, working at petrol stations, refused to serve Sharif and Sirhan when they drove in.

Some friends claim that Sirhan became perceptibly more withdrawn after this first, shaming brush with the law by a member of his family.

Aida's difficulty was much the same sort as Sharif's—personal in nature but the product of conflicting cultural attitudes. Approximately two years before her death from lukemia in march 1965 she moved to Palm Springs to take up a post there as an accountant, in the Sun and Fun Candy Store. What is not generally known is that while in Palm Springs she married an American. Because she knew or surmised that her brothers would disapprove of her marrying a non-Arab, Aida kept her marriage secret from the family, or at least from its male members. Mrs. Sirhan almost certainly knew about it and perhaps Adel, who was closest to Aida in age and affection.

Aida's marriage is the second family happening to which the Sirhans never refer. Though a great many details of the family history were brought out during the course of the trial no mention was ever made of this particular fact.

With the progress of her disease, Aida would come back home to Pasadena to rest for weeks at a time and friends observed that during this period the Sirhans were particularly turned in on themselves.

Leukemia is incurable, so Aida and the family knew that she was dying. They turned to giving her herbal food and medicines but it was forlorn hope.

Hers was a long-drawn-out agony. The disease first manifested itself in 1962 and she was given only half a year to live in the beginning. During the last six months she was almost continually ill at home and since Mrs. Sirhan and Adel were working and Munir was too young and Saadallah and Sharif were otherwise engaged, the task of sitting with Aida and caring for her fell to Sirhan. At times the blood would gust from her nose and Sirhan, with his childhood horror of blood, had to try hard to stop himself from fainting. At such times Aida would be rushed to hospital and, in Mrs. Sirhan's words, "That took all the family and we didn't have any more strength to stand it".

Like her brothers Aida was physically small, pleasant-mannered and well-liked. When, in the last stages of the disease, she was in the hospital and Father Romney visited her there, he was impressed by the quality and weightiness of the books she was reading: "not the usual movie magazines".

Like most people, like her own brothers, Father Paul only learnt that Aida was married at the burial, at which he officiated because the announcement was in her married name. And it was only because of the funeral that her husband visited the Sirhans' house and, for the first time, met his late wife's brothers.

A few days after her death, one of the brothers, more in anger than sorrow, exclaimed against the fact that Aida had kept her marriage hidden from them. But, she had good reason to anticipate their disapproval.

It may be wondered why a brothers' disapproval should carry such weight with a sister. It is not that in the absence of the father, the brothers represented male authority in the family: their objections would have been decisive even if Bechara Sirhan were still in Pasadena. The concept that the son is the defender of the family honour of which the daughter, his sister, is the symbol,—an obligation that carries with it the responsibility of having a say in the sister's private life,—this concept is found not merely in Arab countries but in all the countries around the Mediterranean Sea. The belief is part of a distinctive and surprisingly uniform culture to be found around its shores: along with the vine and the olive and the potent milk-white drink known variously as pernod or raki or ouzo or arak. Crimes of violence committed by brothers in attempts (usually unwanted and half-witted) to defend their sisters are as common in Sicily as in Lebanon. Even after many years of living in the individualistic and permissive social setting of America, a serious and intelligent young woman like Aida Sirhan was not prepared to flout her brothers' opinion on whom she should marry.

Equally significant is the fact that she never discussed the matter with them: she knew beforehand that they would disapprove of her marrying an "outsider." That the family should not become too intimately linked with America was something understood and taken for granted.

Adel, the musician, was personally the best adjusted to the conflict of cultures but this did not mean that he, too, did not feel the weight of family disapproval when it came to the question of marriage. Adel moved from one Arab supper-club to another and back again. When working, he could earn up to $150 a week, the largest salary of any of the Sirhans. And when not playing the oud, he turned his hand to cabinet making or picture-framing. Most of the Sirhan brothers, like their father, can use their hands. Most of them, too, have a streak of the gambler in them. With Sharif, and probably Sirhan, it was the horses; with Adel it was cards. But as one of his friends remarked, "He is a lousy poker player". So it was not unknown for Adel to be skinned the day after pay day and to have to fall back on friendly loans and advances. Both Sharif and Adel were, however, punctilious about repaying their debts.

Over the years Adel has on three occasions had serious connections with young women, all non-Arab-Americans, with marriage being definitely considered. In each case there was a breaking-off, sometimes from Adel's side, sometimes from that of the girl: Adel took these happenings with far more philosophic calm than Sharif did. Some of his Arab-American friends regretted that he did not marry because it might have helped him to settle down.

But the Sirhan family was not of that opinion. On the third occasion when Adel's marriage seemed imminent, Mrs. Sirhan and his brothers appealed to friends to use their influence to break up the connection, so strongly did they disapprove. It was a disapproval in principle, for there was nothing wrong with the young lady of Adel's choice.

The troubles of the youngest brother are suscinctly described in this newspaper account (*The Los Angeles Herald-Examiner,* June 20, 1968):

"The 14-year-old brother of Sirhan B. Sirhan, accused assassin of Sen. Robert F. Kennedy, is fighting a deportation order issued against him after he was convicted of felony narcotics charges, an immigration official has disclosed. Munir Bishara Sirhan, known as Joe, was arrested June 10, 1966, for possession and sale of marijuana. He was tried as an adult and convicted in Superior Court of both charges on Oct. 13, 1966. On Dec. 1 of that year he was placed on five years probation with the first year to be served in county jail, court records disclosed. But on May 15, 1967, the judge set aside the conviction because Sirhan was a juvenile at the time of the alleged crime and ordered him to be turned over to the juvenile authorities, the record showed. The deportation order was issued in 1966, but he appealed to the board of immigration appeals in Washington, which only just now had begun the process of reviewing the appeal, immigration authorities indicated. He based his appeal on the argument that he was a juvenile at the time and the conviction had been set aside for this reason. The Immigration Department apparently contended that the judge had no jurisdiction to issue later orders after the disposition of the case and that the decision to treat him as a juvenile should have been made before, not after, the trial".

In short, if this report is correct, Munir Sirhan theoretically still faces deportation on the basis of an incorrect conviction which has been rescinded but which the Immigration Department contends is still valid. Sirhan contends that Munir would have been deported by now if it had not been for the publicity given to the family because of his trial.

Munir spent some months, in the early part of 1967, at a juvenile correction farm.

Thus during their eleven years in Pasadena, the Sirhan family has had more than its fair share of tribulations. There was the departure of the father after six months, Sharif's trouble in 1963 entailing the loss of his job, Aida's death and the business of her secret marriage, Munir's trial and conviction in 1966, Saadallah's continuing unemployment and the financial and emotional problems of Adel.

Such being the record of the Sirhans' legal and economic troubles, it is surprising that so many people nevertheless liked and respected them. They somehow gave the impression of deserving better things, so that their troubles seemed the unfair visitations of a malign fate. "Life gave them a rough deal" was one expression used; and "they seemed destined to suffer" was another. Perhaps people felt this sympathy because the Sirhans appeared to be caught in a conflict of large impersonal forces. Some of their troubles were entirely self-created, like Munir's trafficking in drugs, but Saadallah's unemployment, Sharif's case, the secrecy of Aida's marriage and Adel's lesser problems, were, almost entirely, due to their refusal or inability to merge politically and socially into America. This may have been a foolish reluctance but it represented a stand on general principles. And it is this that probably evoked the puzzled and compassionate respect of those who knew them.

Typical of this defensive affection was the opinion of Mrs. Frances Rosemond (*Life,* June 24, 1968) "who believes herself to be one of the few friends of the family during their first years in the U.S.": " 'They were in one hell of a bind. They were treated like Negroes. They were Christians but most people didn't know or care; they were intelligent, sensitive, proud—they really didn't belong anywhere. They were really displaced people ... There was an air of elegance about them. They were all very well educated, British schools in Jerusalem, I think. They spoke the King's English beautifully, musically. They complained to me: 'What kind of culture is this when you can't even speak your own language properly? English is not even our language and yet we even speak it better than you!' ''.

And during the sad and shabby happenings of these eleven years, what was the other member of the family, Sirhan Sirhan, doing? He was, in the first place, not getting into any sort of trouble; and secondly, he was, until 1963, putting himself through school and trying to make a living.

Since the school authorities in Pasadena, like those at the Pasadena City College, interpreted the Court Order to give it the widest possible applicability, no information could be obtained directly from them on any aspect of Sirhan's years in school. But a good deal of information about his school years came out in the course of the trial.

The general problems facing Sirhan as an immigrant schoolboy have been aptly summed up by *Life* magazine (July 8, 1968): "Sirhan . . . overcame enormous handicaps—an awareness of his own strangeness in the eyes of his school mates, shyness, a mingled envy and repudiation of the people and the attitudes of garish Southern California. He kept out of trouble, blended, almost as if he were transparent, into the student body . . ."

These were not the only problems he had to face. Because the family arrived in Pasadena in the middle of the American school year, and because of the difference in educational systems and the medium of instruction, Sirhan was placed two grades behind when he entered Longfellow Elementary School; so that he graduated from high school at the age of 19, when in the normal course of events he should have done so when he was 17 or 18.

At the trial an official of the Pasadena School System testified that at the age of 14 years 10 months Sirhan had the mental age of 12 years 8 months, and that at 17 his mental age was 15 years 2 months. Sirhan's overall I.Q. figure was 89, the normal range being 90 to 110. The school's final estimate of his intelligence was that he was slightly better than average on the whole, standing 558 in a class of 829. But this, it must be remembered, is the record of a student for whom the medium of instruction was not his mother tongue. He showed linguistic ability in earning B grades in both Russian and German.

The official testified that in school Sirhan had "no special problems". But he did have the problems of assimilation and integration that face all first-generation Americans. It was in high school that he discovered that because he was brown and poor he would not be accepted as an equal by the white and rich. Feeling himself among an excluded minority, Sirhan resorted to the not unusual response of people in that position—he turned around and despised the "bourgeois" average and the society they represented. It was in high school that he began reading books by authors such as C. Wright Mills who are critical of the American social structure.

Small and brown, without money and without a car, Sirhan could not hope to make a mark on the social life of his school. Some of the tribal customs of the American young frankly puzzled him: he recalls his amused astonishment at his first dance when he saw the vigorously contorted movements of his classmates.

A girl who went to this school with him remembers that she and her schoolmates made fun of Sirhan because he was older than any of them and because he had come from a foreign country, though not specifically because he was a Jordanian. A boy who went through school with Sirhan recalls: "He could hardly speak English. Kids picked on him, telling him dirty words he'd repeat without knowing what they meant [and Sirhan, as we have seen, was unusually conscious of bad language]. He was a very hard worker after school. He sold papers and swept out a coffee shop nearby. He came over to my house a lot to play with me. My parents gave him one of my old bicycles. They often tried to have me behave like him, he was so polite".

By 1963, when Sirhan entered John Muir High School in the 10th grade, he had overcome any early disabilities and he did well there. One of his teachers has described him as "polite, clean and an A-1 student". He won "A" grades and was on the student council both in his junior and senior years. He even joined the officer cadet corps. The memories of his friends are varied but never uncomplimentary: "A taciturn individual who did not say very much . . . friendly, really pleasant, but hard to get to know . . . he was so dark and scrawny but always so neat. The other kids came to school in sweat shirts and jeans, but Sirhan always had a clean shirt . . . a first-rate student . . . he was brilliant. He was studying Russian when everyone else was studying English and Spanish . . . he was calm and well-mannered, nothing evil about him . . . he was withdrawn and alone".

The young man who was president of the school council when Sirhan was a member recalls that Sirhan captured his interest because he seemed so out of things, yet, "if we were working on some class function, such as a dance, he would be very conscientious about it. I liked him. I remember him best as being a very warm person". He remembered one thing which probably made Sirhan feel that he was part of things. "Sirhan, if I remember correctly, won a prize as one of the best in the candy sale".

But clearly it needed more than record candy sales to make Sirhan feel that he was, for good and all, a part of America, because when at school he confided in a friend that he "dreamed of being something big in Jordan after his university studies in the U.S." The ambitious dreams of adolescence are normal enough, but what is truly significant is that Sirhan's ambitions were to be played out in Jordan, not America.

At the same time, Sirhan seems to have had a premonition that he was not going to fulfill any of his big ambitions for he told a school friend that he "was despondent about his failure to do better and feeling that life was taking him nowhere, and that he was not going to make a mark". Whether or not this was just an expression of the usual weltschmerz of youth, Sirhan took a step that showed he could also be realistic in his ambitions. When he was 17 and still two years away from finishing school, he put in an application for job as an exercise boy for horses at the Hollywood Park Race Track.

I enquired amongst those who knew Sirhan in Pasadena about the how and why of his penchant for horses and racing, which seemed to me so out of accord with the rest of his character. The "how" was easily explained: Sharif went to the race track a lot and probably passed on his interest to his younger brother. As to the "why": jockeying, if successful, can be a glamourous and highly-paid profession and one which did not require any special qualifications except the small, light physique which Sirhan, in any case, had. The theory was also advanced that "Arabs love horses"; but a great many Arabs do not, and Sirhan did not come from a horse-riding Bedouin family but from urbanized, farmer stock. So it was probably the economic reason that was determinant.

It was five years before Sirhan returned to the world of horse-racing and by that time it was too late.

In the meantime Sirhan continued as a model student and graduated from John Muir High School in June , 1963.

In June, 1963, Robert Kennedy had been Attorney-General and, virtually, assistant President of the United States, for two and a half years.

Many people have wondered why a good student like Sirhan did not go on to the University of California or that of Southern California and instead went to Pasadena City College which, by any standards, is a second-rate institution. (When I visited it, a display of pictures of distinguished alumni included one U.S. ambassador, sundry business-men and an airline hostess). The answer is fairly simple: Pasadena City College is within easy walking distance of the Sirhan house whereas getting to the distant campuses of U.S.C. or U.C.L.A. would have presented a formidable problem. What is more important is that soon after leaving school, Sirhan had to start working and earning, not to pay his way through school but to help the family budget. It will be recalled that it was six months after Sirhan left school in December 1963, that Sharif lost his job. This meant that the wage-earners in the family were reduced to Mrs. Sirhan, Aida and the somewhat erratic Adel.

It was during that winter that Sirhan took the first of his many humble jobs and discovered that the world was not his oyster. After March 1963 he could not have been anything but a part-time student because he was also earning his living in a variety of jobs; and the entire length of his stay at the college was just one year and five months.

After a reasonably successful spell in high school, college came as a disappointment to Sirhan. The whole approach was impersonal, the lectures were delivered by rote and there was little or no intellectual stimulus or challenge. Pasadena City College, in truth, is little more than a degree factory.

Sirhan's grades in College were not particularly good but this was not due to any mental inability. One of the psychologists involved in the trial, Dr. Seymour Pollack, said that there was "no evidence to indicate that Sirhan was intellectually inadequate or that he was unable at any time to carry on in college". His final mark was a percentile of 22, which means that he would have stood 22 in a class of 100, but this was due either to his boredom, or to the distraction of his jobs or Aida's sickness.

His grades got slowly worse and in his fourth and last semester he had five Fs. But even then he was not dismissed for a poor academic record but for poor attendence: this was in May 1964, prior to the end of the semester.

This was less than eight weeks after Aida's death and the two events were directly connected. Mrs. Sirhan explains, "He had to fill his time at the College but he couldn't do it because he was helping with his sister as there was no one else . . . she was the only sister he had and she was dying. He asked Dr. Pedro for a certificate explaining his absences, he even took it twice from the doctor, but they didn't pay any attention to that. He was really upset when they sent him away: 'They wouldn't reason with me, they wouldn't reason with me', he kept saying." According to Dr. Pollack, Sirhan still remains very angry and bitter over the unfeeling, unimaginative and strictly bureaucratic attitude of the Pasadena City College administration. Indeed there is nothing that can be said in its defence, except that the College is simply a factory and works according to factory rules, with attendance being the most important of these.

Sirhan's comment was, "I gave up my scholastic ambition completely at that time". This rejection marks the definite beginning of Sirhan's slow alienation from American society.

From here on the life of Sirhan Sirhan is one of "the short and simple annals of the poor".

In September, 1964, Sirhan began working for Mr. John Davies who operates a service station close to the centre of Pasadena's business area. When I spoke to Mr. Davies he was busy in the repair section of his Station: he has a lean, lined face with kindly eyes behind his rimless spectacles. He explained that he did not hire Sirhan who, as far as he knew, had been working at the station for about six months (that would be from March, 1964) before he, Mr. Davies, took it over. It was then a 24-hour service station and Sirhan was on the night shift, from 8 p.m. to 4 a.m. Mr. Davies decided to close down at midnight and Sirhan did the last shift, from 4 p.m. to 12. He earned between $1 and $1.65 an hour, a maximum weekly wage of $80.

Sirhan's work, according to Mr. Davies, was solely on the filling station side: he filled cars with petrol, oil and water; washed them down and wiped them off; and at the end of the day, swept out the station "and cleaned the rest-rooms"—that is the semi-public lavatories that most American filling stations provide for their customers. Though I knew by then that Sirhan did things at home and in the neighborhood, like sweeping out a coffee shop, which he would not have done back in Jerusalem, the information that he cleaned out bathrooms gave me a mild shock. It may mean nothing in America, but for an Arab or an Indian, this is considered very lowly work indeed. What must be remembered is this: That while working as filling station assistant was perhaps the best employment that Sirhan, with a high school education, could find, it is the sort of work which in Jerusalem would have been done, and is still done, by illiterates, who have had no schooling at all because it demands no education. And Sirhan would have known this: in Jordan his education would have certainly led him on to better things in life; but in America it meant very little.

"He was a real good worker", Mr. Davies said. "In fact I'd hire him again. He was very polite, courteous and attentive." Sirhan worked for Mr. Davies for ten months and left because he refused to take the needling he got from a superior. "Why the needling," I asked. "Was it because Sirhan was small, or brown, or a foreigner"? Mr. Davies looked unhappy but denied that these were the reasons: "The superior was having trouble at home with his wife and I guess he took it out on Sirhan".

He shifted to another service station, about 50 yards away, run by Ivan Milicic. I never met Mr. Milicic but local papers reported him as saying that Sirhan was "honest and hard-working. If he would come to ask for a job, I would rehire him".

Though his earnings were modest enough, Sirhan had started to bet on horses at Santa Anita race track. After a few weeks with Mr. Malicic,

Sirhan showed him a bundle of money from what he said was a stroke of luck at the race track, and, presumably feeling rich, he quit work.

Sirhan's next job was with an elderly gardener, William Beveridge, who just before I tried to meet him seems to have left his house in a hurry because there were several days' deliveries of milk and newspapers lying on his front porch. Other journalists had met the Beveridges, which was probably the reason for their departure, and Mrs. Beveridge was quoted as saying of Sirhan, "He was a gentleman all the way". The Beveridges liked Sirhan well enough to allow him to live for some weeks in their trailer when he left home after his fight with Saadallah. With Mr. Beveridge Sirhan worked as a gardener watering the plants, an activity in which he was genuinely interested. This and the earlier service station job took Sirhan through the first half of 1965.

After almost two years in this series of dreary jobs, and directly because of his dismissal from college the lure of jockeying took Sirhan again, and perhaps the lure of quick money too. The stewards at Santa Anita advised him that at his age—he was now nearly 22—it was too late to start acquiring the experience or the reflexes that a good jockey needs. And though he was small, five feet-five inches tall and about 120 pounds, he was still a bit too big for the job. He persisted however and worked without salary for two or three weeks so as to get taken on in the stables. His first job was "mucking out" the stalls, that is cleaning them, and grooming the horses. After this "apprentice-ship" later in 1965 and again in 1966, he was licensed as a "hot-walker", walking horses to cool them off after training and also as an exercise boy.

In the summer of 1966, he spent some months, still exercising horses, at Granja Vista Del Rio Ranch in Corona, California. The people in charge of the Ranch were fairly certain that Sirhan would not make a good jockey because even though he liked horses he was frightened of them, especially the thoroughbreds. "But", as one of them puts it, "he had this terrific will—to try and do it well." He had two spills when exercising the horses.

Then, on September 25th, he was thrown, badly, from a filly when, as the riding jargon has it, "breezing her at full speed". Ironically enough this particular accident was not due to Sirhan's lack of expertise. Mr. Millard Sheet, one of the race horse owners using the

Ranch, who was on the track at the time, is quite definite that the accident was due to fog. According to him a horse that is blinded by fog goes wild. Despite the trainer's warning that without visibility it was dangerous to exercise the horses, the other owners were impatient to have their horses worked. The fog lifted just enough for Sirhan and another rider to be sent down the track and then another wave of thick fog came down. Within seconds the horses and their riders were down in a tangled heap.*

Sirhan, knocked unconscious by the fall and with his face all bloodied, was carried away on a stretcher. He was treated in hospital for cut and bruises and the doctors said he should stay at least a week but, as he put it, "I have an aversion to hospitals. I stayed only overnight".

But he still would not give up. He rode again on October 8th and fell again, partially reopening the wound over his left eye. The ranch at Corona would not keep him on any longer but he found a new job as an exercise boy at the Del Mar Race Track in November. On November 25th he took yet another tumble and was told that he would not qualify as a rider. Sirhan angrily insisted that he could gallop as well as anyone but at this point he finally abandoned the idea of becoming a jockey.

One of the trainers he worked for made the most fitting comment on this incongruous ambition that Sirhan nursed, with such determination and courage, for so many years: "He should never have been a jockey. He was too smart".

For a year Sirhan was out of work. The main thing he seemed to have done in the latter half of this period was to pursue a claim of compensation for the injuries he sustained during his last fall.

The details of this tussle are that after the fall he was taken to the Corona Community Hospital where Dr. Richard Nelson reported he had a cut on the chin, bruises and abrasions and "was generally banged up". Dr. Nelson said that Sirhan had complained of general pain, particularly in his stomach, but had said nothing about a head injury. "He was

* This information is given in R. A. Houghton's *Special Unit Senator*, pages 187–189.

suspicious of everything I was doing," Dr. Nelson recalled. "He didn't want any shots. He said that in the old country people told him not to have shots. We finally gave him one for tetanus. But he was in hospital mostly for observation of possible internal injuries. There were none". And after one overnight stay, he was discharged from the hospital.

A month later Sirhan complained of pain, blurred vision and extreme motion in his eyes. He was examined twice, on November 8th and December 20th, 1966, by Dr. Milton Miller, a Corona opthalmologist. Dr. Miller said that his examination showed that "visual activity was normal in both eyes and the eyes looked healthy". He also told Sirhan that "he seemed to be exaggerating". Dr. Miller said that when he refused to write a letter verifying his eye injuries as a basis for a disability claim, Sirhan telephoned him and said that the doctor had "better do what he told me or he was 'going to get me' or I 'would be sorry' or something to that effect".

Seven months later, on July 10, 1967, Sirhan filed a disability complaint for workmen's compensation and hearings were held on October 2 and on February 7, 1968. At the hearings Sirhan's physician, Dr. Maurice Nugent, and the specialist retained by the insurance company, Dr. Albert Tashma, both concluded in their reports that Sirhan had 20-15 vision.

However, the neurosurgeon consulted, Dr. Forrest Johnson, said that there was no way of checking a complaint of head injuries and that a doctor could not discount a complaint of a headache. The claim was settled for $2,000. To the end, Sirhan complained that the settlement was too small.

The representative of the insurance company that eventually paid up, described Sirhan, not unnaturally, as "somewhat surly but definitely sane". Mrs. Anne Toomer, who represented Sirhan, said that "he was just like anybody else. My recollection is that he was a normal industrial accident case".

Later on a great deal was to be said about Sirhan's "personality change" brought on by the head injuries he sustained in his accident. The idea was proven groundless but his family did notice a change in him after November 1966. His mother had the simplest and most adequate explanation for this alleged "personality change": "I begged

him not to go back to the horses because it was too dangerous. But
then it was so hard for him to get a job. He stayed at home for over a
year with no job. Maybe it was from his unemployment, but he became
nervous. He used to go often to the library, if he didn't have the bus
fare to the library he wouldn't ask for it, he would walk. Sometimes he
used to take me to work himself and he used to tell me one day he's
going to let me rest when he got a good job, or he wants me to rest and
him to work, and that's why he used to be really upset very much to
see me go to work and he has no job". According to Munir, his brother
put in several applications through the labour exchange but "there
would always be some sort of an excuse why he couldn't have the job
he applied for. He wanted a professional type thing . . . not a clerk".
The nervousness brought on by this year of enforced idleness is evident
in this exchange during the trial: Sirhan, "I went to the State
Department of Unemployment". Lawyer, "For Unemployment
Insurance?"–"No, no, for . . ."–"For your weekly check?"–"No, no,
no. For an application to get a job"–"Alright"–"And nothing came
from that".

On the 9th of September, 1967, Sirhan went to work at "Organic-
Pasadena, the cryptic name for what is usually referred to as a "health
food" store. On its card it is described as "Pasadena's largest Natural
Foods Center", featuring "Certified Raw Milk . . . Fertile Eggs . . .
Unsulphured Dried Fruits . . . Live Food Juices . . . Fresh Organically
Grown Fruits and Vegetables". The shop is completely undistinguished,
one of a row of Pasadena's usual low wooden boxes. The external
aspect of the shop and the listing of its wares may lead on to suppose
that here one has a combination of the drab and the cranky
characteristics of many of Los Angeles' quasi-religious sects. But that
would be a completely false impression, for the owner of the shop is a
truly unusual man.

In the window of the shop, among the "natural" foods, stands a copy
of a book, "Flee the Captor" by Herbert Ford; it has forewords by Dr.
W. A. Visser't Hooft, first General Secretary of the World Council of
Churches and by Hashell Lazere, an official of the American Jewish
Congress underground and its compassionate leader, John Henry
Weidner". Mr. Weidner is the owner of the shop.

A former Captain in the Dutch Army, John Weidner set up an underground resistance organisation covering Western Europe during the Nazi occupation. His organisation rescued hundreds of Allied airmen, Jews and other likely victims of the Nazis. For his services, he was decorated by four governments, Holland, Belgium, France and Britain, and received a Certificate of Commendation signed personally by President Eisenhower.

The essence of the book and of the heroic operation it describes is contained in these words of John Weidner: "When you want to help people in need you can't be concerned if your hands get dirty, or if your life is in danger, for that matter".

Mr. Weidner is a barrel-chested man with a strong, open face, and once one knows his background, it does not seem odd to find such a man amongst such merchandise as sunflower seed, peewee dates and prunes, and a selection of books containing such titles as "Zen Cookery", "Zen Macro-Biotics" and "Eat Your Troubles Away". Odd or not, Mr. Weidner has prospered in his trade, for he has a branch store in Monterey Park.

He is a devout Christian, a Seventh Day Adventist and a second generation vegetarian.

For nearly six months Sirhan worked for this exceptional person who, perhaps because he himself was a foreigner and had seen a great deal of life, understood him better than any other person in Pasadena. Also because Mr. Weidner went out of his way to try and understand Sirhan.

The long talk I had with Mr. Weidner took place in his narrow office, partitioned off from the rest of the store. Above his head hung the framed commendation from President Eisenhower. One wall was lined with packets of dates and raisins and margarine. The air was filled with the clean, sweet smell of his merchandise and it struck me as odd that in America there have to be special shops to provide the naturally grown fruits and vegetables that were the only kind available in unconsidered piles in the little shops on King David Street where Sirhan passed every day on his way to school.

Mr. Weidner got to know the Sirhans first through Aida, as a customer and then through a friendship based on their religious interests, with Mrs. Sirhan.

He first employed Munir, over two years earlier, but after three weeks, the boy suddenly disappeared: this was when Munir was arrested on his narcotics charge.

In September, 1967, Mrs. Sirhan asked if he would employ Sirhan who, she said, had been out of work for some time. Mr. Weidner went to the Sirhan home to talk about the job with Sirhan who admitted that he had no experience in working in a shop and that his last job had been with horses.

According to Mr. Weidner, Sirhan looked weak and could have been taken for a 15-year old boy.

It was agreed that Sirhan should work for 45 hours in a six-day week at $2 an hour, with two weeks notice for dismissal or resignation to be given by either side. At $90 a week Sirhan was back in the same income bracket as when he had started work four years earlier.

Sirhan's work was to clean the fruit and vegetables, to deliver merchandise to the stores and to check the stock room.

His work was satisfactory, Mr. Weidner said; he was regular and punctual; neat and clean in his appearance; correct with the other employees and polite with the customers.

But he would not wear an apron because that would have offended his pride (it was the same consideration that led Mrs. Sirhan to ask for the job rather than Sirhan himself).

With Mr. Weidner his relations were always somewhat touchy. "He had to take orders, because, after all, I am the boss, but he found it hard to take my orders and he didn't like to have things explained to him. His attitude seemed to be 'I'm as good as you are'. Because I sensed this feeling I discussed with my wife how to handle him; we wanted to understand and help him", Mr. Weidner went on.

"It was obvious that he was completely honest and I had no worries about asking him to deposit the takings of the shop in the bank—a thousand dollars sometimes".

"He was lonely, but not unsociable: he would talk and joke with the girl customers and they with him, but, from what I could see, he had no particular girl friend of his own. He was kind-hearted—I once saw him bringing ice cream for a poor old man. He didn't drink and didn't smoke and he always walked to and from the shop; he said that walking was good for the body. I understood that here was a young man who lived by certain principles; he often said that he would never lie"—an echo of his father's claim.

Working close together, Mr. Weidner and Sirhan came to have many discussions on politics and religion. One of these talks that Mr. Weidner remembers—it was typical of several on the subject of politics—began when Mr. Weidner put to Sirhan the question that so many people did, "Why haven't you become an American citizen?"

"Because I am a Jordanian Arab and because there is no freedom in this country," Sirhan replied.

"It is true that there are many things wrong with America; nothing in life is perfect; but here there are democratic processes to obtain improvements," Mr. Weidner asserted.

"No, in America freedom does not exist," Sirhan insisted.

"Would you say that there is more freedom in America than in Russia or China?" asked Mr. Weidner.

"I would say there is more freedom in Russia and China."

"Then why are there so many refugees from these countries? Haven't you read about the thousands of Chinese who are leaving China to go to Hong Kong?" Mr. Weidner questioned.

"That's a lot of American propaganda," was Sirhan's reply.

"If you went and saw for yourself, you would find it is not propaganda."

"Maybe one day I will go and see for myself," Sirhan concluded.

Mr. Weidner continued, "On another occasion when we were discussing why he had not become an American citizen, he replied by criticising America for helping Israel against the Arabs. 'And I am an Arab,' he said, 'so how can I become an American?'

"It was somewhat frustrating trying to argue with Sirhan because his mind was made up, and one couldn't get him to change.

"We naturally talked about the Negro problem, and he was bitter about the conditions of poverty the Negroes lived in.

"He told me one day that 'rioting is the only way in which the Negroes will get what they want'.

"I answered that of course Negro conditions needed improvement and that it would come; it was already coming slowly. But not through violence. Martin Luther King was a great Negro leader, but he was non-violent."

"But Sirhan insisted, 'It will only come through violence.' "

"He was critical of America's foreign policy. What America was doing in Vietnam was wrong. And, of course, the help America was giving to Israel was completely wrong. I sometimes felt that he had turned against the whole American way of life, and that he was an anarchist in revolt against our society".

"And yet he had his beliefs and principles. Personal honour and his self-respect were important to him. And second only to that he esteemed patriotism. He had strong patriotic feelings for his country. Yes, I would say he loved his country." And from his discussions with Sirhan, Mr. Weidner knew that the reference to Sirhan's country meant Palestine.

"Of course, we talked a lot about the Middle East and the Jews. He hated the Jews: because of their power and their material wealth, they had taken his country from his people who were now refugees".

"Because of Israel, he said, his family had become refugees, and he described to my wife how he himself had seen a Jewish soldier cutting off the breast of an Arab woman in Jerusalem.

"During one of our discussions on the Middle East, he asked me, 'Do you know how the Palestinian refugees have to live now?' I replied that I had seen a great many refugees when I was in the underground and they were mostly Jews. They had nowhere to go and millions of them had been killed. I was glad that they now had a home to go to in Israel. Doing violence would not help the Arab refugees".

" 'Don't you think that the Jews also can be cruel? We have to fight' he said, 'there is no other way to find peace' ".

"I told him that the Nazis had tortured me and that they had killed one of my sisters. But after the war, I did not try and find out who was responsible so as to get them punished. I forgave the Nazis and now I have some German friends.

"Sirhan replied, 'I admire you for what you have done and I would like to be like you, but I can't forgive the Jews for what they have done to the Palestinians—and they are still doing it!'

"I told him that if men did not have the strength to forgive, they should ask God to give it to them.

"Sirhan's answer was, 'There is no God. Look at what God has done for the Arabs! and for the Palestinians! How can we believe in God?'"

Despite Sirhan's categoric statement, Mr. Weidner said that he did not believe that his denial of God was serious or that he was a one hundred per cent atheist.

There were other aspects of Sirhan's personality on which Mr. Weidner was himself categoric: "Sirhan was a completely normal person; and Arab national pride was for him a very important motivating force. I always felt it was there, as if he was saying, 'I'm an Arab—don't push me too hard!' And he loved his mother and was very attached to her.

"We talked a lot together, and yet, in a way, it was never easy to talk to him, and very hard to communicate socially. My wife and I always give a Christmas party for our staff; last Christmas everyone came except Sirhan. He said he couldn't make it, but I suppose he wanted to be able to say 'no' to me just once.

"When Sirhan was given his $2,000 compensation for his fall, he was, naturally, very pleased. I asked him what he was going to do with it and said I hoped he would use it to continue his studies, and that he could start again at college in the fall. He told me that he was not quite sure that he would".

Mr. Weidner's summing up of Sirhan was in these words: "He was an intelligent boy but, of course, his experience of life was not very wide. Because of this combination, he was individualistic and because of that it will be a special agony for him to be in jail. But also because his personality is not yet fully formed, it will be easier for him to repent, and so to earn eternal life".

Before describing the tragi-comic incident which resulted in Sirhan and Mr. Weidner parting company, there are two points in his narration that call for comment. It was not easy for Jean Weidner to forgive the Nazis but, comparatively, it was much easier than the forgiveness he asked of Sirhan. Jean Weidner forgave the Nazis who were broken and beaten, defeated enemies who were no longer a menace to anyone. He asked Sirhan to forgive Jews and Israelis who were still at war with the Arabs and still in occupation of Sirhan's homeland. Their conversation took place a few months after June, 1967, when the Israelis had inflicted a humiliating defeat on the Arabs and had occupied the parts of Palestine remaining under Arab control after 1948-1949. And in Jordan the Israeli victory owed much to their using napalm, not only on the Jordanian Army, but on Palestinian civilians, Sirhan's people. Absolutely innocent civilians, miles from the battlefront, were burnt by Israeli napalm.

Second: to think that American policy in Vietnam and the Middle East is wrong is not necessarily indicative of anarchistic beliefs. There are hundreds of thousands of good American citizens who believe so and they include nine-tenths of all Americans with direct experience of the Middle East. And in Europe, Asia and Africa there are tens of millions of people who would agree with Sirhan, and who are, if anything, strongly anti-anarchistic. Nor do they despair of a change for the better.

The break that came on March 7th, 1968, was based on a misunderstanding that developed into a tussle of wills. That morning Mr. Weidner asked Sirhan to deliver goods at Monterey Park and Downey, in that order. Sirhan did it in the reverse order which Mr. Weidner learnt of when his wife, in the other store in Monterey, reported that Sirhan had been late in arriving.

On his return to Pasadena, Mr. Weidner asked Sirhan why he had used the Downey-Monterey route, and, according to Mr. Weidner, "Sirhan snapped back, 'because you told me to'. I said, 'No Sirhan, I told you to do it the other way around,' and he flared up and said, 'So you call me a liar. I never lie. I'm quitting'. And he walked out of the shop. After a few minutes, he returned and said, 'My conscience is bothering me. I said I would give you two weeks notice so I will stay two weeks'.

"He continued working, though, naturally, relations were a bit strained. His notice expired on a Sunday. On the preceding Thursday there was an argument between us because he had not covered the merchandise that was in the backyard before he left work. Sirhan said that he had no time and that I was not here for him to inform me. He then walked out of my office and into the store. I called him back and told him that he would have to listen to what I said or leave. 'That is unfair,' was his reply, and I told him that he should work properly or quit. 'I'll quit, but pay me now,' he asked. I said I would pay him on Monday and his answer was that I should pay him for a further two weeks in lieu of notice because I was dismissing him. We began arguing about this and he sat down on that table and said he would not leave until I paid him, or he would take the matter to a labour court.

"I called in the police to get him to leave the shop. The police asked him whether he was an American citizen and Sirhan got angry and said, 'You have no right to ask me that. I am a Palestinian' and then showed his immigration card. The police asked him to leave, which he did.

"During the next few days, I received word through friends that Sirhan had said that if I apologised to him, he would return to the shop. I went to his house one morning and told him that if he would apologise to me, he could stay. He said, 'No.' I then told him that I never called him a liar and that I did not think he was one. He said nothing and I left.

"I received a notice to attend a meeting of the labour board. It was held on the 24th of April. Sirhan was friendly to me when we met there and we then put forth our points of view. He argued that he had quit just before serving out his notice. The board decided in my favour and I never saw Sirhan again."

This is a ludicrous story about an unnecessary falling-out based entirely on a verbal misunderstanding, which was not explained away because of a clash of personality. What is significant is Sirhan's resentment at being asked by the police whether or not he was an American citizen, for clearly this had become a sore point with him.

It was very much to the fore during the next, and last meetings he had with Miss Linda Massri. "I was driving along Lake Avenue when I saw Sirhan on the sidewalk. I stopped and asked him to get in. He seemed very upset, and when I asked him what was wrong he told me he had lost his job and had been to the Labour Exchange to find a new one. He said, 'The lady in charge right away asked me not 'are you a citizen' but 'why aren't you a citizen'? I resent this imposition. Don't I have the right to be a citizen or not to be a citizen, if I choose'? I could see that he was very hurt and so for an hour we talked sitting in the car and I tried to explain that such questions were part of the routine and that there was nothing personal in them. He calmed down after a bit but I'm not sure that I convinced him."

The last person to whom I talked, and who gave me an over-all picture of the Sirhan family and of Sirhan himself, operated in a very different setting indeed than the hygenic atmosphere of Mr. Weidner's health-food store. This was Mr. Lou Shelby (the simplified American version of Elias Shellaby), the owner of the Fez Supper Club in Hollywood. The usual barn-like object from the outside, the oriental atmosphere within the restaurant is almost substantial enough to be cut with a knife. I talked with Mr. Shelby after he finished his duties as *compere* for the the floor-show of the evening: a performance by two belly dancers,–an athletic young American girl ("Yasmina, flower of the Orient") and a rather more authentically undulating Egyptian.

Mr. Shelby is of Lebanese origin, born and raised in Boston, who took his B.A. from the University of California and who is in his present profession because he is a musician and because being in business gave him stomach ulcers.

Mr. Shelby's connection with the Sirhans was mainly through Adel and, somewhat, through Sharif. Adel had worked for him as an oud player, on and off, over a period of seven years. He had visited the Sirhans' house several times for musical rehearsals. This year, 1968, Mr. Shelby, with his mother and cousin, paid their first formal social call on the Sirhans at Easter, which was in April.

"The Sirhans always struck me as being a 'weird' family. By that I mean something quite strange and unusual. Perhaps the best way to explain it is by saying that though they were Christians, the general quality, the atmosphere, of their family life was that of a Muslim family: it was serious and heavy and lacking in the adaptability and quickness which most Arab Christian families here have. And there were their relations with their mother: the sons were fond of her, of course, but she had little influence on them and they didn't take her wishes or feelings into account.

"The two elder sons were fairly pragmatic and not too idealistic. They were beginning to adjust to America and of them, Adel was best adjusted to the conflicting cultures. It's true they retained their old nationality but Adel, at least, allowed his Jordanian passport to lapse, and I had quite a job getting it renewed in a hurry when we had an engagement in Mexico.

"This Easter visit was the usual formal affair,—with things served in the correct order—first coffee, then liquors, then sweets. This was the first occasion I talked to Sirhan as an adult. He never came to the supper club on his own. I suppose he is too serious for that sort of thing. I remember him coming with his mother two or three times, when we had some special function on.

"But this time we had a really big argument on Middle East politics. Naturally, Mrs. Sirhan tried to break it up several times but it just went on and on. We switched back and forth between Arabic and English.

"Sirhan's outlook was completely Arab nationalist—the Arabs were in the right and had made no mistakes. I tried to reason with him and to point out that one could be in the right but still make mistakes. But he was adamant. According to him, America was to blame for the Arabs' misfortunes,—because of the power of Zionism in this country.

"The only Arab leader he really admired was Nasser and he thought Nasser's policies were right. The Arabs had to build themselves up and fight Israel, that was the only way. The only outside friend the Arabs had was Russia, but, according to Sirhan, Russia had not proved a good enough friend during last June's fighting."

It is noteworthy that while Sirhan would not accept any criticism of Russia when arguing with an "outsider", like Mr. Weidner, he himself criticised Russia when in conversation with a fellow Arab.

"Sirhan argued well and intelligently," Mr. Shelby went on, "But I think he needed to finish his education to understand the full world situation. He looked at things from just one narrow standpoint, and his ideas were too theoretical and idealistic."

I asked Mr. Shelby his explanation of why after finishing high school and doing well there, Sirhan should not have been able to find anything better than menial jobs. His answer was very direct: "He was a small, brown man and it is not at all unusual for small, brown men to have to accept menial jobs."

Mr. Shelby did not amplify, but it was my understanding that he was referring to the Spanish-Americans and the Mexican immigrant labourers who are very much in evidence in Southern California. The Sirhans, in appearance, could very well have been mistaken for Spanish-Americans or Mexicans and would have been treated like them.

And these groups are among the economically and socially under-privileged in the United States.

I also asked Mr. Shelby that if Sirhan was such a dedicated Arab nationalist how, at this distance from the Middle East, his Arab nationalism was nurtured and kept alive. He gave me another direct answer: "Look it didn't need any nurturing or anything like that. It wasn't necessary. He was a Palestinian, wasn't he? He knew what had happened to him." Mr. Shelby went on, "The F.B.I. came and talked to me, and I told them, 'What in God's name do you expect when America backs Israel?'"

We got on to the general problem of immigrants. "I am an American," Mr. Shelby said. "I was born and raised in this country and it has been difficult enough for me to live with two cultures. One has to try and boil them together to produce a single mixture from two different things. But for a refugee, it must be damnably difficult."

Mr. Shelby's remark about the relationship of the Sirhan brothers to their mother confirms what a good deal of the other evidence suggests—that Mrs. Sirhan may have had to be both mother and father, and to hold the family together, but she was certainly no dominating matriarch. She sometimes asked her Arab-American friends to try and use their influence with her sons to get them to do, or not do, something. She was often not aware of what had happened to them, or even where they were. When Munir disappeared from home, because of his drugs charge, Mrs. Sirhan was frantic to find out where he was. Sirhan did not tell her that he had been briefly in the hospital after his fall, and she has said that after the accident she couldn't "talk to him." Clearly, the basis of the sons' relationship with their mother was love, not obedience.

5

The Reciprocal Rejection

A cross-section of the personality of Sirhan Sirhan on his 24th birthday in March, 1958, would show a hard, clear political core surrounded, in contrast, by quite blurred, uncertain elements.

The drive of his ambition had been considerably blunted by five years of trivial tasks, failure as a jockey and by unemployment. Earlier he had been reported as wanting to become a journalist, a diplomat, or a teacher; to be something big back in Jordan; to do something to give expression to himself: his ambitions were not so much to promote himself as to further a cause. But when he was recovering at home from his fall, he told Linda Massri, during a talk they had on Freud and psychological motivations, "I'm not motivated by anything." And when Mr. Weidner approached him about working in his shop, Sirhan suggested that he first try and find some other more suitable person. Lacking outlets for his ambitions, he seemed to have abandoned ambition.

The other characteristic that his friends noted was that he was not particularly attached to material things. He had to work for his living and to help the family. He was careful with his money and saved it. But he never seemed directly and emotionally involved in his family's financial problems. As one friend put it: "He lived in a world of his own and in his world he never seemed to feel poor, but rich. I suppose it was because he read a lot and was interested in many things."

This is not to suggest that he did not bear his fair share of the family worries. Almost the first thing Mrs. Sirhan said when given the news of Sirhan's arrest was: "He's a good boy, He's taken everything on his back." But he gave the impression of, somehow, keeping family affairs and his real interests in separate compartments.

One of these interests was religion. He may have denied the existence of God, but he could not possibly shed the accumulated effect of long years of intense religiosity. Many people, when they abandon organised religion but still retain a sense of the Holy, whether as a genuine feeling or as a residue, incline towards semi-mystical cults that are half-way houses between complete belief and atheism. This is what seems to have happened to Sirhan.

Early in 1968, he applied, by mail, to become a member of the Ancient Mystical Order of Rosae Crucis. The Rosecrucians claim that their order dates back to 1350 B.C. and the heretic Pharoah Akhnaton who repudiated the formalised state religion of Egypt and became the world's first known propagator of monotheism. The Rosecrucians are a world-wide order which, in their own words, "expounds a system of metaphysical and physical philosophy that is intended to awake the dormant faculties of an individual whereby he may utilise his talents and become more aware of the world around him and lead a more useful life."

Whatever these words may mean, or apply to, the Rosicrucians do not charge much for passing on their ancient wisdom—a modest four dollars a month. Sirhan clearly took them seriously, for when in jail he asked for his outstanding membership dues to be paid.

From his cell, Sirhan asked to be provided with two books, very substantial ones, on theosophy: *Talks on 'At the Feet of the Master'* by C. W. Leadbeater and *The Secret Doctrine* by Madame H. Blavatsky. Theosophy, the world headquarters of which is at Adyar, near Madras in South India, is not so much a doctrine in itself as an attempt to try and distill the common elements from all religions and to fuse these essential and enduring truths into a pure and spiritualised creed.

That someone like Sirhan, who in his master-passion of politics was down to earth, should turn to such marginal mystical sects may seem strange. But not if one considers his strongly religious upbringing, with the emphasis his parents placed on Bible reading and the direct and personal interpretation of the Scriptures: it is only a step from this protestantism to the intense individualism of the mystics. And one has only to break through the rigid structure of any formalised religion to collapse into the safety-net of aesthetic theosophy.

In a way, too, one should see in this tendency the triumph of the Southern Californian milieu, with its addiction to strange sects, over the simpler faith that Sirhan brought from Jerusalem. He seems to have rejected most things that America and California stood for but perhaps, spiritually, the Los Angeles of the bearded guru and the exotic prophet got under his shield.

Earlier on, his reading was confined to books on Middle East politics and history. These were the sort of books he brought home from his school library and which he is recorded as having borrowed from the Pasadena Public Library. He did not borrow many books from the Library, but he went there frequently enough for the staff to remember him and, as always, to comment that he was courteous and polite.

He used the library during the years when he was working, which showed that he had not, yet, accepted that he was merely a filling station hand or a jockey.

It was his interest in politics and in the Palestine Problem that kept him interested in current happenings and world affairs. As we have seen, his brothers, though to a lesser extent, were also involved in the Palestine issue. So too was Mrs. Sirhan, characteristically, from a religious angle: she would quote chapter and verse from the Bible to show that the Jews were not the Chosen People or at least not the only Chosen People, and that all true believers were Chosen.

Anyone who has spent time in the Middle East would have come across many young Palestinians who are as obsessed with the tragedy of their country as Sirhan obviously is. Only the fact that he should feel so strongly after eleven years away from home, and in far-distant California, is somewhat initially surprising, but not on later reflection.

To observe at first hand the evolution of America's Middle East policy, and to read daily, and to see on TV, American coverage of Middle East events would be the greatest possible challenge to any patriotic Palestinian.

As has been said, American Middle East policy after the 1956 Suez crisis reverted to its traditional line of generous financial and diplomatic support of Israel. This assistance was increased unprecedentedly, though without provocative fanfare, during the term of office of President John Kennedy.

The late President was much admired by the Arab peoples, as he was by the whole of Afro-Asia. He carried on a correspondence with President Nasser which showed that he was trying to understand the Arab point of view and was prepared to grant that there was such a point of view. Yet during his term the United States gave a greater volume of financial aid to Israel than ever before. And late in 1962, President Kennedy sanctioned the secret negotiations that led to the first American commitment to supply Israel with advanced weapons and the sale of Hawk missiles in 1963.

If President Kennedy was pro-Israel he was not openly anti-Arab; as far as his pro-Israeli stance would allow, he tried to be pro-Arab.

Under President Johnson American Middle East policy became both pro-Israeli and anti-Arab.

One policy innovation of the Johnson Administration was directed specifically at the Palestine refugees. Ever since 1948, America has been contributing about 25 million dollars to the annual budget of UNRWA—a very modest sum for a country like America to contribute to the upkeep of a million people. After 1964, the American contribution was reduced by about 3 million dollars, that is by one-eighth, and further cuts were threatened.

In 1966, the sale of surplus wheat to Egypt was stopped, as an act of deliberate reprisal for Egyptian criticism of U.S. policy, not in the Middle East but in Vietnam. Whatever the Administration in Washington, there have always been a certain number of influential American

Jewish advisors or experts near to or in the White House. But to the Arabs it seemed an act of gratituitous provocation when President Johnson appointed Mr. Arthur Goldberg to be America's Permanent Representative to the United Nations, because Mr. Golberg had publicly avowed himself to be a Zionist, that is an active supporter of Israel, and the Arab-Israeli conflict was a constant subject of discussion by the Security Council and the General Assembly. A former Cabinet Minister and a former Supreme Court Judge, Mr. Goldberg not only expounded U.S. Middle East policy, he helped to frame it; with his direct access to the White House, he ignored the State Department officials who, from time to time, tried to be even-handed.

Soon after he succeeded President Kennedy, President Johnson announced that America would cooperate with Israel in building a nuclear power plant to desalinate sea water. Even the nuclear know-how from the peaceful use of atomic energy is always useful.

It was, however, in May and June of 1967 that the full extent of President Johnson's pro-Israel, anti-Arab commitment became apparent. When the crisis over the Gulf of Akaba was building up, President Johnson issued a statement asserting that America was committed to the national sovereignty and territorial integrity of all states in the Middle East, and President Johnson, personally, asked President Nasser not to strike the first blow. Yet when Israel struck the first blow, President Johnson, despite pressing requests from Prime Minister Kosygin, refused to ask Israel to halt its advance until it had reached all its military objectives; he refused to describe the Israeli attack as aggression even though American (and British and Russian) radar units in the Mediterranean picked up the Israeli planes on their way to attack Egypt; no attempt was made to warn Egypt; and subsequently he refused to condemn Israel for aggression and to ask it to withdraw from territory seized through aggression. Several columnists writing from Washington, American and foreign, have reported that when Israel went to war it was with the clear understanding that America would intervene militarily if ever the territorial integrity of Israel were threatened. Also that Israel had 72 hours in which to act before the U.S. would ask for a "cease-fire" at the U.N.; which is what actually happened.

In the debates at the U.N. during the summer of 1968, the U.S. was one of a small group of 15 states, and the only Great Power in it, which consistently supported every resolution that the Arabs opposed, and opposed every resolution that the Arabs approved.

When 101 member states asked Israel not to incorporate the Arab sector of Jerusalem, Sirhan's home town, into Israel, no state opposed it, but the United States was the only Great Power amongst 13 countries that abstained on the vote.

These acts of commission and omission of the Johnson Administration, all anti-Arab, are widely known; even the "secret" commitments have now been publicly reported in the press. Any Arab in America, remotely interested in politics, would know about them.

Writing in his Dairy* as far back as 1901, Theodore Herzl, the father of Zionism, noted that one of the main tasks facing the Zionist Movement was "to capture the communities,"—that is the Jewish communities throughout the world. Zionists have been capturing the communities, one by one, ever since and the fact that Zionism had captured the bulk of the Jews of the United States and other countries was evident in June, 1967.

The battle for the American Jewish community was won and lost in the early 1920s—won by Weizmann, later to be the first President of Israel, and lost by Supreme Court Justice Louis Brandeis. Brandeis was a Zionist too, but he believed that a Jewish national home in Palestine should be more a cultural than a political entity, and that the Jewish community in Palestine and the Jewish community in America should cooperate but not be indissolubly linked. Weizmann believed that the American Jewish community, along with Jewish communities in every country, should identify whole-heartedly with Eretz Israel, the Land of Israel, and his point of view ultimately prevailed within the American Jewish community, with but a few noteworthy exceptions.

In the meantime, American Jews had acquired very considerable influence on American publicity media—the press, films and later TV, and book publishing.

When American politicians sought Jewish support, it was not only for the Jewish vote (which as a bloc vote is important in New York City

* *Diaries*, p. 347.

and other urban centres) but also for favourable presentation in Jewish-influenced publicity media. The fact that the bulk of the Jewish communal organisation in the U.S. had been captured by the Zionists has brought the American politician into direct contact with the World Zionist Organisation.*

Just how great this influence is was amply demonstrated in June, 1967. First, the media were saturated with news coverage of the fighting in the Middle East. Secondly, the presentation was almost wholly pro-Israel and anti-Arab.

The ordinary American reader or viewer discovered that the Middle East war, in which not a single American was involved, was far more important than the war in Vietnam, in which half a million Americans were fighting. Then, he discovered that the Arab was the enemy not only of Israel but of the American press, radio, and TV on which the Arabs were denounced and derided.

For several weeks in the summer of 1967 and since then, the Arab supplanted the Russian, the Chinese and even the Viet Cong as a hate-figure for America. Very few Arabs in the Middle East know that they have been designated as America's Public Enemy Number One, but most Arabs in the United States, like Sirhan, were regularly reminded of this fact.

The Sirhans, we know, had a TV set and took in both the Pasadena and Los Angeles newspapers. What did they read and see? The largest newspaper, *The Los Angeles Times,* is wholly committed to Israel. Its editorial on June 6th, said that America had an obligation to maintain the territorial integrity and independence of Israel which would imply U.S. military intervention in defensive terms. For the week starting Monday, June 5th, this paper gave two whole pages to war coverage, quite apart from articles critical of the Arabs and cartoons depicting the Arabs either as savages or as figures of fun.

We have no documented record of what TV stations presented, but we do know that they presented a great deal. Station KXTV, for example, presented no less than seven Special Reports on the Middle

* See Chapter 7, "Zionism and Christian America;" Chapter 8, "The Politics of Zionist Fund Raising;" and Chapter 10, "Zionist Propaganda" in *The Political World of American Zionism* by Samuel Halperin, Detroit, 1961.

East on Tuesday, June 6th, apart from news bulletins, news flashes and relays of the debates at the U.N. What we do know from viewers, American and Arabs, is that American TV coverage was overwhelmingly pro-Israel.

The Arab governments are partly to blame for this overbalanced presentation. Because they were losing the battle, they deliberately made it very difficult for newsmen to operate.

It was not only in the news on radio and TV that the Arabs were belaboured and berated. Even so-called comedy programmes picked up the theme and soon anti-Arab jokes and references to General Dayan's eyepatch were the order of the day. Nor was American euphoria at Israelis victory over the Arabs limited to the publicity media—it found expression on hippy posters and in men's fashions.

It was a bitter, galling period for the Arabs in America to have to live through and I know of some who, a few days after June 6th, switched off their radios and TVs and stopped reading the newspapers—except for *The Christian Science Monitor,* when they could get it. As one of them, an Arab college professor, put it: "Here we felt we were behind the enemy lines. But what harm has any Arab government done to the American government, or the Arab people to the American people, that there should be this hatred for the Arabs?"

In September, 1967, another Arab professor in the United States, Dr. Michael Suleiman published an essay entitled, "The Arabs and the West: Communication Gap"* in which he wrote of "the Arabs' basic frustration at their inability to communicate with Westerners" and he reached this conclusion: "The Arabs, denied most of the ordinary channels to communicate with the West, have consequently resorted to the articulation of their interest through anomic groups [that is, violent groups] . . . Under such circumstances, the wonder is not that so many Arabs have turned to the Soviet and Chinese camps for solace, but rather that such a large number of Arabs continue to attempt to communicate with the West."

It may be of interest at this point to look at the other side of the coin,—to see what American Zionist Jews thought of their own activity

* In "Il Politico," University of Pavia, 1967, XXXII, No. 3.

in May and June, 1967. A masterly analysis was provided by Professor Leonard J. Fein of the Massachusetts Institute of Technology in an address he gave to the National Conference of Jewish Communal Studies in Detroit in June, 1968.† The Professor begins by reporting that in May, Jewish communities debated whether they should arrange public rallies in support of Israel and sing "Hatikva" (the Israel national anthem). He continues: "In the event, of course, we lost our cool completely. By June 5 we had tossed aside the manuals, and were behaving in unprecedentedly disruptive ways. We begged, we pleaded, we demanded, we insisted, we threatened, we promised, we were aggressive, petulant, temperamental. We threw a tantrum. And, against all predictions, the roof did not cave in. There was no outpouring of anti-Semitic sentiment. There was no serious backlash . . . The lesson is that we have been more defensive than we need have been . . . that there is far more room for assertiveness than we dared suppose." In the past, Dr. Fein says, the American Jews achieved much "in our elevation from a paltry three per cent of the country's population to a full partner status in its religious community—one third Catholic, one-third Protestant, one-third Jew. From three per cent to thirty per cent, what more could we have sought?" He concludes by asking whether, despite these gains, the American Jew should continue with "the New Militancy" of May and June. Some Jews "argue that we had best not risk our miraculous success, that we had best not push our luck too far." He is not of this opinion: "I must answer that we may die of success just as surely as we may die of struggle; that to suppose that America cannot contain a Jewish community that dares to assert itself, in all its distinctiveness, is to sell this country short . . . is to ignore the leading lessons of last June . . ."

This analysis has been quoted at some length because here, eloquently expressed by one of the challengers, is "the challenge" that Arabs in America had to face, in especially active form in June, 1967.

They were not only harrowing weeks for the Sirhans—the brothers were angrily critical of American publicity media to their Arab-American friends—they were anxious weeks too, because they had

† Reproduced in *The Jerusalem Post,* July 2, 1968.

relatives and friends in Jerusalem, where there had been fighting, and in Taibeh, near where there had been fighting. Ramallah is about ten miles from Taibeh and at Ramallah, as reported in the world press, a Jordanian Army hospital was bombed.

As my questions to Mr. Shelby indicated, I had wondered how Sirhan, in Pasadena, kept in touch with news from home, and how he maintained his spirit of Arab nationalism.

As regards the first question, the answer is simple: there were letters from friends to Mrs. Sirhan and there was the coverage provided by the American press, radio and TV of happenings in the Middle East. Because of the interest of the American Jewish community, this coverage is quite extensive. For the same reason, it is one-sided.* The representatives of most American newspapers, news agencies and radio and TV stations in Israel, are Israelis, whereas the far fewer representatives they have in Arab countries are Americans. The same is true of the British and French media.

The partisan nature of this news coverage by itself provides part of the answer to the second question—of how Sirhan's Arab nationalism was kept alive. But there were other sources too. The family subscribed to a weekly Arabic newspaper, *Al Bayan*, which is published in Brooklyn and which has been in existence for close to 50 years. It is only an eight-page publication but the editor gives at least a two pages summary of the week's happenings in the Middle East. And in his editorials he takes the straightforward Arab nationalist line.

There has been much speculation that Sirhan was in touch with various organised Arab groups and especially with the Organisation of Arab Student in America. *The Washington Post* stated this as a positive fact, but a few days later carried a denial from the O.A.S. itself in which the Organisation stated that there was no record of Sirhan ever being a member of any of its chapters in the Los Angeles area. There is no chapter of the O.A.S. in Pasadena City College. On paper, the O.A.S. sounds like an impressive organisation with 110 chapters, a membership of 7,000 Arab students and a quarterly publication called *The Arab Journal.* But in fact, its organisational structure is weak, so that its

* In his paper, Dr. Suleiman provides detailed statistical proof of this in an analysis of seven major American publications.

activities vary greatly in intensity from campus to campus and from year to year. As it happened, it has never been very active in the Los Angeles area and, as I have described earlier, I had great difficulty in trying to get in touch with any of its officers. All that I could discover was that its activities were limited to two or three meetings a year.

A leaflet put out by the Zionist Organisation of America entitled "Anti-Israel Forces on the Campus" by James H. Sheldon purports to show that the O.A.S. is dangerously active in spreading extremist and violent ideas. But anyone who has tried seriously to study the activity of the O.A.S. will know that the nightmares that Mr. Sheldon conjures up are not nightmares but chimeras.

What is true, however, is that since last June, and quite distinct from the O.A.S., the Palestinian resistance organisation, Al Fatah, has undertaken some publicity activity in the United States. This has been reported by the Middle East correspondent of *The Christian Science Monitor* from Beirut. These activities have been fairly vigorous on the West Coast—Arab students and Arab-Americans have, for instance, been receiving copies of Al Fatah statements and communiques.

Whether Sirhan was on the Al Fatah mailing list is not known. As we have seen, the family generally held itself aloof from the local Arab organisations. Enquiries have shown that they did not even take part in the humanitarian efforts of various Arab-American organisations and groups that raised funds for Arab "expellees" during and after June, 1967.

The best answer to my second question, on the source of Sirhan's continuing Arab nationalist feeling, was that given by Mr. Shelby, "He was a Palestinian. He knew what had happened to him."

The earlier question, "Why did the Sirhans stay on in America? Why did they not return to Jerusalem?" may now be answered.

By 1968, indeed for many years before, it was quite apparent that they were not going to accept America as their second country. They remained Jordanians because the hope of going home was always there. In the Palestinian Diaspora, as in the earlier Jewish Diaspora, the belief in The Return is fundamental.

As we have seen, it was not that they may have wished to return because of their economic problems in America but that they had economic problems because they wanted to return.

They were unable to give their loyalty or love to America, and America had not turned out to be the Promised Land of economic opportunity. They had no real reason for staying on, and it would have obviously been better for everyone if they had not tried to make the best of a bad job that showed clear signs of not getting better and perhaps of getting worse. Yet they stayed.

It was not that they lacked the money to pay for their return home, as was the case for their outward journey. The sale of the house would have produced adequate funds.

Perhaps the main reason is that they did not have anything very much to go back to, beyond the feeling of once more being "at home." (And after June, 1967, they would certainly not have felt "at home" in a Jerusalem under Israeli control.) The only one who had really benefited from the stay in America was Sirhan; Saadallah, Sharif, Adel and Munir had not acquired any new or useful skills or experience. Finding work in Jordan would have been as difficult for them as in America.

We know that Mrs. Sirhan was, despite everything, reasonably happy and settled in America; so was Adel. To go back to Jerusalem would have meant for her the third family uprooting, and at her age, she would be understandably reluctant to undertake yet another transplanting.

Sirhan's attachment to his mother and the hopes she placed in him ruled out the possibility of his going back home. The Sirhans fled to the Old City because they had nowhere else to go. They stayed in Pasadena because of the force of habit and inertia.

So they stayed on in Pasadena, when it would have been better for them to return to Jerusalem where they could have managed to make a new life, without the constant feeling that they were like a Palestinian woman of long ago who, too, was "sick for home" and "stood in tears amid the alien corn."

Let us pull back and, from a certain distance, look at Sirhan Sirhan.

On the outside he is a small, brown man. On the inside he is aloof and lonely; sensitive and touchy to the point of being prickly; with more than a touch of melancholy and emotionalism; spiritually adrift but questing earnestly for a new religious faith; studious and serious-minded. He had ambition but was unable to make any sort of a career. Five years after leaving school, what, in terms of the values of American society, was Sirhan Sirhan?—an utterly obscure nonentity, a squashed cabbage-leaf. But if, like Eliza Doolittle, he refused to accept that he was a squashed cabbage-leaf, it was because he had a fierce pride in his personal honour and an even fiercer patriotism.

He lacked the assurance given by membership in a happy and united family. He lacked the assurance of having a country of his own. In formal terms, he was a Jordanian Arab but he was really a Palestinian, and Palestine was no more.

Two things made him the way he was. The first was his unusual family. There was the aloofness and the strong religious feelings of his parents. And there were his brothers, with the series of misadventures into which they fell. Sirhan's code of behavior was puritanical and perhaps, in reaction, he was the only one of them "to go straight."

The second factor was his inability and unwillingness to adjust to the demanding American way of life.

He was unable to adjust to it because it was too different from the sort of life he had been brought up to admire by his parents. This rejection came from Sirhan.

He was unwilling to adjust to it because America, or rather, the political leaders of America, among whom was Robert Kennedy, gave more importance to the wealth and power of their Zionist co-citizens than to the right to exist of the small and hapless Palestinian people. This rejection came from America.

PART II

THE SECOND VICTIM

6

Character is Fate

Robert Kennedy might have been alive today if Israel had not become a major factor in American internal politics and especially in American Presidential campaigns.

A cursory examination of current electioneering speeches, television debates, and the 1968 party platforms will show that Israel, a small country of less than three million people at the eastern end of the Mediterranean is given more importance than the United States' immediate neighbours, Canada and Latin America; than America's old ally, Britain, or France or Germany; it is more important than India or China. Only Russia and Vietnam are given greater attention, and in a very different way. The talk is what the U.S. can do "about" or "with" Russia and Vietnam, but what the U.S. can do "for" Israel. Of the 121 member states of the U.N. Israel emerges as America's most favoured nation.

All American politicians, with few, if any, exceptions give Israel this strange and disproportionate importance because of the wealth and power of American Zionists. Robert Kennedy was not among the exceptions, but his support for Israel was not solely due to political and propaganda calculations. These were probably his main reasons, but, in addition, he supported Israel because of certain qualities in his character which we also find in the popular image of Israel's national character.

Writing on "The Qualities of Robert Kennedy" in *The New York Times* (June 7, 1968), the well-known columnist, James Reston, observed: "In many ways the personal characteristics of Robert Kennedy were very much like the dominant characteristics of the American people. We are an ambitious, strenuous, combative, youthful, inconsistent, abrupt, moralistic, sports-loving, non-intellectual breed, and he was all these things."

Mr. Reston also said of Kennedy: "He was an all-or-nothing man and he lost everything in the end . . . He was prepared to choose between defeat at home and defeat in Vietnam, and between Israel and the Arabs, as few politicians and few Americans are, and this cost him not only the leadership of his party but his life."

Mr. Reston does no more than state a plain fact when he says that Robert Kennedy's choice between Israel and the Arabs cost him his life. He did not feel the need to state that Kennedy's choice was for Israel rather than the Arabs: he assumed that his readers knew it. But Mr. Reston is incorrect when he suggests, as he seems to, that few politicians and few Americans are prepared to choose between Israel and the Arabs. On the contrary, almost all American politicians, on the record, and many non-politicians have made this choice for Israel. Perhaps what Mr. Reston meant to imply is that few politicians and few Americans are prepared to back their choice with the all-or-nothing commitment that characterised Kennedy; but even this is only partially true. If for Robert Kennedy the Arabs were marked zero and Israel 100, his commitment to Israel was a hundred per cent, for other American politicians it has been at least ninety per cent.

If the qualities listed by Mr. Reston identified Robert Kennedy with the American people, there were other qualities—and they have been considered among his salient characteristics—that led him to identify himself with the popular image of Israel, and to feel a personal empathy and sympathy for the Israelis.

A recent biographer of Kennedy, Margaret Laing, who spent three weeks with the late Senator in 1966, has written,* ". . . the Jews had the qualities he admired most. And as time passed, his emotional commitment to them was to grow. He increasingly believed he could communicate with them."

Miss Laing has noted that Robert Kennedy's first public statement on a public issue was a series of newspaper articles in which he wrote admiringly of the Israelis.

Exactly 20 years later almost to the day, a passing reference in a television programme to these early articles was to lead to his assassination.

The four articles, based on a brief visit Robert Kennedy paid to Palestine, appeared in *The Boston Post* from June 3, 1948, but he was in Palestine around Easter, which was in April. This was just before he graduated from Harvard—the paper describes him as a "Harvard senior," and he was 22 years old at the time. The assignment was obtained for him by his father, to whom the *Post,* now defunct, was indebted.

The four articles are reproduced in full in the Appendix because they record Robert Kenndey's first contact with and evaluation of a problem that was to crop up time and again in his later career, and which ultimately led to his assassination. They are also among the few of his published writings that we can be quite sure he actually wrote himself. Ghost writers contributed so greatly to his later articles, books and speeches that the correspondent of the London *Observer* told the Senator that this was one of the things that was wrong with his political campaign.

Even making allowances for the fact that these articles were Kennedy's first attempt at journalism, and that he was just leaving college, they are singularly undistinguished pieces of writing: shallow, disjointed and naive. They also contain major inaccuracies of fact, and these have been corrected in a note to the Appendix because some of them are still being repeated. These articles are more interesting for what they tell us about Robert Kennedy than what they tell about Palestine in 1948.

Palestine in April, 1948, the last month of the British Mandate, was

* *The Next Kennedy,* New York and London. 1968.

in a state of near chaos with Arab and Jew preparing for the showdown. Kennedy, in an attempt at objective journalism (though there has never been and cannot be any such thing) states both cases in his first article. But the second, third and fourth articles are only about the Jewish effort, which is scarcely surprising because by his own choice he lived on the Jewish side and went on forays with Jewish soldiers. By the fourth article his underlying admiration for the Jews comes clearly out into the open.

In the second article, Kennedy describes how he was shown round a kibbutz by "a Jew who 40 years ago was in Boston making speeches for my grandfather." One can always find Jews in Israel who have such links with every major country in the West because they came from the West and remain part of it. Neither Kennedy nor anyone else would find many, or any, Arabs with such familiar connections. And on this circumstance is based the fundamental, unspoken, presupposition of Westerners about Israel and about the Arabs—for Westerners, the Israelis are "us," the Arabs are "them." For Asians, of course (and Israel is in Asia), the roles are reversed—the Arabs are "us," the Israelis are "them."

One thing Kennedy understood very clearly was the bitter hatred that divided Jew and Arab, and the Arab determination never to have a Jewish state in their midst: "they are determined that a seperate Jewish state will be attacked and attacked until it is finally cut out like an unhealthy abscess ... if it [Israel] does become a reality it will never have as neighbours anything but hostile countries, which will continue to fight militarily and economically until victory is achieved." Ten years later, in January, 1958, when he was counsel for a Senate committee enquiring into labour disputes, Kennedy visited a town in Wisconsin that was also divided by hatred and he remembered Palestine: "The loathing and hatred between Arab and Jew was an all-consuming thing. It was impossible in those days to talk to any representative of either side without becoming immediately aware that every person on both sides had been caught up in the conflict. Men had lost their reason." * In those later years, Kennedy knew that the Arabs

* *The Enemy Within* by R. F. Kennedy, New York, 1960. Popular Library edition.

(like Sirhan) continued to hate Israel, as they had told him they would. He therefore knew that by supporting Israel he had taken a position on one side of a front-line of hate.

He admits, in the first article, that it is precisely "because there are such well-founded arguments on either side [that] each grows more bitter toward the other." But it is not the arguments on the Jewish side that drew him to it. He all-too-readily concedes that "there is no country or group of countries that would ever consider taking 800,000 Jews" and that the Jews had suffered graviously from Nazi persecution. And so, the Jews have to have Palestine. But he did not even begin to explain why Palestine should have to pay for the anti-Jewish feeling of the West, directed even against the survivors of Nazi persecution.

What evokes his admiration for the Jews are the qualities that he admired then and that he exemplified in his own life later on: the Jews are "an immensely proud and determined people . . . these indications of spirit and determination . . . the Jews who have been lucky enough to get to Palestine are hardy and tough;" they have "an undying spirit that the Arabs, Iraqi, Syrians, Lebanese, Saudi Arabians, Egyptians and those from Trans-Jordan can never have. They are a young, tough, determined nation and will fight as such;" the Jews "with 101 per cent morale, will accept no compromise . . . they will fight and they will fight with unparalleled courage." Tough and determined, determined and tough, the words are an admiring refrain.

Kennedy's admiration for the forceful aspects of the Israeli character came to be better known than the despatches themselves. Two of his biographers, referring to these articles, quote him in praise of the Israelis but in words he never actually used. Thus, one says that Kennedy wrote that the Jews had "much more spirit and discipline and determination than the Arabs, that they were tougher inwardly and outwardly" * and another says that "he admired the Israelis' 'spirit and zest and determination and discipline.' " † But Kennedy could very well have used these words on his favourite theme.

The young Kennedy gives only one practical reason why the U.S.

---

* R. de Toledano, *RFK: The Man Who Would Be President*, New York, 1967, Signet.
† D. Schaap, *RFK*, New York, Signet, p. 64.

should favour the establishment of a Jewish State; it is the same geopolitical consideration that motivated the framers of the Balfour Declaration 20 years earlier: "The United States and Great Britain before too long a time might well be looking to a Jewish State to preserve a toehold in that part of the world." The Western Powers have since found that toehold, though perhaps "bridgehead" would be a better word.

Two of Kennedy's statements, read now, have a ring of historical irony. The first is when he quotes the Jews as saying that "if a Jewish state is formed it will be the only stabilizing factor remaining in the near and middle east." The opposite has proven true.

And his words: "If the American people know the true facts, I am certain a more honest and forthright policy would be substituted for the benefit of all." This is a hope that the Arabs, with their belief in the essential goodness of the American people, still cling to, despite present day American Middle East policy. But very few Arabs have any hope of getting "the true facts" through to the American people across a wide, "communications gap."

From these articles one senses that Kennedy not only understood but shared the hatred for the British that he ascribes both to the Palestinians and the Jews. He obviously sees the Jews as a small, persecuted people standing up to the might of the British Empire—perhaps a remembrance of Kennedy's Irish ancestors standing up to their hated British overlords. Yet Kennedy failed to see that the original inhabitants of Palestine were engaged in exactly the same sort of battle—against the British and later against the power and wealth of Zionism.

Throughout his articles he never refers to the natives of Palestine as Palestinians, but only as "Arabs." Thus, in his mind, they became part of the vast Arab world, the Goliath to Israel's David. This politico-semantic confusion has continued down to the present. The Arabs, as a whole, did much to create and perpetuate this mistake; the Palestinian people have been the victim of this particular example of the tyranny of words.

There was one other quite personal reason why, after his visit to Palestine in 1948, Kennedy should not feel kindly towards the

Palestinians. One day while preparing to get a lift from Tel Aviv in a convoy to Jerusalem, he met a tank captain who offered him alternate accommodation. He chose the tank, and when he arrived in Jerusalem he learned that the convoy had been wiped out by Palestinian fighters. That he narrowly escaped being killed by "Arabs" might under-standably thereafter have created a certain prejudice against them in Kennedy's mind. He frequently referred to his escape from Palestinian bullets when talking to Jewish audiences.

The quality of "toughness" was so important to Robert Kennedy that he not only admired people who were tough but he also ascribed toughness to the people he admired. Thus, in the Conclusion of *The Enemy Within* he wrote, "The great events of our nation's past were forged by men of toughness, men who risked their security and their futures for freedom and for an ideal" and, "It seems to me imperative that we reinstill in ourselves the toughness and idealism that guided the nation in the past." * But some of the great makers of the American nation, Jefferson and Lincoln, were not "tough" men in the Kennedy sense of the term; strong, yes, but not "tough."

Toughness, determination, discipline, a combination that was synthesised into a favourite Kennedy word—"vigorous"—these were some of the qualities Kennedy admired in the Israelis and tried to exemplify in his own life. His acts of daring and endurance are well known—on the football field and in canoing, swimming and mountain-eering. All his biographers say that his drive for physical achievement sprang from the fact that he was physically smaller than his brothers: "remember that he was the runt of a pretty competitive family. It's a matter of a couple of inches in the tibia."†

Reading about Robert Kennedy's life and recalling the impressions I had gained of Israelis from several visits to that country and years of professional interest in its past history and present activities, I felt that there were other qualities that they had in common which would have led him to have a special soft spot for the Jewish State.

There was the determination, instilled in all the Kennedy children by their parents, that they must win at all costs and whatever the means. It

* *The Enemy Within*, pp. 306–307.
† W. Nicholas, *The Bobby Kennedy Nobody Knows,* Greenwich, Conn., 1967, the pages of this book are unnumbered.

is because of this determination to win that Robert Kennedy was so frequently labelled "ruthless." And ruthless he was, with no great regard to means, in the election campaigns he organised for his elder brother and for himself.

The goal to be won in politics was power, and the Kennedys, on occasion, applied it totally to achieve their objectives. An example of this was the crushing of the American steel companies when they dared to raise their prices against President Kennedy's wishes: this operation, which involved the F.B.I. knocking on journalists doors in the middle of the night, was mounted under Robert Kennedy's supervision. Discussing the backing and filling that characterised Cabinet meetings, he said: "What is really needed is a minor dictator who listens to everybody involved, then decides and says, 'Well, this is what has to be done now, and this is what you are going to do.'" After he became Attorney General he once orated to a meeting of college coaches: "Except for war there is nothing in American life—nothing—which trains a boy better for life than football." War, the total expression of power, was transmogrified into the Great Trainer for Life.

There was, inevitably, in Robert Kennedy a good measure of arrogance. At the 1960 Democratic Convention he bluntly told an undecided state caucus: "We are a young group and we are going to take over America." At the same Convention he demanded that Hubert Humphrey deliver the delegations pledged to him "at once, or else." And during the Bay of Pigs crisis he ordered Chester Bowles, whether he liked or not, to give public support to that venture.

Strange as it may seem, there is no word in the English language for one of Robert Kennedy's principal characteristics—his total commitment to a cause. "Persistance," "determination," "dedication," "relentlessness" do not capture the quality of character that was behind his total involvement in the campaign to elect his brother, or his long-drawn-out effort, a real man-hunt, to destroy James Hoffa, the trade union leader. There is in French the word *"jusqua'a bout"*—"to the end" and "jusqu'a boutism" is what Robert Kennedy had and what he admired in others. It was this quality of total driving commitment that drew him to Senator Joseph McCarthy and his anti-communist witch-hunting. Robert Kennedy worked for the Senator against the advice of his elder brother and he retained a personal loyalty to McCarthy to the very end: he was one of the few public figures who attended his funeral.

His grudging, reluctant admiration for the jusqu'a boutism of the Vietcong, plus their toughness and determination, was one element in his policy advocating a negotiated peace in Vietnam; something akin to de Gaulle's "peace of the brave" in Algeria. How, he once asked a reporter, could one lightly dismiss the Vietcong, those little guys with fantastic guts who stormed the U.S. Embassy on a suicide mission?

Even a nodding acquaintance with recent events in the Middle East will be sufficient to provide numerous examples of Robert Kennedy's characteristics put into action by Israel: the arrogance of defying the condemnation of the Security Council and the unanimous wish of the General Assembly not to incorporate Jordanian Jerusalem; the total application of force against the Palestinian "expellees," the will to win by any means, including the bombing of hospitals, like the August Victoria in Jerusalem, and the widespread use of napalm by the Israelis. Many of Israel's positions were Robert Kennedy's personal qualities raised to the level of national policy.

A single-minded, and simple-minded, admiration of muscular virtues can have serious personal and political consequences. Except perhaps towards the end, Robert Kennedy, as one of his sisters said, never felt the tremors of self-doubt and he had little patience with the defeated. His wife, Ethel, is reported to have said of him (a report she later denied) that "he has no patience with the weak and the hesitant." And after a calamitous meeting that Kennedy had with a group of Black intellectuals—calamitous because of a total inability to communicate with each other—the author James Baldwin remarked: "he just didn't get the point. He was naive. He doesn't know pain. He just doesn't know."

It must, however, be pointed out that these were not the only qualities of Robert Kennedy. He was not only the proponent of "vigour." There was great compassion in him. He loved children and they loved him. And Mrs. Jacqueline Kennedy, who could judge Robert Kennedy better than most, said of him, "This is the one I would put my hand in the fire for;" a rare tribute.

Yet the essential colouration of his character was that of the man of "vigour." Merely because of what he himself was, it would have been virtually impossible for Robert Kennedy to balance his admiration for the "Superman," Nietzschean qualities of the Israelis with any compensating sympathy for the Palestinian people because they were weak, they suffered, they were defeated.

Because of his character, Robert Kennedy was fated to be anti-Palestinian.

The Palestinians were, therefore, his Blind Spot. In theory they should not have been. He once said: "We believe men and nations will not willingly choose to submit to other men from other lands."* That is the heart and core of the Palestinian struggle. He sympathised with the weak and downtrodden in the United States. But the Palestinians are not American voters and have no powerful American friends, and one wonders how much of a difference this must have made.

* R. F. Kennedy, *A New Day,* New York, 1968. Signet, p. 119.

7

Bitter Coffee, or the Demands of Politics

"German Documents Allege Kennedy Held Anti-Semitic Views"—this was the wording of a leaflet distributed in Jewish districts in the election for a Massachusetts Senate seat between John Kennedy and Cabot Lodge.

"I was elected by the Jews of New York and I would like to do something for the Jewish people:" President John Kennedy to Prime Minister David Ben Gurion of Israel in May, 1961.

Soon after June, 1967, Senator Robert Kennedy was addressing a meeting of Jewish trade unionists. He coughed to clear his throat and said, "I've just drunk a cup of bitter Arab coffee and have not had time to wash my mouth." The audience was much amused.

These three statements, the first a threat, the second pro-Jewish, the third anti-Arab, sum up the curious relationship of the Kennedy family with American Zionism. According to some biographers, the second and third statements were the result of the first; that is the pro-Jewish promise and the anti-Arab joke were the end-results of the anti-Semitic accusation.

Even if this hypothesis were only partly true, it is remarkable that one of the most, if not the most powerful of political families in America could be moved towards a certain policy by charges that were based on the most slender of foundations.

The Kennedy who allegedly held anti-Semitic views was Joseph Kennedy, Senior, the father of the former President and of Robert. The grandson of an Irish immigrant, he amassed millions, by methods that do not bear too close scrutiny, from such diverse products as films, real estate and whiskey. From 1937 to 1940 he was U.S. Ambassador in London. Joseph Senior was very much an Irishman and therefore anti-British. He was an isolationist and a believer in Fortress America who hated to see America entangled in foreign wars. And he made coarse remarks about Jews. He was not an anti-Semite. But in the pre-war years, his views could be made to seem anti-Semitic by those Americans, Jews and Gentiles, who wanted America to intervene actively against the anti-Semitic tyranny of Hitler. The elder Kennedy was no appeaser of fascism. His despatches from London, in the volumes of documents released by the State Department, simply show that he took a very gloomy view of Britain's prospects of survival in 1939 and 1940. His appraisal was realistic but unimaginative because he clearly failed to understand the character of the British people and the impact of Churchill's leadership. Hence he thought Hitler was going to win. But nowhere did he give the impression that he wanted Hitler to win. And so Ambassador Kennedy, who did not want his country to come into the war at all, particularly objected to it supporting what he believed to be the losing side. One personal reason given for his anti-war position was that he had four sons and he did not want them killed in any foreign war. In the event, his eldest son was killed and the second eldest only narrowly escaped death, so his apprehensions were justified.

It was Joseph Kennedy who had instilled in his sons an admiration for success, for toughness and for "vigour." The political danger of this simple-minded admiration is that when these qualities were applied to an analysis of the pre-war scene, it was the Nazis who appeared tough and successful and the democracies that appeared weak and hesitant.

Whatever his real views were by 1940, the pro-Nazi, anti-Semitic labels were firmly passed on to Joseph Kennedy, Senior. An example of the sort of accusation made against him is the story by Ben Hecht, then pro-Zionist but later bitterly repentant, who in his autobiography wrote that Kennedy "had spoken to fifty of Hollywood's leading Jewish movie makers in a secret meeting at one of their houses. He told them sternly that they must not protest [against Nazi atrocities] as Jews . . . Any Jewish outcries, Kennedy explained, would impede victory over the Germans. It would make the world feel that a 'Jewish War' was going on." As late as 1964, it was reported of "the liberal Jewish community" of New York that "they believe old Joe bought the ovens [in the death camps] ." *

For Joseph Senior the word "Jew" could be used as a term of abuse and he seemed to have distrusted Jewish influence in American politics and, in particular, the Jewish impact on the political careers of his sons. There was the one, well-documented occasion when Joseph Senior shouted at political collaborators, "You and your sheeny friends are trying to destroy my son." (John) and he went on to charge that "the Liberals, the labour people and Jews were out to destroy" him.† This form of ethnic abuse the father seemed to have passed on to at least one of his sons for when Robert Kennedy once lost his temper with a journalist he dubbed him a "Stevenson Jew."‡

In time, of course, Joseph Senior's anti-Jewish terminology became well-known within the American Jewish community. This was to prove a very heavy liability to his sons. To quote the words of two Kennedy biographers: "He [Joseph Senior] knew that he had endowed his sons with enemies as well as friends. Much of the liberal suspicion of the Ambassador was in fact unfounded. While it is true that his conversation at times reflected the ethnic antagonisms that had long character-ized East Boston and Massachusetts this hardly made him an anti-Semite." § The other biographer is rather less urbane: "This smear [of anti-Semitism] based on half-truths, conjecture and a scattering of fact,

---

* P. Kimball, *Bobby Kennedy and the New Politics,* New Jersey, 1968, p. 104.
† V. Lasky, *JFK, The Man and The Myth,* New York, 1963, p. 141.
‡ de Toledano, *RFK, op. cit.,* p. 153.
§ T. Sorenson, *Kennedy,* New York, 1966, Bantam, p. 35.

attached itself to the Kennedy boys, who worked that much harder in their maturer years to 'prove' their freedom from Joe Sr.'s presumed ideological taint."* Robert, obviously, was the one who worked hardest at cleaning himself of the alleged anti-Semitic taint.

de Toldeano refers to "a scattering of fact" to back the charge that Joseph Senior was anti-Semitic. Apart from dubious anecdotes like that of Ben Hecht, there seems to be precisely one single document, likewise of dubious authority, to support this accusation.

When, in the 1960 Presidential campaign, John Kennedy's opponents revived the accusation of his father's alleged pro-Hitler anti-Semitism, *The New York Times,* on September 1, 1960, published a thorough study of the whole question written by the well-known correspondent Homer Bigart.

Homer Bigart reports that there was apathy among Jewish voters with respect to both the candidates, Nixon and John Kennedy, because they regarded both "with varying degrees of distrust." There was, in particular, a division among "the so-called Jewish group" on whether John Kennedy was pro-Israel or anti-Semitic. Part of this feeling sprang from an active Jewish dislike of Joseph Kennedy, Senior, which one Democratic Party worker went so far as to call "a personal revulsion."

When Bigart tried to pin down the precise cause for this personal revulsion, the Jews he interviewed told him that they had heard of the existence of a letter in which Joseph Kennedy was supposed to have expressed approval of the Hitler regime. Rumours about this letter had been given wide circulation. The general belief concerning this all-important letter was that its contents "discounted the necessity of a firm stand by the United States against Hitler and suggested that the Roosevelt Administration overrated the influence of the American Jewish community." This, then, was the supposed documentary basis for Jewish dislike of Ambassador Kennedy. However, the Anti-Defamation League of B'nai B'rith said that it knew nothing about the existence of any such letter. Nor did it have knowledge of any official American documents to substantiate the charge of anti-Semitism made against the elder Kennedy.

---

* de Toledano, *op. cit.,* p. 35.

Bigart reports that Nixon also came under scritiny because, in the 1950 Senatorial campaign in California, he was alleged to have remarked of his opponent, Mrs. Helen Douglas, that she was the wife of the film star, Melvyn Douglas, "whose real name was Hesselberg," meaning that he was a Jew. B'nai B'rith put a team of no less than seven men for no less than five months on to the task of tracking down rumours that Nixon had uttered those five anti-Semitic words. Nixon was cleared.

So when B'nai B'rith declared that it had no direct documentary evidence of Joseph Kennedy's anti-Semitism, we can safely assume that this clearance was given after an equally thorough investigation.

But there was one piece of indirect documentary evidence, the "German documents" of the 1952 Republican leaflets. In fact, there was only *one* document. This was a report from Herr Herbert von Dirksen, the German Ambassador in London during Ambassador Kennedy's tenure, to the German Foreign Office of a talk with Kennedy which was published, along with other captured German documents, by the State Department in 1949. Von Dirksen's letter said: "The Ambassador (Kennedy) then touched upon the Jewish question and stated that it was naturally of great importance to German-American relations. In this connection it was not so much the fact that we wanted to get rid of the Jews that was so harmful to us, but rather the loud clamour with which we accompanied this purpose. He himself understood our Jewish policy completely; he was from Boston and there, in one golf club, and in other clubs, no Jews had been admitted for the past fifty years. His father had not been elected Mayor because he was a Catholic; in the United States, therefore, such pronounced attitudes were quite common, but people avoided making so much outward fuss about it."

When this document was published, Joseph Kennedy described it as "complete poppycock." Herr von Dirksen, he said, "must have been trying very hard to set himself right in Germany by telling the German Foreign Office the things he thought they'd like to hear;" and sychophantic reporting, as is well-known, is, fortunately, one of the weaknesses common to all dictatorial administrations. The von Dirksen report is, in any case, self-contradictory because if Ambassador

Kennedy did say that he himself had experience of minority discrimination, this would have made him not anti-Jewish but pro-Jewish.

This von Dirksen report has been quoted at some length because it has a certain historical value. On the narrow base of this one captured enemy document, plus some coarse jokes and crude oaths, was erected like a huge inverted pyramid, the scaffolding of "Kennedy anti-Semitism" in which were enclosed Joseph, John and Robert Kennedy, one of the most powerful families there has ever been in American politics. The elder son John, in his Senatorial campaign in Massachusetts in 1952 and in his Presidential campaign in 1960, and the younger son Robert, in his Senatorial campaign in New York in 1964 and in his brief Presidential campaign in 1968, because they felt they had to counter and disprove the anti-Semitic accusation made against their father, had to take a strongly pro-Jewish, and therefore a pro-Israel, stance.

According to Homer Bigart, Jewish voters were distrustful of John Kennedy for other reasons too—that he was a member of the "authoritarian Roman Catholic Church and that the family had been friendly towards Senator Joseph McCarthy. But many other groups in America, besides Jewish voters, had their doubts about Kennedy for these two reasons. What really mattered for the Jewish voter was the charge of anti-Semitism.

One cannot but wonder why the von Dirkson report was given so much credence and importance while little notice was taken of another comment on Ambassador Kennedy from a far more important German source. On February 25, 1939, Doctor Goebbels himself denounced Ambassador Kennedy for serving President Roosevelt's "war-baiting policy."

Attention was concentrated on the von Dirksen report not only by Jewish groups but by the Kennedys' non-Jewish political opponents. For instance *The New York Times* reported on November 3, 1960, that the "New York Young Republicans for Nixon and Lodge" were circulating pamphlets about Joseph Kennedy's anti-Semitism, just as was done in 1952 in Massachusetts.

In the competition for Jewish votes and the support of powerful Jewish publicity organisations, American political parties and candidates try and outbid one another. This, as we shall see, was true of John Kennedy's campaigns in 1952 and 1960 and equally of Robert Kennedy's campaigns in 1964 and 1968.

The Kennedys were never allowed to forget the original taint of anti-Semitism and so their bids and counter-bids had to be all the more emphatic and conspicuous.

During John Kennedy's 1952 Senatorial campaign, the Kennedy camp felt the need to organise a "Jewish Committee for Jack Kennedy." Not only was his father's anti-Semitism held against him but he was also reminded of the fact that he had proposed an amendment in the House of Representatives which would have had the effect of cutting down U.S. aid to Israel. Aware that what was called "the vital Jewish vote" was in danger, a friend of the Kennedys', Congressman John McCormack, took the extreme step of calling a meeting in Boston's heavily Jewish Fourteenth Ward where he announced that it was he and not Congressman Kennedy who had proposed the "anti-Israeli" amendment to stave off another Congressman's efforts to slash even more funds. This story was a complete invention but indicates how desperately anxious the Kennedys were to retain Jewish support.

When John Kennedy ran for the Presidency in 1960, the Jewish voter had yet another complaint against him. This was the fact that in July, 1957, he had made a speech criticising the French government for its attempt to suppress the Algerian national movement and the Eisenhower Administration for not lending its weight to the cause of Algerian independence. As an enemy of the Arabs, Israel consistently opposed the granting of independence to any Arab territory. At the U.N., Israel consistently voted against the Afro-Asian bloc on all questions relating to the freedom struggle in Tunisia, Morocco and Algeria.

John Kennedy's pro-Algerian speech was held against him for years after and as late as July, 1968, I was told in Jerusalem that this speech was one reason American Jews were inclined to be suspicious of his younger brother, Robert.

During the 1960 campaign, Joseph Kennedy's alleged anti-Semitism was, of course, once again given a hearing. At the nominating convention, Kennedy's opponent, Lyndon Johnson, and the columnist, Drew Pearson, were among those who publicised the Senior Kennedy's anti-Jewish remarks. In the campaign itself, Ambassador Kennedy was "assailed in a barrage of New York newspaper advertisements as an anti-Semite."‡ Nevertheless, John retained the majority of the traditionally pro-Democratic Jewish votes.

It was this support that probably prompted his ramark to Ben Gurion—that he had been elected by the Jews of New York and that, consequently, he would like to do something for the Jewish people. And so he did. As has been said, U.S. financial aid to Israel rose to unprecedented heights during his term of office.

Furthermore, soon after his election, early in 1961, President Kennedy sent Myer Feldman, who was his advisor on Jewish affairs, on a secret mission to Israel. Feldman was authorised to pledge the support of the U.S. Sixth Fleet (based in the Mediterranean) to Israel in the event of any Arab attack on the Jewish State. It has been stated that Feldman also made a bargain with the Israelis that they should stop work on a nuclear bomb in return for an offer of Hawk anti-aircraft missiles, which were finally delivered in 1963. Feldman has confirmed that the pledge of involving the Sixth Fleet was made but denies that there was any other bargain.*

Mr. Feldman has himself reported† that he was present at a meeting, held in Palm Beach "late in 1962" between President Kennedy and the then Israeli Foreign Minister, Mrs. Golda Meir. The latter put the question, "What would the United States do if Israel's neighbours challenged the territorial integrity of Israel?" Mr. Feldman records, "The answer of the President was firm and unequivocal. He reminded Mrs. Meir that for practical, strategic and historical reasons the United States had a special relationship with Israel not unlike our relationship to Great Britain. He pointed out the United States could not afford to sit idly by if Israel was invaded, and we would come to her assistance instantly. . . . He underlined this comment in a personal, still-unpublished letter to Prime Minister Ben Gurion in the spring of 1963."

‡ Sorenson, *op. cit.,* footnote to p. 235.
* *Parade* magazine, New York, June 16, 1968.
† In an article in *The Los Angeles Times,* Part II, page 5, June 6, 1968.

Yet, though President Kennedy kept his promise and did a great deal for Israel, he refused to adopt the attitude that American friendship for Israel necessarily meant American hostility towards the Arabs; for him there was no either-or choice to be made between Israel and the Arabs. He initiated a friendly correspondence with President Nasser and it was well-known that he hoped to meet with him, as one of the leaders of the Third World, in Washington. That the Third World was of increasing importance in world affairs was one of the fundamental points in President Kennedy's foreign policy. But the Third World had excluded Israel from its ranks, largely because of Israel's pro-colonial voting record at U.N.

Therefore, President Kennedy's friendly approaches to President Nasser and to the Third World in general continued to be viewed with doubt by American Jews.

This was one other obstacle that Robert Kennedy had to overcome when, in his turn, he tried to win Jewish political and publicity support in 1964.

Thus, when he began to campaign for a Senate seat in New York, Robert Kennedy had to contend against his father's reputation for anti-Semitism; his elder brother's support for Algeria and friendliness towards President Nasser and the Third World; and his own connections with Joseph McCarthy who had always been hated by Jewish liberals.

There are two and a half million Jews in New York State, 15 per cent of its population, but their influence is far greater than their figures indicate. It is they who give New York City its distinctive character and since this community is quite solidly Zionist, New York is a major factor in Middle East affairs. No politicians can attain office in New York City or State without the backing of the Jewish community.

Robert Kennedy set about winning that support with his characteristic energy and efficiency.

Prominent Jews such as Senator Abraham Ribicoff, David Dubinsky, the trade union leader, and the comic writer Henry Golden were enlisted in the campaign: Golden's special task was to tell jokes and extol Kennedy's virtues in Yiddish. According to one of his admiring biographers,* "Bobby himself tried to heal the wounds about his father by telling of his father's liking for Jews. Once, at a Jewish resort, Bobby told his audience; 'My father spent a lot of time in Hollywood in the thirties and got to know many Jewish families. He knew the Warner Brothers and Sam Goldwyn and admired the way they taught their children respect for their parents and love for each other. My father liked that and decided to bring his own family up that way. That's the way the Kennedy family was brought up." Another, slightly less admiring biographer comments,† "Since there were very few parallels to be drawn between Kennedy family life and Jewish family life, this kind of talk didn't always go over."

But he persisted. In the words of Nicholas, "Bobby plumped down for more aid to Israel, chastised the Soviets for anti-Semitism and was photographed [in a synagogue] wearing the Jewish skull cap, the *yarmulke*. But Bobby also made some political errors as far as the Jews were concerned. He failed to show up for a Manhattan Zionist convention . . . Bobby also stated that he favoured continued shipments of surplus American food to Egypt, an enemy of tiny Israel . . . The fierce competition for the Jewish vote fortunately had a humourous break. The city's leading Arab organisation picketed the headquarters of both candidates, but announced that Kennedy was the lesser of two evils. The political damage of Arab endorsement was too much to bear, so Kennedy's press secretary, Debs Myers hurriedly sent a wire to the Arab office, disavowing, in Kennedy's name, any support from those Arab countries which are engaged in war-like activities in the Middle East. (A photograph of Kennedy discussing this telegram was specially taken). 'Good lord,' sighed a Kennedy aide, 'that's all we need now, the Arab vote.' "

That this incident should be regarded as "humourous" is significant. What is far more important is that it marks the beginning of Robert Kennedy's positive and public repudiation of the Arabs in favour of Jewish support. Another Kennedy aide "later laughed, 'I didn't know there were any Arabs in New York.' " That, in truth, was the point of

* W. Nicholas, *op. cit.*, page unnumbered.
† L. J. Quirk, *Robert Francis Kennedy*, Los Angeles, 1968, Holloway, p. 259.

the "joke"—the Jews were powerfully present, the Arabs only marginally, and pathetically so.

The photograph of Robert Kennedy seated in a synagogue wearing the traditional skull cap evidently did not go down well either at the time or even in retrospect. The captions given to it in the laudatory commemorative books produced after his death are all rather unkind. Perhaps the religious ploy was too patently political. One caption reads, "He wears a skull cap in a synagogue in an effort to win votes;" a second is, "Bobby had a ticklish time allaying the suspicions of many Jews;" and a third caption describes it bluntly, "A further, less convincing attempt to alleviate the doubts of the Jewish community."

Another skull-capped appearance in another synagogue was to be of supreme importance in the life, and death, of Robert Kennedy.

Soon after he was elected Senator, the Kennedy family donated $1,450,000 to Yeshiva University, described as "the pride of all Jews." But rumours of this gift to a Jewish institution were in the air earlier, during the election.

A summing-up of Robert Kennedy's approach to the Jewish voter, and a somewhat more genuinely humourous incident it provoked, has been given in one of his biographies:*

"He did not handle the ethnic issue well . . . Bobby openly discussed the ethnic vote, which is a gross breach of political etiquette, yet had great difficulty playing to it, which is accepted political procedure. He seemed uncomfortable munching a *knish* or wearing a *yarmulke* in a Jewish crowd . . . During Rosh Hashanah, the Jewish New Year, he campaigned on Manhattan's West Side, a heavily Jewish area; his advisers told him he had to offer each Jewish voter New Year's greetings. 'How can I?' said Kennedy. 'How will I know which ones are Jewish.'

" 'Look at them,' suggested one adviser, who was Jewish himself.

" 'It won't help,' Kennedy confessed. 'I can't tell that way.'

"His staff improvised. They assigned Al Blumenthal, a state legislator, to walk with Kennedy; each time a Jewish voter approached,

* Schapp, *op. cit.,* p. 109.

Blumenthal would say 'Now,' and Kennedy would grab the voter's hand and say 'Happy New Year.'

"The strategy worked perfectly until a policeman accidentally stepped on Blumenthal's foot. 'Ow!' said Blumenthal, whereupon Bobby stuck out his hand and said 'Happy New Year' to an understandably startled young Negro."

As a candidate, Robert Kennedy, naturally, did much more than seek identification with Jewish groups: he made speeches to Jewish audiences and told them what they wanted to hear. In one of his early speeches he stressed the themes he was to repeat later on. On September 18, 1964, *The New York Times* reports that "the Democratic candidate recalled that as a newspaper correspondent he had become 'involved' in Israel's War of Independence. He said he had ridden a tank from Tel Aviv to Jerusalem when Jerusalem was beseiged by the Arabs. Mr. Kennedy contended that he had been among the first to see that the Jews were going to defeat the Arabs in Palestine . . . he said the United States should make it clear that in case Israel were attacked, 'we will stand by Israel and come to her assistance' . . . he backed Israel's plan to use Jordan River water in the Negev, and that he favored a joint United States–Israel attempt to desalinize Mediterranean water for use in the desert." In later speeches, he recalled that Israel had received more American aid during the Kennedy Administration than at any other time; and cited his role in the decision of the Kennedy Administration to send Hawk missiles to Israel. He frequently said that American commitments to Israel were part "not of a Jewish problem but a problem for all Americans." The incessant questioning by Jewish audiences about Israel finally irritated him, for he told one such group to "care about the world and not just take an interest in Israel."

Israel figured prominently in Robert Kennedy's maiden speech in the Senate (June 23, 1965) when he proposed that Israel, and other countries with nuclear potential, should renounce their nuclear programmes in return for guarantees against nuclear blackmail.

In subsequent speeches, during 1965 and 1966, Kennedy stressed that Israel should receive arms from America to maintain its military balance with the Arabs; he quoted a statement by the late President Kennedy that "friendship for Israel is not a partisan matter—it is a national commitment."

During the period of crisis in May and June, 1967, he spoke repeatedly in support of Israel. *The New York Times* alone records him as giving five pro-Israel speeches between May 24 and June 23. In them he mentioned the need for America to give Israel "whatever food or economic assistance she requires" so as "to repair the ravages of war within her borders." These words sound almost sarcastic, since the ravages of war were all on the Arab side and Jordan and Syria had to receive a sudden influx of 300,000 "expellees." He spoke in flowing terms of Israel as "a tiny outpost of Western culture and ideals," as "this gallant democracy" equipped with "arms and courage."

In the three preceding years, Senator Kennedy never referred to the Arabs, but in 1967 he did have a few words for them: "the people of the Arab world are largely illiterate, wracked by disease and poverty, without the education and organisation to enrich their harsh desert lands . . . For decades, irresponsible leaders have turned their people's frustrations outward toward the West and Israel;" they were "victims of irresponsible leadership."

During May and June, 1967, Senator Kennedy frequently referred to America's national commitment to defend Israel. At the time, this assertion puzzled many observers. The Israeli Foreign Minister, Mr. Abba Eban, is said to have surprised President Johnson when he asserted, late in May, that Israel had a written undertaking from the United States to come to its defence. The Administration later let it be known that no such document was to be found in the archives of the White House or of the State Department.

Clearly what Senator Kennedy was referring to was the late President Kennedy's promises to Mrs. Meir and Ben Gurion, which had so far been kept secret. Mr. Feldman referred to them publicly only on June 6. And even he notes that many people "question the scope of the commitments" because they were based on "verbal guarantees" given to Israel "privately." What Robert Kennedy was evidently trying to do was to bring the promises out into the open and to convert personal promises into a national guarantee that would have the effect of a formal military alliance between the U.S. and Israel. This, however, had not yet come about despite American military, economic and diplomatic assistance to Israel, since June, 1967.

It was in the post-June period that Robert Kennedy made his "humourous" reference to his choking on a cup of bitter Arab coffee.

These words of his gave more offence to people throughout the Arab world than any other pro-Israeli or anti-Arab statement he ever made.

They were taken as a deliberate insult, by him personally, to Arab hospitality and to the Arab way of life.

Hospitality is one of their traditions of which the Arabs are, justly, proud, and it is symbolised in the small cup of coffee (which can be served bitter, medium sweet or sweet) that is served to all guests as a matter of course. It was a tradition that was observed, as we have seen, by the Sirhan family in Pasadena.

For a political leader to say publicly to a Jewish audience that he had to wash his mouth out after drinking Arab coffee had the same effect on the Arabs as would a remark by a speaker to an Arab audience, that he had just finished eating an unappetising dish of pork with Jews, would have had on the Jews.

In American, British or French terms it was akin to an Arab speaker gaining a cheap laugh by blowing his nose in a handkerchief made in the design of the Stars and Stripes, the Union Jack or the Tricolour.

After Robert Kennedy's death, comments by Arabs and letters to the editors of Arab papers, even when they deplored the killing, harked back, over and over again, to the crudity and hurtfulness of the bitter coffee remark, which was widely publicised throughout the Arab world.

The fact that after June, 1967, the Arabs were smarting under their military defeat and diplomatic set-back made them all the more sensitive to this crack at their way of life. For scores of thousands of Arabs this single, off-hand remark was the last straw on the camel's back.

Robert Kennedy almost certainly did not know the larger significance that would be attached to this joking comment, though it was in conformity with his whole approach to the Arabs for whom he, clearly, had little liking and less respect. He ate *knishes* and attended *bar-mitzvahs* and wore a *yarmulke,* but he could not drink Arab coffee.

It may be argued that by making his blatant appeal to the Jewish community Robert Kennedy was doing no more than playing the game of ethnic politics, which is a recognised feature of American public life.

And ethnic politics has come to be accepted because politicians do not seem able to resist the temptation of picking up votes by making the easy emotional appeal to the sectional loyalties of Irish-Americans or Italian-Americans or Polish-Americans or Jewish-Americans or Black Americans; but, not, it would seem, Arab-Americans.

It can also be argued, however, that Robert Kennedy, because of his *jusqu'a boutism*, carried ethnic politics to dangerous lengths, that he played this game, as he played all games, roughly and to win, irrespective of the rules—and of the consequences. In his final, brief campaign he used the appeal of ethnic politics to an extent that no other candidate did.

Since the United States is a nation of immigrants, who have yet to be fused into a single American people, a certain amount of ethnic politics is inevitable. It even has its defenders: "ethnic politics—for all its demagoguery and ticket balancing excesses—lent a certain richness and dependability to American politics."*

Because the Republican Party spoke for the White-Anglo-Saxon Protestants, the WASPs, it was left to the Democratic Party to represent the hyphenated ethnic minorities and the Catholics, Jews and Negroes. One writer has referred to the Democrats as "a federation of American minorities" or "the minorities coalition of the Democrats."† After the Depression it was left to a great Democratic President, Franklin Roosevelt, to broaden the popular support of his party by basing his popularity on class rather than on ethnic or minority loyalties. It was still a sectional appeal, but it was a far wider one than what the Democrats had got used to.

Perhaps because the Kennedy brothers came from a Catholic and Irish family and one that had had to claw its way up the economic ladder, in their politics they reverted to the older ethnic politics of their party. In Robert Kennedy's campaigns, especially, the slogan was "A majority of the Minorities."

Beginning with John Kennedy's Senatorial campaign of 1952, which Joseph Senior organised, the Kennedy's concentrated on the sectional

* Kimball, *op. cit.,* p. 13.
† T. H. White, *The Making of the President, 1960,* New York, 1961, Pocket Book, Pp. 345–437

approach. They organised committees to appeal to the needs and prejudices of every ethnic group, every profession, every religion. By the time Robert Kennedy took over the running of his brother's Presidential campaign, the card index and the computer were pressed into service, and one piece of information that was always recorded, on hundreds of thousands of personal cards, was ethnic background.

It is now common knowledge that religion, John Kennedy's Roman Catholicism, played a major part in his Presidential campaign and in his narrowly won victory. It was injected most skilfully—people were incessantly reminded that they must forget about the candidates' religion.

A whole book has been written on the subject of *Bobby Kennedy and the New Politics,* the "New Politics" being defined as "the contemporary contest for political power characterised by primary reliance on personal organisations in preference to party machinery, emphasis on consolidating voters rather than on dividing them along traditional lines of class or religion, projection of political style above issues and exploitation of the full range of modern techniques for mass communication."* Robert Kennedy was an exponent of the New Politics in respect of the first and the last two points but he definitely did not try to consolidate "voters rather than [divide] them along traditional lines of class or religion."

He did nothing but this in his 1964 New York campaign with his ethnic approach to Jews, Blacks and Italian-Americans.

Robert Kennedy did much for the Blacks when he was Attorney-General but his interest in their cause was not something that sprang from a sense of personal compassion or sympathy for the underdog. If it had, he would have become interested in the Negro question long before he actually did so. He himself confessed that "before 1961 I never lost much sleep over civil rights." He became involved when civil rights emerged as a major part of his job as Attorney-General; and even then the Kennedy Administration took time to really throw its weight behind the Black struggle: "an inadequate approach" in the words of the late Martin Luther King.

* Kimball, *op. cit.,* pp. 1–2.

By 1964, of course, the Negro problem was a major political issue and nowhere more so than in New York City with its major Black ghetto in Harlem. Therefore Robert Kennedy gave time and attention to the Black Americans as he did to New York's Jews.

By 1968 Kennedy was able to evoke great emotional support from the Negro community. But whether, from his side, the motivation was genuine feeling or political, sectional calculation, is an open question. On the one hand, there are stories of Kennedy keeping white politicians waiting while he talked with Blacks,* while, on the other, there are stories of him keeping Blacks waiting while he talked with white politicians. *The Los Angeles Times* reported one such incident† under the heading, "Lessening Negro Support for Kennedy Seen:" the complaint was made that Kennedy felt that he had already won the Negro community and so did not need to bother about Black politicians.

Whatever the motivation, here was another old-style Democratic Party appeal to a minority group—traditional ethnic politics.

In the description, already quoted, of Kennedy's handling of ethnic politics in New York the author observed that "he did not handle the ethnic issue well . . . Bobby openly discussed the ethnic vote, which is a gross breach of political etiquette." Ethnic politics has its rules of etiquette, one of which is that ethnic politics may be used but not openly, self-consciously referred to.

If this is hypocrisy, it is necessary hypocrisy. The pretense that in America there is no ethnic vote is the homage that the vice of ethnic politics pays to official policy of the separation of religion from politics. Much of ethnic politics is also religious politics because most of the hyphenated American groups are Roman Catholics and, in addition, there are the Jews.

If the religious aspect of ethnic politics were to be stressed then one of the fundamental principles on which the American Republic is based would come under dangerous challenge. Robert Kennedy overdid his ethnic politics. And with no community did he do it so blatantly as with the Jews.

* *Time* magazine, Atlantic edition, May 24, 1968, p. 14.
† May 28, 1968.

We have seen that as part of his 1964 New York campaign, Robert Kennedy entered the hall of worship in synagogues wearing the traditional skull cap. No other candidate made such an openly politico-religious approach. We have also noted that this particular move by Kennedy did not receive very favourable publicity. Could it be that the Jews did not like open political emphasis being placed on the fact that they were of a different religious and ethnic group? Or because Kennedy, unwittingly perhaps, was reminding others that the Jews were an especially different minority?

Unfortunately, Kennedy did not learn anything from his New York campaign, or at least not in this regard, because in 1968, he made even more strenuous efforts to harness minority-religious feeling, specifically that of the Jewish community, to his political ambitions.

8

The Trigger

After January, 1968, the race for the American Presidency, hesitantly at first, began to gather speed and with the quickening pace the grip of American Zionists on the contestants began to tighten.

On no other candidate did this grip tighten more uncomfortably than on Robert Kennedy.

Since his last campaign in New York in 1964, his younger brother had created yet another obstacle to Jewish support for Robert Kennedy. Senator Edward Kennedy was chairman of the Special Senate Subcommittee on Refugees and Escapees. In that capacity he made a tour of Palestinian refugee camps in Jordan and Lebanon in 1966. At the conclusion of this tour the Senator expressed his support for the U.N. resolution that called for the repatriation or compensation of these refugees. This resolution had been passed in December, 1948, and has since been reaffirmed by vote of the General Assembly every time the refugee situation has been discussed. The Senator's stand was, therefore, unexceptional and wholly unadventurous. But Israel, for

20 years, has refused to implement this resolution, and so the youngest Kennedy's statements greatly upset the Israelis and American Zionists.

Hence, in 1968, Robert Kennedy who, in his quest for Jewish support, had to overcome not only his father's alleged anti-Semitism, his elder brother's alleged "softness" for the Arabs, his allegiance to Joe McCarthy, was now faced with yet another hurdle: his younger brother's open-minded approach to the Palestine refugees, who are at the heart of the Arab-Israeli problem.

Because of his family, Robert Kennedy's task to convince the American Jewish community of his friendship for Israel did not become easier with the passage of time.

Furthermore, he had to contend with other candidates who were prepared to make equally pro-Israeli statements and promises and who were not burdened by the alleged anti-Israeli attitudes of any members of their families. Therefore Robert Kennedy had to work that much harder to win Jewish confidence.

Even for someone accustomed to the large part played by ethnic politics in American elections, the great importance given to Israel in the 1968 Presidential campaign is a strange phenomenon. The candidates did not feel the need to issue policy statements about Ireland or Italy or Poland, though large blocs of voters hailed from these countries. But, over and over again, they did have to make statements about Israel, even though some of their Jewish voters did not come from Israel and were, in fact, refraining from going to Israel despite appeals by Israeli leaders.

All such statements were, of course, strongly in support of Israel and therefore necessarily, in the circumstances of 1968, strongly anti-Arab.

The decisive move in the campaign to commit Presidential candidates to a definitely pro-Israel line came in May when "the American Israel Public Affairs Committee invited the leading Presidential candidates to express their views on the Near East crisis." These views, of Messrs. Humphrey, Kennedy, McCarthy, Nixon and Rockefeller, were published in the May issue of *Near East Report* published in Washington.

As an editorial note puts it, in highly euphemistic language, "all candidates stated that there is a U.S. commitment to the preservation of Israel. All would like to see early Arab-Israeli negotiations. All would like to see friendship between the United States and all the peoples in the Near East. All the candidates are agreed that Israel should receive military assistance from the United States."

The official policy of all the Arab governments rejects every one of these four points.

In January and February, 1968, when he was still standing hesitantly on the sidelines of the campaign, Robert Kennedy made at least three statements recommending arms aid to Israel. On January 8, he said that "the U.S. should supply Israel with whatever weapons it needed to offset whatever Russia was supplying the Arabs so that Israel 'can protect itself.' " He specifically included the 50 supersonic Phantom jets the Israelis have been seeking. He said much the same thing the next day after meeting with Israeli Prime Minister, Levi Eshkol.*

In his statement to the American Israeli Public Affairs Committee, Senator Kennedy had something to say about the Arabs. He maintained that there could not be peace in the Middle East "while proud Arabs suffer in unspeakable poverty beside a flourishing neighbour" and while "some hostile Arab neighbours have turned their backs on peace for their own private and personal gain." He believed that "Arabs and Israelis must meet, and mix, and trade with each other."†

Senator Kennedy did not explain how this idyllic situation was to be brought about in the face of continuing Israeli occupation of Jordanian, Syrian and Egyptian territory and in the face of the continuing presence of over a million Palestinian expellees. Besides, his hopes for a peaceful settlement contrast strangely with his advocacy of arms aid to Israel.

In March, just before he declared his candidacy, the Senator presented a five-point "peace" plan at a United Jewish Appeal dinner. The audience being what it was, the plan was, naturally, fully in accord with Israel's wishes. Indeed it went further, because in his fifth point Robert Kennedy suggested the setting up of "foreign assistance funds—through a special U.N. development fund—for use in the

* *The New York Times,* January 9 and 10, 1968.
† *Near East Report,* February 8, 1968.

occupied [Arab] territories." Not even Israel went so far as to ask for this, because it would have meant United Nations recognition of her occupation, and while leaving Israel in occupation, the plan would have relieved her of any consequential economic burdens.

In the meantime, mass expulsions, the elimination of villages from the map, the exiling of political leaders, protest strikes and demonstrations and arrests—all the usual sequels of military conquest and armed occupation were going on in the occupied territories which international—U.N. funds were to develop, according to the Senator's proposition.

The Israeli occupation was brought home to the Sirhans when, on April 4, a passenger bus was stopped by an Israeli police jeep a few miles east of their native village of Taibeh, and three youths were taken from it and shot by the Israeli policemen in the nearby fields; two of the victims died.*

One of the first acts of Kennedy after he declared his candidacy was to send Mr. Feldman to Israel "conveying messages" to "Premier Levi Eshkol, Defence Minister Moshe Dayan and other officials. Mr. Feldman said he was not at liberty to discuss the terms of the messages but he emphasized that 'Israel could not have had a better friend' than the Senator."† One thing discussed by Mr. Feldman was a probable visit to Israel later in the year by Mr. Kennedy. It will be recalled that Kennedy had already met with Prime Minister Eshkol in January, 1968. Why, soon after announcing his candidacy, did Kennedy feel the need to send secret messages to Israeli leaders: was it to try and convince them to convince the American Jewish community that he was indeed a good friend of Israel and therefore deserving of their electoral and publicity support?

It was during the primary contests in Oregon and California that Robert Kennedy, on three well-publicised occasions, expressed his policy of total, military support of Israel. And on two of these occasions his appeal was frankly ethnic-religious, pro-Jewish and anti-Arab.

* *The New York Times*, April 5, 1968, Report by James Feron.
† *The New York Times*, June 7, 1968.

The contest in California, according to *The Times* of London, found "Senator Kennedy struggling with Senator McCarthy for the crucial Jewish vote in Los Angeles."* Therefore, on May 20, he went to one of the principal synagogues in that city, Temple Isaiah, and in the sanctuary, wearing the *yarmulke,* he spoke on his proposal for a U.S.-Soviet agreement to stop the shipment of arms to the Middle East. In the prepared text of his speech Kennedy emphasised that until such an agreement was reached, the U.S. "must fully assist Israel—with arms if necessary."†

On May 27, he went much further. In Portland, Oregon, he once again spoke in a synagogue, the Temple Neveh Shalom, wearing the *yarmulke* and once again from a prepared text, which had been given to the press beforehand (the vote in California was still a week away).

In this speech, Kennedy outlined a precise programme of American aid to Israel which went further than anything said on this subject by any other American politician.

In his text the Senator said that the United States must defend Israel against aggression "from whatever source." He continued, "our obligations to Israel, unlike our obligations towards other countries, are clear and imperative . . . Israel is the very opposite of Vietnam. Israel's government is democratic, effective, free of corruption, its people united in its support.

"The Soviets have sent supersonic fighters to the Arabs. Soviet planes and pilots they have trained are on Arab soil. Forty Soviet warships are in the Mediterranean, and their advisers are in Arab nations."

He said that the United States could not permit such an imbalance.

Therefore, "the United States should without delay sell Israel the 50 Phantom jets she has so long been promised."

Furthermore, the United States should immediately cut off economic aid to Arab countries that is used "in support of aggression against Israel." In which connection he recalled that he had voted in the Senate for a law suspending all economic aid to Egypt.

He went on to advocate "direct negotiations" between the Arabs

* *The New York Times,* June 7, 1968.
† *The New York Times,* May 21, 1968.

and Israel which should, among other things, settle the position of Jerusalem where "everyone, for the first time, has free access to the Holy Places of their religion," which is as clear an indication as possible of his approval of Israeli control of the Holy City.

And he ended by criticising anti-Semitism in Poland.

The text of this important speech was prepared by the Harvard Scholar, Dr. Nadar Sarbin, who was Robert Kennedy's advisor on Middle East Affairs. Dr. Sarbin, a former Israeli citizen, fought in the Haganah in the First Battle for Palestine in 1948.

All these politico-military statements, it must be remembered, were made in a place of worship, something Kennedy's opponent in Oregon and California, Senator McCarthy refrained from doing.

A photograph of the skull-capped Senator Kennedy addressing the congregation at the Temple Neveh Shalom appeared across two columns at the top of page three of *The Independent* of Pasadena on May 27. This was the daily paper subscribed to by the Sirhans. That photograph is reproduced here on page vi.

On the day before, May 26, the same paper carried a comment by the well-known columnist, David Lawrence, entitled "Paradoxical Bob" in which Mr. Lawrence had little difficulty in pointing out the paradoxes, or rather the contradictions, in Kennedy's position towards Vietnam—where he advocated disengagement—and towards Israel—where he advocated engagement and commitment. In this column, Mr. Lawrence was merely applying to Kennedy a discovery that many people had made the previous June: that the liberal-minded "doves" on Vietnam were "hawks" on the Middle East. This is probably because many of the Vietnam doves are Jewish, a fact that prompted a disgruntled Johnson to comment that if the American Jewish community wanted his support on Israel, it should not be so critical of his policy on Vietnam.

The following excerpt from the David Lawrence column is significant; it begins: "Presidential candidates are out to get votes, and some of them do not realize their own inconsistencies. Just the other day, Sen. Robert F. Kennedy of New York made a speech in Los Angeles which certainly was received with favour by Protestant, Catholic and Jewish groups which have been staunchly supporting the cause of Israel against Egypt and the Arab countries." Lawrence then goes on to quote Kenned'y speech at Temple Isaiah about America not accepting an imbalance against Soviet arms in the Middle East, yet, he noted, no Presidential candidate had demanded economic sanctions against the Soviet Union. Lawrence observes that Senator Kennedy had said that America should use its power "only as a strategic reserve against the most serious of threats"—and that Vietnam was not a threat to America. Lawrence goes on: "Lots of people, however, think the situation in the Middle East is not nearly as dangerous as the situation in Southeast Asia. Also there are many members of Congress who feel that, it is proper for the United States to render military support to Israel in the Middle East, it is just as necessary to protect the countries of Southeast Asia against aggression." Lawrence observed that Kennedy had said that America should exercise its power but with a decent respect for the opinions of mankind, while at the same time he "recommended a stern policy in the Middle East." Lawrence concluded by giving his reasons for this paradox—the fear of the draft taking young Americans to Vietnam, on the one hand, and on the other, the fear that "a large number of people in this country are deeply concerned with the events in the Middle East, particularly with the fate of Israel. Hence the political candidates see a big advantage in proclaiming their support of American intervention in the Middle East." Robert Kennedy was the Second Victim of the Kennedy-Sirhan tragedy,—a victim partly by choice, partly by compulsion, of the pursuit of this "big advantage."

In pursuit of this "big advantage" Robert Kennedy repeated his paradoxical positions in the last statements he made about Israel, in a television debate with Senator McCarthy on June 1st.

Both the Senators agreed that the U.S. should lighten its foreign commitments, but Kennedy then went on, "I do think we have some commitments around the globe. I think that we have a commitment to Israel, for instance, that has to be kept. But what I don't think is that we can be the policeman of the world." Later on the interviewer said to Kennedy, "You, this past week in Portland, proposed that we send 50 jets to Israel." Kennedy replied, "Phantom jets;" and Senator McCarthy then joined in to say that America has "to rebuild the strength that they [the Israelis] lost in the recent war. If that means 50 jets, then it is 50 jets." The Israelis claim to have lost 18 jets in the June fighting.

Even though both candidates mentioned planes for Israel, they were talking about two quite different propositions. Robert Kennedy was speaking about a new consignment of 50 Phantoms while Senator McCarthy was limiting himself to a replacement of planes lost in action.

During the preceding three months Israel showed that it could make effective use of the jet planes it already had. On March 23, a full scale air and land assault was launched, across the Jordan River, into Jordanian territory, at the village of Karameh, allegedly a "terrorist" base. In this attack 40 civilians were killed and Israel was condemned by the Security Council. On June 4th, the day before Robert Kennedy was killed the Israeli Air Force bombed the Jordanian town of Irbin, 20 miles beyond the Jordan River, and in this attack 70 civilians were killed. This news reached Los Angeles on the afternoon of June 4.

The Los Angeles Times of June 5th that carried the news of the Kennedy assassination also carried on its front page, the headline "Israeli Jets Rip Jordan as new Fighting Erupts."

When Sirhan Sirhan was apprehended in the kitchen of the Ambassador Hotel in the first hour of June 5th, he had in his pocket a clipping of the David Lawrence article from the *Pasadena Independent*.

Somewhere in the latter half of May, during which Robert Kennedy was making his statements in synagogues about supplying Phantom jets to Israel, Sirhan Sirhan had scribbled in his diary "Robert F. Kennedy must be assassinated before 5 June 1968."

This meant that Sirhan's generalized disillusioned antagonism towards and rejection of the United States quite suddenly focused on the person of one particular American politicians. But that this should have been Robert Kennedy was, even for Sirhan, a surprising development.

Here too, once again, anger was the product of disillusionment. Sirhan has often spoken of his admiration, respect and even his love for President John F. Kennedy because he was the first American leader who seemed to be trying to understand the Arab viewpoint, and who took the trouble of establishing personal contacts with Arab leaders. He was saddened, though not overwhelmingly so, when the President was assassinated. Yet when Robert Kennedy made his belated entry into the Presidential race much of the approving feelings Sirhan had for the elder brother were transferred to the younger one. Obviously unaware of Kennedy's consistently pro-Israeli record he merely saw him as the champion of the underdog.

The disillusionment came with abrupt finality on May 15th and was caused by the excessive pro-Israeli zeal of some of Robert Kennedy's Jewish friends in the publicity media.

That evening a half-hour documentary film entitled "The Story of Robert Kennedy," made by a Jewish film producer, John Franken-heimer, for the Columbia Broadcasting System, was presented on television in Los Agneles. Sirhan was watching this programme and during it the commentator made the point, which Kennedy himself did so often, that as a young journalist he had been with the Israelis in Israel when they were establishing their state in 1948. The TV commentary went on, "He wrote his dispatches† and came to a decision;" then for the next 30 seconds the Israeli flag flying in the breeze was on the screen while the commentator intoned, "Bobby Kennedy decided his future lay in the affairs of men and nations." There is no logical connection between this statement and the Israeli flag but it was an oblique emotional connection that the producer was seeking to establish, a connection between Kennedy's political career and the State of Israel. This ploy was clearly directed at the Jewish voter and he certainly would have made the desired connection. It just happened that the same connection was made by one particular Palestinian viewer.

This is how Sirhan described his reaction to this programme:* It presented Kennedy, he said, "as being for the underdog and also being for the disadvantaged and for the scum of society, that he wanted to help the poorest people and the most prejudiced and the weakest and at that moment, sir, they showed on the television where Robert Kennedy was in Israel helping to, so I thought, helping to celebrate the Israelis, sir, there, and the establishment of the state of Israel, and the way that he spoke, well, it just bugged me, sir, it burned me up and up until that

† These dispatches are reproduced *in toto* in the appendix, see p. 259.
* Pages 4970 et seq. of Testimony.

time I had loved Robert Kennedy, I cared for him very much, and I hoped that he would win the Presidency until that moment, sir. I hoped that he would win the Presidency but when I saw, heard, he was supporting Israel, sir, not in 1968, but he was supporting it from all the way from its inception in 1948, sir. And he was doing a lot of things behind my back that I didn't know about and, until that time when I watched him on teleivision, it burned me up, sir. And that is most likely, sir, the time I had written this." Question: " 'Robert F. Kennedy must die' and did you feel Robert F. Kennedy must die?" Answer: "At the time, sir, that was the way I felt about it, and if he were in front of me, so help me God, he would have died right then and there."

A few days later on the radio Sirhan heard that Kennedy, during his election campaign, visited a Jewish social club in nearby Beverly Hills and, far more important, heard that he had committed himself to supplying Israel with 50 Phantom bombers; "that was on KFWB, sir, the All News. My mother liked to listen to that."

As proof of his determination to stop Kennedy, Sirhan, after this radio news, went to his room and began one of his mental exercises. He looked into his mirror and concentrated on Kennedy: after a time Kennedy's face replaced his face in the mirror.

Those concerned with denying that Sirhan had any political or Palestinian motivation have tried to find a discrepancy in the fact that whereas Sirhan later on said he wanted to kill Kennedy because of his promise on the 50 bombers he had written down this resolve on May 18 which was two days before Kennedy spoke of supplying arms to Israel. It is difficult to see where the discrepancy comes in. Sirhan himself said in court that, on May 18, he would have killed Kennedy "right then and there" because of his discovery that Kennedy had been pro-Israeli since 1948. Kennedy's pledge on the bombers only reinforced this prior determination and gave it new urgency. To all Palestinians "1948" is a "trigger" year and it would be even more so for Sirhan who, in 1948 in Jerusalem, suffered so much and saw so much bloodshed. The fact that Kennedy in that dreadful year was backing the Zionist enemy was, entirely by itself, more than enough to make him the enemy of any Palestinian nationalist. It was enough for Sirhan. When to this initial provocation was added, eight days later, the further provocation of

Kennedy supporting the granting of offensive weapons, of bombers, to Israel, then, for Sirhan, who knew so much about bombs, Kennedy became someone who had to be stopped.

One sentence in Sirhan's description of what happened on May 18 has a special significance and poignancy. These are the words, "And he was doing a lot of things behind my back that I didn't know about." Here he was expressing his disillusionment, his disappointment with someone whom he had loved. He already felt that America had misled him and betrayed his hopes and now, once more, he found himself misled and betrayed by an American leader. Of course, Sirhan should have known about Kennedy's attitude to Israel, but the fact is that he did not, and that his discovery was not just a surprise or a shock but a deep disappointment.

According to Sirhan admiration for and antagonism towards Kennedy alternated in the next 18 days. On the one hand, he was writing in his notebook: "My determination to eliminate RFK is becoming more, the more of an unshakeable obsession;" and "Kennedy must fall, Kennedy must fall. Please pay to the order of SS the amount of SS. Second group of American sailors must be disposed of. We believe that Robert F. Kennedy must be sacrificed for the cause of the poor exploited people." According to one of the lawyers in the trial,* Sirhan, during this second fortnight of May, "was disturbed that both his mother and his brothers did not see, didn't perceive Senator Kennedy as the same destructive and malvolent and dangerous person as Sirhan perceived him to be; and I gather that he and his family, his mother and brothers, had some arguments about this." Sirhan was also practicing with his pistol. He went six times to gun ranges before June 4th. He was practicing on a range on June 1st and he went again on Sunday June 2nd but was unable to shoot because the range was reserved that day for big bore weapons.

Yet, on the other hand, on that same day, Sunday the 2nd, he drove to downtown Los Angeles to attend an "open house" meeting with Robert Kennedy at his campaign headquarters in the Ambassador Hotel. (Sirhan at first denied that he attended this meeting). He had to

* Page 7569 Testimony.

wait awhile and jostle through the crowds but he did finally get to see and hear Kennedy making an impromptu speech.

Sirhan during his trial described his reactions thus: "When I saw him that day, he looked like a saint to me." Question: "You honestly mean that?"—"I honestly mean that, sir."—But, obviously, Sirhan had other and stronger feelings too. Question: "Did anything happen in the meantime (the 2nd to the 4th June) to change that point of view?"—"I don't know, sir, because his willingness, his commitment to send those 50 Phantom jet bombers to Israel was still solidified in my mind."—"You still had in the back of your mind, though, about the fifty bombers;"—"Yes, sir, I did. I didn't like that at all."

Even in his testimony in court the ambivalence of Sirhan's feelings towards Kennedy come through. Thus his continuing feeling of disappointment is evident when he said that Kennedy's pledge "was unfair; was not worthy of him."*—Question: "You still thought he was going to do it?"—"I don't know if he . . . he kept saying that he would, yes."—"Even after you saw him on June 2nd?"—"The Zionists in this country do have the policy, sir, of holding every Presidential candidate to his word when he commits himself to them."—"So even after June 2nd you still felt that he was going to send these bombers?"—"It was a part of American politics. He knew where his best interests lay, sir, in American elections."

According to Kennedy those interests lay in outbidding every other candidate in his appeal to the pro-Israeli sentiments of Jewish voters. And that appeal was intolerable to someone who felt himself, and his people, to be victims of the Israelis.

Sirhan has admitted that his philosophy of life incorporated the saying, ascribed to the Arabs, "The friend of my enemy is my enemy." During his campaign Robert Kennedy felt the need to publicise his long-standing support for the Israelis and his determination to put even more powerful and destructive weapons into their hands. This, for Sirhan the Palestinian, was the final pressure on the trigger.

* Testimony page 5309.

PART III

THE ASSASSINATION
AND ITS AFTERMATH

9

The Assassination

The fatal intersection of the lives of Sirhan Sirhan and Robert Kennedy took place in the sixteenth or seventeenth minute of June 5th, 1968, the first anniversary of The Second Battle for Palestine.

In the Los Angeles area, June 4th was a grey day with low clouds and fog and "only light smog." The sun never broke through. Mr. and Mrs. Kennedy and six of their children spent the night of the 3rd-4th at the home of a friend on Malibu Beach. Soon after noon, Senator Kennedy went for a swim and at one point the father plunged through heavy, rolling surf to rescue one of his sons who had got caught in the undertow. The family frolicking continued in the swimming pool. Because he had no work to go to Sirhan woke fairly late on the morning of June 4th, not much before 9 a.m. He must have looked at the morning papers because, according to his testimony, he decided not to go to the races that afternoon since the horses running did not look attractive. Instead he decided to carry on with his pistol practice. Having had something to eat he drove to the shooting range of the San

Gabriel Gun Club in Fish Canyon, in the foothills of the Angeles National Forest some miles east of Pasadena. He arrived there about 11:30 a.m. and he stayed at the range the whole day till the time it closed at 5 p.m. Two young men who were practicing next to him noticed him because Sirhan was doing rapid firing which was normally not permitted on the range. They got into conversation and discussed their weapons, with Sirhan identifying his as an "Iver Johnson." In the course of the afternoon an attractive young woman started firing, hesitantly, near Sirhan and he went over to her and, with a touch of gallantry, explained how she should handle her pistol. He had a slight altercation with the rangemaster when he was told to stop firing at 5 o'clock.

During the five to six hours he was on the range Sirhan fired seven or eight hundred rounds.

In the afternoon the Kennedys moved to their suite in the Ambassador Hotel.

By 6 p.m. Sirhan was at Bob's Big Bay Restaurant on Colorado Boulevard in Pasadena where he had a meal of hamburger and lettuce, a salad and coffee. He met an acquaintance, an Indian exchange student, Gaymoard Mistri, and they drank their coffee together and talked about horses. Sirhan paid for his friend's coffee and at about 6:50 p.m. the two of them walked across the street to the Pasadena City College cafeteria.

There they met with three Arab students and talked about summer courses. They had a chocolate for which, again, Sirhan paid. He and Mistri left the cafeteria together and Sirhan challenged Mistri to a couple of games of pool, but Mistri declined. Mistri bought a newspaper because he wanted to look through the section of classified advertisements. He gave the rest of the newspaper to Sirhan and in looking through it for the racing section Sirhan saw an advertisement by the local Zionist organisation about a parade, celebrating the anniversary of the Israeli victory over the Arabs, to be held on Wiltshire Boulevard "tonight." Sirhan took this to mean the night of the 4th but this was an early edition of the next morning's newspaper and was referring to the night of 5th June.

Unaware of his mistake Sirhan parted company from Mistri and drove into Los Angeles to watch "the Jew parade," as he called it. Of course, he did not find it.

At this point, Sirhan recalled that a girl he knew in high school, Kathleen Rafferty, would perhaps be at the election-night headquarters of her father, Max Rafferty, a Republican senatorial candidate. This was in the Ambassador Hotel where, Sirhan knew, Robert Kennedy also had his headquarters.

Sometime after 9 p.m., perhaps later, Sirhan went to the Ambassador Hotel, parking his aged pink-and-white DeSoto a couple of blocks away. A Mexican and a Puerto Rican claim that they met him outside the Venetian Room of the Hotel from where he had been gently eased out of a party celebrating the primary victory of Max Rafferty. Sirhan angrily criticised "the rich Rafferty people who step all over the poor" and when one of the others said that Kennedy might help the poor, Sirhan is alleged to have burst out, "Kennedy! He should never be President. You think he really wants to help the poor? Kennedy helps himself. He's just using the poor. Can't you see that?" This incident, if it did take place, happened about 9:45 pm. Sirhan had bought himself two drinks at the Rafferty party—Tom Collinses, the first of which he drank down quickly and the second more slowly.

From 10 p.m. on the primary election results began to come in, both from California and from South Dakota, which voted on the same day. The tension in the Kennedy suite mounted, particularly because the crucial California results were slow in coming in due to a computer failure. The Senator, looking very tired, took refuge in the bathroom to get a few minutes of peace and quiet but was pursued even there.

From 10 p.m. to 11 o'clock Sirhan drifted around in the area of the Kennedy party. He drank two more Tom Collinses.

According to his account, during the trial, at about 11 o'clock Sirhan decided to go home and walked out to his car but found himself too drunk to drive. This, he claimed, was his last conscious memory of what happened on the night of June 4th. Under hypnosis he spoke of going back to the hotel to get himself some coffee that would help to sober him up. He had left his pistol on the back seat of the car and, fearing that the Jews might steal it, he stuck it into the top of his pants.

In the half hour between 11:15 and 11:45 Sirhan drank several cups of coffee and moved around some more: he spent some time watching the teletype working in the Press area in the Colonial Room, adjacent to the main ballroom.

At about 11:45 it was known that Robert Kennedy had won in both states: in Dakota by 50 per cent to the 30 per cent of Hubert Humphrey, and in California by 46 per cent to 42 per cent for Eugene McCarthy.

At that time it was decided that the Kennedy party should move down to the Embassy Room, for a speech and a victory celebration, and then on to a fashionable nightclub, called The Factory, for a private victory party. It was originally planned that the candidate should go from the Embassy Room downstairs to a second ballroom to give another victory speech to the overflow of 15 or 18 hundred people who were unable to find place in the main ballroom, but this was cancelled because of the lateness of the hours. It was, instead, decided that after the one speech, the Senator should have a brief meeting with the press in the Colonial Room, and then move on to The Factory.

A little after 11:45 p.m. the Kennedy party decided to go down to the Embassy Room. Because of the crush in the ballroom, Robert Kennedy made his way to the podium by a back entrance through a corridor that is used as the hotel's serving kitchen. He shook hands with cooks and kitchen helpers on his way to the stage.

Since this serving kitchen passage now has a modest place in history, it merits a brief description. Looking along it, in the way Robert Kennedy must have done on his way to the ballroom, and as Sirhan did when awaiting Kennedy's return, it appeared much larger to me than the impression given by photographs: it was both longer and wider than I had expected it to be. In actual measurements, it is 65 feet long and 16 feet wide. Buried in the depths of the hotel, it is a gloomy claustrophobic tunnel, poorly lit by cold blue flourescent tubes set in the ceiling. Most of the right-hand wall is lined with a series of three tables, steam tables or warming counters, where food is placed after being brought from the kitchen, which itself lies behind the right-hand wall, and before being served in the ballroom to the left. Along the left-hand wall, not opposite but somewhat beyond the steam tables, is a tall row of icemaking machines. On the night of June 4th, and on the day when I visited the scene, a tray-stacker stood alongside the first ice-making machine: this is a contraption of four upright rods standing on a base meant to hold a pile of trays.

The main kitchen and the serving kitchen were in use that night so that there were empty plates and cups filled with cigarette butts on the steam tables and, underfoot, the floor was damp. The stale smell of cooking has soaked into the walls of the passage and is a permanent presence; the colour of the walls matches the smell. A grey, grimy, malodorous place.

Some sort of a security check was supposed to have been in force to keep unauthorised persons out of the serving kitchen but, in fact, just about anyone who wanted to drift in from the ballroom or the pressroom could have done so.

One witness has said that he saw Sirhan come into the passage along with the Kennedy party on its way to the ballroom. He was, in any case, in the passage sometime before midnight. He was dressed in pale blue jeans, a white shirt and a loose blue sweater. He held, sometimes with one hand sometimes with both, an object that looked like a rolled-up poster, twenty-four inches long and three to five inches wide.

During the 15-odd minutes or so while Kennedy received the cheers of his delighted supporters and made a light-hearted speech, about 10 or 12 people stood around in the serving kitchen. They were mostly workers from the kitchen hoping to see and to shake the hand of the candidate. They stood behind or in front of the steam tables. One of them was approached by Sirhan who repeatedly asked whether the Senator would go out along the passageway: the kitchen helper replied that he did not know.

It was, however, known that Kennedy was to go from the ballroom podium to the press area in the Colonial Room. Alastair Cooke, the correspondent of the B.B.C. and of *The Guardian* has described how, daunted by the crowd in the ballroom during the speech, he was turning away to leave the hotel when he was recognised by a Kennedy helper and told of the press conference. For some reason it was assumed by him and by other pressmen that Kennedy would not come to the Colonial Room directly across and through the crowded ballroom but would once again skirt round it through the passageway as he had on his way in.

This is why Cooke and Robert Henly, political editor of the

Globe went into the serving kitchen as Kennedy's speech drew to a close.

As the passageway began to fill, Sirhan moved over, away from the steam tables, to the tray stackers on the left. Being short, and thus unable to look over the heads of the increasing number of people, he climbed on to the tray stacker and held on to one of its rods with his left hand. In his right hand, pressed into his stomach, he held the roll-up object; he was in a semi-crouching position as if someone had hit him in the stomach.

On the tray stacker he was joined by a young woman in a polka-dot dress whose good looks during the preceding few minutes had attracted the attention and favourable comment of the young kitchen workers. Sirhan and the girl continued the conversation they had struck up earlier.

On the ballroom stage, after the candidate had spoken, there was some confusion as to where Kennedy was to go next. Senior members of the hotel staff, unaware of the change of plan, thought that he was to go downstairs to the second ballroom. But the Kennedy staff were concerned only with how to get the Senator quickly to the pressroom. One of his guards suggested that they go through the crowd. But the Senator himself chose the passageway and pushed through the curtains at the rear of the podium. He passed through an anteroom and if he was to go to the other ballroom he would have then turned left, but he turned right and passed through swinging doors into the serving kitchen.

As he came abreast of the icemaking machines, he began to shake hands with the hotel staff.

Some remark in the conversation between Sirhan and the young woman standing together on the tray stacker caused them both to smile; and at this point he stepped down from the tray stacker.

By then enough people had gathered in front of the approaching Kennedy so that only his head was visible above their shoulders. There were 20 to 30 people in his party coming behind him.

Sirhan pushed through the people in front. He brushed past Karl Eucker, the *maitre* of the hotel, who was on Kennedy's right hand, and turned just behind him.

As he did so Robert Kennedy turned away half-left to shake the hand of yet another kitchen helper standing near the steam tables. Sirhan pulled a revolver from above his left hip and from three or four inches away shot into Kennedy's head just behind his right ear.

In that brief second, in the flash of flame from the pistol barrel, the lives of the Palestinian and the American intersected with tragic results.

Sirhan continued to fire at Kennedy who had begun to fall back. By the third shot, Karl Eucker had swung back and left and had clamped his left hand on Sirhan's right wrist while he wrapped his right arm around the front of Sirhan's neck. They struggled across the passageway and onto the top of the steam table.

During this struggle Sirhan kept pressing on the trigger and shot off eight rounds in all, wounding five other people. The flashes lit the passageway and there was a smell of cordite in the air. Sometime during those first twenty to thirty seconds—for it did not take longer for the eight shots to be fired—just before and just after he was being grappled with—Sirhan was heard to call out: "I can explain . . . let me explain . . . I did it for my country . . . I love my country."

From the first shot the crowded passageway erupted into chaos and frantic movement.

On the left, on the floor, for the first few seconds, the great Senator lay alone—people held back from approaching him. Then the spasm of shock and fear broke and people rushed to his aid.

On the right everything was movement—a tight knot of bodies and arms and legs flailing around on top of the steam table. It took eight people to blanket and finally subdue the assailant. The revolver was finally snatched out of his clenched fingers: there was one bullet left unfired.

A very few minutes later policemen, holding Sirhan horizontally, propelled him out of the front entrance of the hotel.

A little later, on a stretcher, Robert Kennedy was carried through the kitchen and a back entrance into an ambulance. Twenty-six hours later he died. It was a tragic end to one of the most dynamic lives in the history of contemporary American politics.

When, under hypnosis, Sirhan relived the two or three minutes of the actual shooting, he said, over and over again, "You can't send the bombers."

There is a surprising number of similarities between Sirhan Sirhan and the two young Jews who killed Lord Moyne in Cairo. Like Sirhan, Eliahu Bet Zouri was below medium height, and though he made friends, he always maintained a certain reserve; like Sirhan, Eliahu Hakim was touchy and once lost a job because he refused to obey orders; all three kept diaries, though in desultory fashion.*

But there was one all-important difference between the Palestinian and the Jews—they planned and attempted to escape after their shooting; he did not. Bet Zouri and Hakim had been ordered by their superior in the terrorist organisation to which they belonged, "This is not a suicide action. You are to make a reasonable plan for retreat," and, if necessary, to wait one or two months to obtain a get-away car.† They gave much thought to this problem and planned carefully for their escape. In the event, they were shot down trying to get away on bicycles. Sirhan, however, did not seem to have planned an escape. Rather, he seemed to have decided to sacrifice his life for his action.

The late Senator had said in 1962: "The nearest thing to an incident in Indonesia occurred as I entered the hall at the university. The place was completely surrounded, as was always the case everywhere we went in this country, by troops and police. As I stepped onto a porch at the entrance, a tall, skinny young man, clad in summer white, stepped suddenly through the lines of soldiers. He took a full windup and let fly at my face with a piece of hard-shelled fruit. It hit me on the bridge of the nose, but aside from the sudden jolt of it, I was unhurt and continued into the school building to deliver the address. Police seized the youth and hustled him away.

"In one way it was a cowardly act since I was, for the moment, defenseless. And yet, thinking back on it, I was struck by his complete political dedication and the difficulties we in a democracy have in

* *The Deed*, pages 52, 176, 174, 209.
† *Op. cit.*, p. 213.

matching it. Here was a young man who knew his efforts to injure me would result in immediate arrest. Still, his desire to do anything he could to take a blow at an 'American imperialist' overshadowed everything else."*

What an irony.

* R. Kennedy, *Just Friends and Brave Enemies,* New York, 1962, Popular Library Edition, p. 88.

10

The Muffled Echo

Massively irrelevant—those are the only words that can be used to describe the editorial reaction of most of the world's newspapers to the Kennedy assassination. There was one outstanding exception.

After any murder the immediate, most obvious, question asked is "why"? Even the most amateur of detectives first tries to establish the motive. Yet that was the last thing attempted by the world's editorialists. Indeed most of them never attempted it at all. They contented themselves with the mechanical, but self-righteous repetition of platitudes that were only obliquely relevant to the case of Robert Kennedy.

And this in spite of the fact that the accused himself gave his answer to the question "why." The world press did not contest his reason: it simply ignored it and the words in which he expressed it. Seemingly, the press was totally uninterested in the motive of an act about which it otherwise wrote at great length.

This strange reaction prompts another question. Robert Kennedy was killed because he was a Gentile who, for a variety of reasons, personal and political, became an over-enthusiastic defender of the cause of Israel. The question then was why the inexplicable refusal of the world press, with the one exception, to perceive, accept and report this simple fact?

Similarly the descriptions of Sirhan and his family given by various newspapers were singularly full of inaccuracies, which will be referred to later. Having myself often had to produce a despatch at high speed, I can understand how some of these inaccuracies came about, though not all of them.

But for the editorial writers there is no excuse.

The news of the assassination broke too late on the night of the 4th-5th June, for there to be any editorial comment: 12:30 a.m. in Los Angeles is 3:30 a.m. in New York, 6:30 a.m. G.M.T., 8:30 a.m. in Cairo and 12 noon in New Delhi. But by 10 a.m. in Los Angeles the identity and the nationality of the assailant was announced and these facts, along with the words he called out, made it possible to give an interpretation, and one interpretation only, of the motives of his action. This news broke in New York at 1 p.m., at 4 p.m. G.M.T., 6 p.m. Cairo time and when it was 9:30 p.m. in New Delhi. Therefore editorialists in West Asia and in all of Europe and America had ample time to produce editorials for newspapers dated June 6th, that would have been thoughtful and perceptive analyses of the assassination and its motives.

As far as any Middle East motivation was concerned, Sirhan, instead of being a Palestinian, might just as well have been an inhabitant of the moon, angered at Robert Kennedy's support for the American project to land a man on the moon.

Before dealing further with this quite extraordinary phenomenon a word needs to be said on the aftermath, at the popular level, of the death of Robert Kennedy. It produced a deep wave of shock and sadness that rolled right around the world. The tributes paid to him by the highest and the humblest went far beyond anything due the American Senator and Presidential candidate. Clearly for a great many people something more than Robert Kennedy died in Los Angeles and more than the third Kennedy son was mourned in New York and Washington.

When he was alive it was often said of Robert Kennedy that he had become the symbol of the Kennedy myth or the Kennedy legend. In his death, he apotheosised the legend. And it was probably buried with him.

The emotional heart of this legend would seem to be an aching nostalgic regret for gifted youth cut off before it could fulfill its promise. One of the constitutents of the grief felt for John Kennedy was that people did not want to believe that he was no more, they only half accepted that he was dead and buried beneath the restless flame in Arlington cemetery. But in that same cemetery on the night of June 8th, 1968, under the glare of arc lamps, the spirit of John Kennedy was finally laid to rest along with the body of his younger brother. An earlier grief was revived and then, at last, assuaged. The funeral train—utilitarian and unromantic—was, in truth, the final cavalcade with lowered lances winding down the hill from a fallen Camelot.

There are several reasons why the world press should set aside the Palestinian context of the assassination of Robert Kennedy and, instead, insist on seeing it exclusively in the context of a violent America.

Much of the world, older and poorer, loves to nag at the younger, richer United States and the death of Kennedy, just two months after the shooting of Dr. Martin Luther King, gave the world justification for lecturing America on its wicked ways. That is precisely what editorial writers did, from China to Peru; and in the process, the much simpler political motivation of Sirhan was buried, or covered up.

Much of this sociological head-shaking was either misplaced or hypocritical. There is much violence abroad in America today, but in fact that country is less violent now than it was a century ago. And in many another country there is more daily violence than in the United States: in India, to name just one.

Yet it was sermons on violent America, or sick America, or even mad America that rolled off the printing presses of the world. One read through column after column of turgid prose without finding a single reference to the word "Palestine."

In the news bulletins of the World Service of the B.B.C. from

London one heard the muffled echo becoming ever more muffled. In the first few broadcasts after Sirhan's identity was established, he was described as "a Palestinian" or "a Palestinian immigrant." This description was fairly soon changed to "a Palestinian Arab" and the following day, Sirhan became, and has remained, "a Jordanian Arab" or "an Arab immigrant." After all, if he was, truthfully, described as "a Palestinian," awkward questions might be asked about "whatever happened to that country."

It was embarassment about their own role in Middle Eastern affairs that predisposed some European countries to say that Kennedy's death was due to the state of America society rather than to the injustice of the American approach to the Palestine problem. How, for instance, could any British commentator, on this occasion, deplore the tragic results of American Middle East policy when Britain's policy has been the same and, at times, even worse? The same held true of countries like France or Italy or West Germany.

Having decided on the dismemberment of Palestine at the United Nations in 1947, it is too much to expect that European or Latin American leaders, or European or Latin American leader-writers, could say "that national tragedy has led, twenty years later, to this personal tragedy." Instead of accepting their share of the blame, it was altogether easier for the Europeans and the Latin Americans to throw all the blame on a "sick," "violent," "mad" America.

In no other part of the world was this shifting of blame more noticable, or nore necessary, than in the Communist countries of Eastern Europe. These countries, led by Soviet Russia, played a very large part in the creation, and then in the initial arming, of the State of Israel. They have, of course, completely changed their policy since then, but the responsibility remains. It is, therefore, ironical but effective propaganda for Moscow, speaking as a friend of the Arabs, to say that it was positively wrong to emphasise the Arab origins of the assassin. "The cancer of violence" in America was the consistent theme of communist analysis of the death of Kennedy. And the poet Yevtushenko was moved to write in a long poem,—

"The eyes of murders peer out alike from under hats and caps,
"The steps of murders are heard at all doorways
"And a second of the Kennedys falls."

The one notable exception to this world-wide obliquity, was the editorial in *Le Monde* in its issue of June 7th. Under the heading "One Year After the 'Six Day War,'" *Le Monde* wrote: "Whether the murderer of Robert Kennedy acted of his own volition or whether he was the unwitting instrument of a dark conspiracy, the criminal act of a Palestinian nationalist on June 5th, the anniversary of the 'Six Day War,' has a symbolic importance. A year after the victory of the troops of General Dayan, twenty years after the creation of the State of Israel, never has despair and hatred been so intense among a people that believes that it has been robbed of its homeland. Sirhan Sirhan is, precisely, one of the hundreds of thousands of Palestinians who have had to leave their homes, some to find shelter in a neighbouring Arab country, others to settle in a foreign land. The resolutely pro-Israeli declarations of Robert Kennedy in the course of his electoral campaign, his appeals for an increase in the supply of American arms to the government of Mr. Eshkol could have exasperated this young, twenty-four year-old man who, like so many of his compatriots, dreams only of revenge and 'liberation.' "

This editorial raised a storm of anger in Israel. The Israeli Embassy in Paris even protested to the French Government, but received a dusty answer both from the Quai d'Orsay and from *Le Monde* itself.

The Economist of London in its June 8 issue carried the following subheading to an article: "The Man Charged with Killing Senator Kennedy is a Palestine Arab. When are we all going to tackle the root of the refugee problem?"

If the press in countries outside America indulged in an orgy of accusation, wholly divorced from Palestine, the press inside America, providing a still more muffled echo, plunged into an orgy of breast-beating and self-flagellation, equally divorced from the real issue.

From the first hours, the American press, with rare unanimity, agreed that the motive for the assassination was to be found in a sick America, or perhaps in a sick Sirhan—in anything except America's Middle East policy.

Some observers felt that this unanimity of the press, in steering clear of the Middle East context, was not perhaps wholly spontaneous. For example, the Washington correspondent of *The Jerusalem Post,* Charles

Fenyvesi, reported in its issue of June 7th under the heading, "U.S. Jews deeply concerned": "In a nation stunned by the tragedy of Sen. Robert F. Kennedy's assassination, Jews are more stunned than others.

"The 'Jewish angle'—the possible intent of the assassin to kill a friend of Israel and the reported 'virulent anti-Semitism' of the suspect—is in the focus of attention here.

"The press has been careful not to put too much emphasis on the national origin and the possible nationalistic motivation of the suspect.

"The State Department was in close touch with the Los Angeles Police Wednesday. Its advice may have been behind the gradual way in which the news of the suspect's identity was announced. First the police said that the suspect would not speak. Then it was disclosed that the suspect was talking, lucidly and volubly, but not about the shooting. Officials refused to reveal what he discussed. Reporters were told that the suspect is Jerusalem-born. This caused a flood of anxious telephone calls to Jewish organizations inquiring if the man could be Jewish.

"One hour later, it was revealed that the suspect had been born in the former Jordanian sector of Jerusalem. But Mayor Yorty declined to identify the suspect's national origin or religious affiliation."

The same point is made in *The Jewish Observer and Middle East Review* of London, in its June 14th issue (page 9): "The Kennedy killing is certain to leave a deep scar on America's relations with the Arab world. But the short-term picture is less clear. The State Department is sparing no effort to play down Sirhan's Arab origins. This is also reflected in many editorials which focus on the internal sickness of American society rather than on the foreign overtones of the incident. Similarly, all members of Congress avoided reference to the Arab-Israeli war in their speeches."

Neither of these Jewish journalists hazards a guess as to why the State Department and the American press and members of Congress should all combine to ignore "the foreign overtones of the incident."

Whether or not the cover-up was co-ordinated between the State Department, the press and Congress, it is a fact that the press and Congress did steer clear of "the foreign overtones."

Why should they have done so? The State Department may have

feared a deterioration in the relations between the U.S. and the Arab states through American criticism of the Arabs. But these relations are so uniformly bad and American criticism of the Arabs has been so comprehensive that nothing could have been said that could have brought about much further deterioration. There may also have been a fear that reprisals would be taken against the Arab-American community, and, in fact, an Arab-American was killed in Chicago a few days later, in apparent revenge for Kennedy.

Perhaps these reasons for caution also applied to the press and to Congress.

On the other hand, it is possible that all three agencies avoided the foreign overtones because otherwise the whole basis of American policy towards Palestine would come under question. Questions might have been asked as to why a Palestinian should so bitterly resent the American approach to his people; and that, in turn, may have led to pressures for a more just and equitable Middle East policy. This, however, would have been most upsetting, especially to powerful Zionist groups, in an election period.

Hence the Palestinian overtones of the Kennedy assassination were effectively buried, covered-up, or ignored. Hence one looks in vain for any mention of the Middle East angle in the editorials of America's most influential paper, *The New York Times*. *The Washington Post* went further, denouncing any attempt to suggest a Middle Eastern connection. In an editorial on June 7th, *The Post* said: "The evidence suggests the murderer was a man acting only upon his own intense grievances and warped impulses. . . . Meanwhile, those who are attempting to exploit the Arab link for a political purpose—either to demean the Arabs or to demonstrate the folly of American support for Israel—are guilty of a mischevious cynicism. They serve neither the memory of Senator Kennedy nor the continuing American interest in peace in the Middle East."

The Times and *The Monitor* did, of course, carry despatches from their Middle East correspondents which dealt with "the Arab link." And the Associate Editor of "The Times," James Reston, even went so far as to mention such a possibility. He wrote on June 8th: "Killing Robert Kennedy to avenge the hatred of the Arab states for Israel—if that was the assassin's motive—was a wholly irrational act. He had nothing to do with Israel's spectacular victory in last year's war. He had no influence on President Johnson or Secretary of State Rusk on Middle Eastern policy—or any other policy for that matter. He was not on his way to the presidency, where he might have directed American foreign policy, and he was certainly not the favorite political darling of the Jews in New York or anywhere else. Yet he is gone."

Having thus dismissed "the Arab link," Mr. Reston seems more at home in a "News Analysis" entitled "World Morality Crisis" in which he contended that the Senator was a victim "of Lawlessness Threatening Modern Public Order"—everywhere. Thus the culpability of a sick America becomes the culpability of the whole wide world.

In the meantime, American newspapers, flogged "the sick society" and "sick Sirhan" hypotheses for all they were worth. *The New York Times* brought off a neat double-barrelled salvo when it wrote on June 5th, "though the act could only have been that of an insane person, it is another horrible expression of the age of violence. . . ." Dr. David Abrahamson, described as "a psychiatrist and a governor of the Limberg Center for the Study of Violence at Brandeis University" said (*The New York Times,* June 6) that Americans condone violence: "We love it. We love to fight." In the same issue of the same newspaper, the historian Arthur Schlesinger opined that the United States was a land of "violent people with a violent history, and that the instinct of violence has seeped into the bloodstream of our national life." Other academics predicted still more assassinations. In *The New York Times* of June 9th, Amitai Etzioni of Columbia University prophesied that "there will be more assassinations and attempted assassinations of political leaders in the United States in the next several years."

After being thrown from a horse in 1966, Sirhan was thoroughly examined and declared fit. But after June, 1968, the fact that he may have sustained brain damage was revived. In this connection, Dr. Nathan Malamud of the University of California Medical School said that it is possible to have "lesions to the brain that might not disable but may cause violence." (*The Wall Street Journal,* June 24). While Dr. Robert Heimburger of Indiana University said that 40 per cent of persons referred to him for violent behavior had organic brain damage.

The psychoanalysts also had their say. Dr. David Rothstein of the Medical Center for Federal Prisoners, Springfield, Missouri, said (*The Wall Street Journal,* June 25) that 27 prisoners who had threatened American presidents had in common "youth, unhappy home environments and, typically, an upbringing by a dominant mother while an ineffectual father stood aside."

Even the amateur psychologists put their oars in. James Reston, for instance, said that "the pressures of all this [the World Morality Crisis] are too much for weak and demented minds."

It was left to Robert Kennedy's home town newspaper, *The Boston Globe,* to produce the *reductio ad absurdum* of the "sick Sirhan" theory. In its editorial of June 6th, it said, "So now it develops that Sirhan Bechara Sirhan was a mad man, truly mad.... 'I did it for my country. I love my country,' Sirhan is said to have cried out as he watched Sen. Kennedy fall. And thus he proved his madness, for this deluded young Jordanian from Jerusalem, a victim of the senseless conflict in the Middle East, is in truth a man without a country to love anymore...." The line of this argument is: Sirhan killed Kennedy because he is mad, proving his madness when he spoke of his country when he does not have a country. That Sirhan should have killed Kennedy simply because he had lost his country and not because he was mad was evidently too simple a thought-process for *The Boston Globe.*

One person would not have accepted "the sick society" hypothesis, and that was Robert Kennedy. In an interview with *Time* magazine in the last week of his life he said stoutly, "basically, we are a spiritually healthy people."

It is strange that more sense on Sirhan's motives was spoken by representatives of the non-intellectual right than of the intellectual left. Governor Reagan of California blamed the permissive attitude which "has been spurred by demagogic and irresponsible words of so-called leaders in and out of public office."

And Mayor Yorty of Los Angeles said that Sirhan was trying to import some of the violence of Middle East politics into America. He was right on target.

When the former decathlon champion, Rafer Johnson, one of Kennedy's bodyguards, slammed Sirhan on to the steam table he screamed at him, "Why did you do it? Why"? The athlete put the only question that mattered, The world press, with few exceptions, completely failed to do so.

Two American communities, the Black Americans and the Jews, were particularly concerned about the killing of Kennedy—the Black Americans because they were affected by the loss of a friend, the Jews because they were involved in the event.

Many people, both in America and in the Arab world, felt that one of the worst effects of the assassination would be to produce a gap between the Arabs and the Blacks, who were beginning to show sympathy for the Arab cause. This actually did not come about because the militant black groups had little time for Kennedy, and because the ordinary Black American was distracted from the Kennedy affair by the arrest of the killer of Dr. King on June 8th, the day of Kennedy's funeral. *The New York Times* reported that in Harlem the news of the arrest turned a sad day "into an almost happy day," "carrying with it a sense of relief bordering on joy." In Washington, Black Americans turned off their TV sets carrying the funeral telecast to talk about the arrest.

In the Middle East there was also another fear concerning the assassination aftermath—that the very effective Zionist publicity apparatus in America would use Sirhan's nationality to widen the gap between Arabs and Americans. There were some, however, who thought that the Zionists would not commit the mistake of drawing Palestine to the attention of the American public, and this proved to be the case. To emphasise the Arab angle would have been to emphasise, at least, the dangers of American pro-Israeli Middle East policy.

The Jewish Observer (June 14) noted: "American Jewish leaders have shown no inclination to make political capital out of the killing. Nor is this just because they are still extremely shocked and saddened by Kennedy's death. When the shock recedes, this caution is expected to continue at the senior, more responsible level." *The Jewish Observer* does not say why "more responsible" Jewish leaders should show "caution" on Kennedy's death. Any more open, vocal Zionist identification with Kennedy would have provoked the comment that the

Zionists bore a certain responsibility for what happened. Hence *The B'nai B'rith Messenger* of Los Angeles (June 14) reports that the messages of condolence from American Jewish groups and individuals stressed "the common theme . . . that the incident reflected the spirit of violence and disobedience of law in the land and of the hatred that is consuming America."

When American Zionists did depart from this deliberately generalised regret, it was to try and fix the blame on the Organisation of Arab Students for spreading anti-Semitic hatred among its members, among whom, facts to the contrary, they included Sirhan.

In only one Zionist publication was there some reference to Robert Kennedy's speech in the Portland synagogue.

It was not so easy for the Israelis to say that the assassination had nothing to do with them, though the attempt was made. In its messages of condolence to the Kennedy family, the Israeli government scrupulously refrained from any special word of thanks or regret, or establishing any special identification with Kennedy. At least one newspaper tried to deny it. *Al Hamishmar* (June 7) wrote, "Senator Kennedy—with all his declared sympathy for Israel—was not the ideal personification of pro-Israel zeal. Willy-nilly one must therefore reach the conclusion that the Israel-Arab background was artificially foisted upon the assassination." *Hamodia* (June 9) attacked the *Le Monde* editorial because it "blames Israel for not permitting Arabs like Sirhan to commit murder and slaughter of Israel citizens every day." *The Jerusalem Post* seems to have been particularly hard put to find an acceptable explanation. On June 6th, it said, referring to Sirhan's words that he did it for his country: "Such a grotesque conjunction of the tragedy of the Kennedy family and the political conflict of our region—a conjunction which an Arab spokesman in the U.S. had the unbelievable temerity to justify—drains any words of comment of meaning." The following day, it went a little further: "It is of little solace to the American people that the assassin was apparently motivated by a political fanaticism which has no direct relevance to the social or political issues of their society. The absurdity of the murder only heightens rather than lessens the tragedy."

Thus the reaction, at least in public, of Israel, one of the main parties involved in the incident, was that even if the assassination did have something to do with the Middle East, it was of no special concern to Israel.

Ironically, in no other area was there more misunderstanding and misrepresentation of Sirhan's action than in the area from which he came, the Arab world. Having become used to ineffectual speech making, ineffectual military action against Israel and, as yet, largely ineffectual guerilla activity inside Israel, Arab leaders, the Arab press and some sections of the Arab public found it difficult to come to terms with the full significance of what Sirhan had done. Their initial reaction was one of confusion and fear. It took about a week for them to recover their balance. Only the majority of the Arab people seemed to understand Sirhan's action, and their reaction, one of pride, was mingled with some regret that the Second Victim had to be a Kennedy.

It was the sheer daring of Sirhan's deed that confused the Arabs: the fact that it was carried out in America and against a world-famous figure who had been the Number Two personality and who might have become Number One in the most powerful nation on earth. The Arab fear was similar to that which might have motivated the State Department: that it could cause great harm to Arab-American relations.

The fear felt by the Arab-American community was of an altogether simpler nature. They feared physical violence, especially in the Los Angeles area, and after the murder in Chicago their fear was not unjustified. Yet it is interesting to note what one Arab-American in Pasadena said to me, "Sirhan was not thinking about us when he did this thing."

The Arab governments expressed the usual polite protoclaire regrets. This was especially necessary for Jordan, of which Sirhan was a citizen and which was also heavily dependent on America for all its arms and much financial support.

The initial Arab press reaction was on the usual "sick America" and "sick Sirhan" lines. The two were combined when several newspapers made the point that Sirhan could hardly be called an Arab when he went to America at the age of 12 and had stayed there for 12 years during which there was ample time for him to become infected with the violence of American society. Thus, in a sense, the Arab press disowned

Sirhan. *The Daily Star,* the English-language newspaper in Beirut which caters for the mainly American foreign community, even entitled its editorial "The Outcast."

Arab political thinking, with some reason, is dominated by the concept of the plot and the conspiratorial idea of history. It was therefore soon declared that Sirhan was the victim of the Zionists, of the Central Intelligence Agency, of the capitalists and imperialists, and of the same people responsible for the killings of President Kennedy and Dr. King. The official mouthpiece of the Syrian government, *Al Baath* (June 6) said that Robert Kennedy was the victim of "the conflict of American monopolies."

American Zionists had tried to link Sirhan with the Palestine partisan group, Al Fateh. But Al Fateh, in an official statement, said that "the assassin could only be a tool in the hands of international Zionism, capitalism and American intelligence. . . . The commandoes of Al Fateh attack only Israeli forces and military installations." Al Fateh has since changed its mind about its targets, after scores of civilians were killed in Israeli air raids on Jordanian towns.

The publicity media of the United Arab Republic reacted very cautiously to the event. Cairo Radio did not announce Sirhan's name or nationality for more than 12 hours after it was broadcast around the world. All the Cairo newspapers joined in condemning the method of political assassination, while the semi-official *Al Ahram* described the assassination as a "painful incident." It said the Senator would have been an ideal presidential candidate had he adopted as fair an attitude towards the Palestine issue as he did towards Vietnam.

The one journalist in the Arab world who, from the start, put Sirhan's act squarely into a Palestinian context was Michel Abu Jaudeh, a well-known columnist of the Beirut newspaper *Al Nahar.* On June 6th, he asked, "How can the murder of the Palestinian Arab homeland be conveyed to the White House, and from there to the mind and heart of every American? For them there is Israel only, and nothing but Israel." On June 7th, he commented, "If the American loves his homeland to the extent of dying for it, so does the Pales-tinian . . . Palestinians place American politicians at the same level of importance as Arab leaders. From this stems the need for American leaders to recognise the existence of the Palestinian people and to seize this historic occasion to reopen the Palestine case."

Similarly, *Al Dastour,* the most influential newspaper in the Jordanian capital of Amman, said (June 7th) that Sirhan was "a simple Palestinian who had lost his homeland and who has not been able to make his complaint reach the heads of America because of the blockade and the walls erected by Zionist propaganda, which made him despair—and he resorted to bullets as a means of expressing his despair."

On June 9th, Arab newspapers reported an assurance given the day before by Ambassador Arthur Goldberg to Arab representatives at U.N. that the U.S. government did not hold the Arab governments in any way responsible for the assassination, even though the assassin was an Arab.

This statement removed the fear of American anger that had distorted the analysis of Arab editorialists and it produced a notable change in their reappraisal of Sirhan and what he did.

Akhbar el Youm in Cairo wrote that "Sirhan's family would have hardly emigrated to the U.S. if Israel had not been established thanks to U.S. help."

From Baghdad, *Al Shaab* observed: "America rubbed his wound every day and developed his determination for vengeance. Day after day, America showed him that its hands were stained with our, Sirhan's and his family's blood. . . . But we also regret that Kennedy died in this manner, at the hands of an Arab."

In Beirut, the Arab nationalist newspaper, *Al Anwar* that had earlier condemned Sirhan, said on June 10th: "regardless of everything, Sirhan's blood-stained bullets have carried Palestine into every American home. The act may be illegal, the price high and the assassination unethical. But American deafness to the cause of the Palestine people is also illegal, unethical and carries a high price."

Thus, within a week the Arab press cast off its initial fear and confusion and saw the assassination as the act of a Palestinian patriot, regrettable though it might be. When a Beirut weekly opened a defense fund for Sirhan contributions flowed in from ordinary people in the four corners of the Arab world—from Morocco, the Sudan, Yemen and the Persian Gulf. Now the Arabs claimed Sirhan as one of their own.

If the Arab man-in-the-street had this opinion of Sirhan much earlier than his leaders and newspapers, it was, to some extent, from the statement issued in New York on the morning of the assassination by Dr. Muhammad T. Mehdi, the Secretary-General of the Action Committee on American-Arab Relations. Dr. Mehdi said, "Sirhan's action reflects the frustration of many Arabs with American politicians who have sold the Arab people of Palestine to the Zionist Jewish voters." These words were carried in several of the early news bulletins of the B.B.C. and they gave the event its most logical interpretation.

11

The Missing Words

"Let me explain. I can explain. I did it for my country. I love my country."

These four sentences were shouted by Sirhan as he fired the revolver and as he grappled with his captors in the kitchen passageway. They are all-important, because they make clear that Sirhan's was a political action undertaken from patriotic feelings for his homeland, Palestine. They provide the motive; they answer the question "Why?"

It was, again, the news bulletins of the B.B.C. that sent these words around the world during the first few hours, when millions of people were listening eagerly to every newscast.

I began to wonder about these words and to note that they were becoming "the missing words" as I started to read accounts of the assassination in the British and American press. They were not reported by the London *Times*. They were not reported by *The New York Times*. They were not reported by *The Christian Science Monitor*. They were not reported by *Time* Magazine; nor by *Life;* nor by *The Observer* nor *The Sunday Times* of London.

One of my tasks in Los Angeles was to trace those missing words and to find out how they were reported to the world. I could not discover why these, and other publications, chose *not* to report them.

During my brief stay in the United States, I carried out an informal "poll" in Los Angles, in various towns in Michigan, in Boston and in New York and discovered that more than half of the people I interrogated had not heard about these words—and some of them were journalists, one of them an editor. Those who did know about the words said that they heard but not read them; in short, they had got them from their TV or radio sets and not from the newspapers.

The words were reported by both the United Press and the Associated Press. The U.P.I. account said that "Dr. Marcus McBroom of Los Angeles, an eyewitness" said "the man who was captured was yelling about saving the country or something. What he said was something like, 'I did it for my country.' The guy was yelling. But I don't know what he was saying."

But *The New York Times* (June 6) stated categorically, "Nothing that he might have said could be heard."

Yet, whatever the confusion, what Sirhan said *was* heard.

I asked Dr. McBroom, a Los Angeles psychiatrist, about what he had heard and he reported that "when the shots were fired all hell broke loose." He heard someone say, "Got him, but he's not dead." He heard Sirhan, while being subdued by several people say, "I did it for my country. I can explain everything."

That is one source for the words.

The second source, reported by the Associated Press, was Mr. Jesse Unruh, the Speaker of the California Legislature and Kennedy's campaign manager in California. He was one of the persons who grappled with Sirhan in the passageway and heard what he called out at that time.

According to *Newsweek* magazine (June 17, page 30), Mr. Unruh heard them again from Sirhan in the police car that took him to jail. "I did it for my country, he told Unruh on the way to the lockup. 'Why him'? cried Unruh assuming Sirhan meant America."

The official police version of this crucial exchange of words is as follows:* Officer Placencia read the Miranda admonishment to Sirhan as the car sped along. Then Unruh asked Sirhan why he had done it. Sirhan replied, "You think I'm crazy so that you can use it as evidence against me"? Unruh asked Sirhan again why he had done it. "I did it for my country," Sirhan said. "Why him"? Unruh asked. "It's too late," was Sirhan's reply. The time was 12:28 a.m. on the 5th June 1968.

In spite of this precise testimony of where and when Sirhan said these words there are still those who, perhaps, trying to play down the Palestinian and political aspect of the assassination, still contend that Sirhan probably never said these words at all.

The first reports of Sirhan's words, as reported by Dr. McBroom and Mr. Unruh, went out to the world in the first flashes put out by the United Press and the Associated Press. But in the subsequent rounded-out stories put out by both these agencies, the words were not reported. This is the reason many small-town American newspapers did not carry them, since they took the more finished, but actually less complete, later reports.

As for the local newspapers, Sirhan's home-town newspaper, *The Pasadena Star News* did not report what he said. Nor did *The Los Angeles Times* in its eyewitness account.

It was probably the reliance on dramatic eyewitness stories rather than on the agencies' files that led to many of the more important newspapers missing the crucial words. There were not all that many journalists in the passageway, though a surprising number were. And those who were there were caught up in the confusion and reported only what they personally saw and heard.

Only astonishingly bad editing by the news desks in the main offices can account for so many important newspapers not reporting perhaps the most important aspect of the entire incident. In the case of the London *Times,* this editing was done, without haste, on the following day. So there is little excuse for the omission. *Time* Magazine actually

* R. A. Houghton, *Special Unit Senator,* page 295.

reported Sirhan as saying, "I can explain," but not the rest of the missing words.

In contrast, the TV networks did not miss on Sirhan's words. Walter Cronkite, of the Columbia Broadcasting System, told his listeners several times during June 5th, that Sirhan was "a Jordanian and that he had said he had done it for his country."

12

The Other Sirhan

Of the late President Kennedy it has been reported,* "The consistent inaccuracy of contemporary press accounts caused him to wonder how much credence they would someday be given by those researching his era." I wonder if we journalists are sufficiently aware of our own responsibilities to History and to future historians.

Much of the time journalists have no time to feel any such responsiblity. And, as I have said earlier, the need for speed was probably the cause of many of the inaccuracies about Sirhan. They hardly deserve repetition, for it is of no great importance that Sirhan was variously reported as being anything between five-foot two-inches and five-foot six-inches tall and weighing from 115 to 130 pounds. But a few of the major inaccuracies deserve to be reported for they seem to be deliberate and *mal fide.*

The worst example is a report put out by the United Press from

* *Kennedy* by T. C. Sorenson, p. 4.

London on June 13 which said, "An Arab government has passed 'new and startling' information to American officials on Sirhan Bechara Sirhan, accused assassin of Sen. Robert F. Kennedy, the *Evening Standard* reported today.

Evening Standard correspondent Jon Kimche who claims close contact with Arab governments, said the information is the result of an intensive investiagion into Sirhan's background by an Arab government, which he did not identify.

"Mr. Kimche said the investigation disclosed:

"Sirhan's full name is Sirhan Bishara Abu Khatar.

"He was first brought to the United States from Jordan at the age of four in 1948, not 1957 as reported.

"He returned to Jordan in 1957 and was married at the age of 13 to Leila Jussef Mikhael on June 27 that year in Greek Orthodox Church at Es Salt, 15 miles west of Amman.

"Sirhan returned to the United States later that year and his wife joined him three months later.

"He returned to the Middle East in 1964 for seven months, four of which he spent in Damascus. He returned again in 1966, spending five months in Cairo, and returned to the United States at the beginning of 1967 . . ."

This story is, of course, a total fabrication. A spokesman for the State Department formally announced on June 13 that Sirhan never left America after his arrival in 1957.

The one mildly humourous point in this story is that Mr. Kimche "claims close contacts with Arab governments." Mr. Kimche was for 12 years the editor of *The Jewish Observer* in London, and there is not a single Arab government that would not like to lay hands on him.

There is also the report in *The Jerusalem Post* of June 7 on statements made by the headman of Taibeh village, Mr. Fayez Mu'addi: "The family's link with the Jehovah Witnesses actually began much earlier, Mr. Mu'addi said, since it was their sect who helped the mother to go first to the U.S. in 1957. The four sons and one daughter, Aida, who is said to have died in the U.S. four years ago, followed a few months later, with the father coming over last.

"Another close friend of the family added that the mother had actually left for the States in 1957 in the wake of a family dispute. When the children followed her, the husband filed a divorce suiter (sic.) in the Greek Orthodox Religious Court. He withdrew it later, after declining to go to the U.S. himself the same year, but actually he never joined his family in the States and lived most of his six years there in New Jersey. The *mukhtar* [Mr. Mu'addi] added that another part of the Sirhan family lived in Texas."

And likewise we have the report—from Israel also—of an aunt of Sirhan who has said that Sirhan never witnessed any violence in 1948 and that the family were not refugees.

There is a memorial booklet on Robert Kennedy entitled "Tragedy!" and produced by Smifty Inc., of Sunset Boulevard in Hollywood. Its last section (the pages are unnumbered) deals with what is called the "despicable assassin" and set out to prove that over a period of years, Sirhan was in close contact with drug addicts and drug peddlers. After providing precise dates and places in apparent confirmation, the magazine says: "You'll notice that no claim is being made here that Sirhan was, himself, a drug user or seller."

Some far more reputable publications indulged in some twisted reporting. In fact, "twisted" seems to be a favourite word to apply to Sirhan. The Middle East correspondent of *The Los Angeles Times,* Joe Alex Morris wrote (June 6) of "the twisted logic of the Arab fanatic." *The Sunday Times* (June 9) has "his twisted ambition." And *Life* (July 8) carries the headline, "The Subtle Twisting of Sirhan Sirhan" and in the text refers to "the slow, subtle and inexorable twisting of one human being."

For one so thoroughly twisted, Sirhan seems to have created a strangely favourable impression on his professional captors. The very capable and experienced chief of the Los Angeles Police, Mr. Thomas Reddin, after having talked with Sirhan "about many things" said that he found Sirhan "very cool, very calm, very stable and quite lucid. If I were to judge him strictly on the lines of our conversation, and that were the only basis, I would say he was a gentleman."

13

The Trial and a Summation

"Thou shalt not kill; but needst not strive
Officiously to keep alive."
—A. H. Clough, *The Latest Decalogue*

"The Lost Significance of Sirhan's Case," such is the title of a pamphlet on the trial put out by the Organisation of Arab Students in California. It reflects the dissatisfaction felt by everyone concerned with the way in which this trial was handled.

So confused was the argumentation, especially by the team of defense lawyers, that in the end the prosecution gave a better presentation of Sirhan's case than did his own lawyers. This topsy-turvy situation was the result partly of a rather mediocre level of legal competence, partly of the helpless bewilderment of Sirhan and his family, and partly of the impact of domestic political pressures.

The trial, for the most part, was a long, drawn-out boring affair, mainly because the lawyers on both sides argued in plodding, pedestrian fashion. They may have been brilliant practitioners of the law and have performed brilliantly in other cases, but in this one they gave the impression of simply not having their hearts in it. This does not mean that they did not work hard and long, and some of them did so without fee. All this notwithstanding, the only possible objective assessment of their actual performance in court is that it was mediocre.

Perhaps this was because they did not face the ultimate legal challenge which can impart high drama to court-room proceedings. They were not under challenge to prove guilt or innocence, to have a man convicted or have him set free; they merely had to sway the jury between one or other degree of guilt.

This was so because of the all too obvious fact that Sirhan Sirhan had indubitably killed Robert Kennedy. Sirhan's mother, with her mother's love, hoped for an acquittal which could only have happened if he had been certified insane. But it was obvious that Sirhan was, and is, no lunatic. All that was in doubt was whether he had pulled the trigger with both premeditation and malice of forethought, which amounts to first degree murder, or only with malice of forethought, which makes it second degree murder. Second degree murder carries the sentence of life imprisonment or for a long jail sentence; the penalty for first degree murder, in California, is the death sentence, although no one has been actually executed in California for the past many years. So the element of fearful suspense was almost wholly absent.

For Sirhan's lawyers their main responsibility was to avoid the theoretical possibility of his judicial execution: as they saw it they had to "strive officiously to keep alive." To win from the jury a finding of second degree murder they entered a plea, peculiar to Californian law, of "diminished responsibility" under which "the defendant is held responsible for a lesser crime than he would be if there were no mental illness or incapacity."

The mistake they made was that they interpreted "diminished responsibility" in a narrow medical sense—Sirhan had to be shown as being mentally ill or incapacitated in conventional psychiatric terms. In ordinary laymen's language, he had to be shown to be just a little mad. All his experiences were, therefore, drained of their political significance and were presented simply as disturbing, upsetting happenings which added up to a totally disturbed and upset mental condition. Sirhan's lawyers did not ignore all that Sirhan had passed through in Palestine, but they handed over his defense to the psychiatrists and for these gentlemen it was incidental, even irrelevant, that the early experiences of Sirhan were those of a Palestinian during the first battle for Palestine, and that Robert Kennedy had made himself a participant in the continuing battle for Palestine on the opposite side. According to the defense lawyers, and especially the defense psychiatrists, these past experiences would not have aroused and kept alive Sirhan's patriotism but would have merely crippled his psyche. Because Sirhan's defense was mainly psychiatric, he was, in effect, abstracted from the dust and blood of the struggle for Palestine and laid out on a couch in an asceptic consulting room.

This is how the defense, with the best of intentions, striving "officiously to keep alive," deliberately pushed aside the real and true significance, the political significance, of Sirhan's trial.

The trial was unsatisfactory for Sirhan as well as for his lawyers and for the prosecution, both in its conduct and in its result. The jury returned a finding of first degree murder and recommended the death sentence. This was a blow for Sirhan and a disappointment for his lawyers; nor was it wholly satisfying for the prosecutor even though he had won his case, because the impression prevailed that the jury had somehow been perverse and unduly harsh in not accepting a mass of mitigating circumstance.

The result was a double blow to Sirhan because his death, if it came about, would have little or no political value, especially in America where he wanted it to count. His lawyers had concentrated so heavily on his psychiatric disorders that the overwhelming final impression was that he was neither a cold blooded murderer nor a hot blooded martyr but simply a half-crazed individual who killed Robert Kennedy when in a trance—a pathetic nut case. He objected to this presentation during the trial but he was overborne.

His lawyers were dissatisfied that their elaborate psychiatric presentation was not accepted because, in professional terms, this meant that the "doctrine of diminished responsibility" was weakened.

The case for the prosecution was also curiously broken-backed. The prosecution lawyers emphasized Sirhan's experiences in Palestine and the effect they had on his personality. But it was only obliquely that they made the crucial point that for a person with such a background Robert Kennedy's statements were a sufficient "trigger," a sufficient provocation. Perhaps if the prosecution had established that there was a firm link between the Palestinian tragedy and Phantom bombers for Israel, Sirhan could have benefitted from a diminished responsibility plea based, not on psychiatric considerations, but on more substantial and understandable political motivations. As it was, the prosecution presented all the personal and political evidence but failed to draw the clear conclusion that emerges from it.

It was left to the members of the jury to make the obvious connection of the Palestinian struggle and Kennedy's promises, and to decide that because of that struggle the Palestinian Sirhan shot Robert Kennedy with premeditation and with malice of forethought.

14

The Leila Khaled Story

by Leila Khaled *as told to the author*

On August 29th, 1969; an airliner of Trans World Airlines on a flight
from Rome to Athens was hijacked by two young Palestinians and after
flying over Tel Aviv the plane landed at Damascus airport where it was
partially blown up.

Having written about Sirhan Sirhan, the young Palestinian who far
from home performed an act of violence for his country, I was
interested in finding out how and why another young Palestinian, Leila
Khaled, carried out her daring action high above the Mediterranean, in
order to draw attention to the Palestinian cause.

I had the chance of meeting her and this was the story she told me
of the flight and what led up to it. The reader will note some
remarkable parallels between the stories of Sirhan Sirhan and of Leila
Khaled.

* * *

"Isn't it something awful that I could see my hometown again only
when I hijacked a plane? But there it was—Haifa—away on the left just

234

past the pilot's head as I sat behind him looking out of the cockpit windows. As we came down to 12,000 feet for the approach to Lydda airport the whole lovely coast of my country, occupied Palestine, which some people call Israel, came into sight, from beyond Haifa in the north almost to Gaza in the south.

"It was a fine clear day, except for some heat haze, but I had little time to enjoy the view because we were approaching the most exciting and dangerous point of our adventure. I controlled this plane and the pilot had done everything I had told him to do. But, in spite of everything, would he, somehow, land the plane at Lydda? Or would the Israelis be able to force us to land?

"It had all begun two days earlier in Rome. This was my first visit to Europe and Rome is a wonderful city. I was very tired when I arrived and slept for ten hours solid. Then the evening before the flight I walked through the city from the Borghese Gardens and the Via Veneto to the Fountain of Trevi. Of course, I threw the traditional coins in the fountain which means, I hope, that I'll see Rome again: but will the Italians let me in next time? There was a woman singer in a cafe near the fountain and I just sat and listened to her for two hours. The only other things I did were to buy myself a bottle of French perfume and to confirm by booking for the flight the next day to Athens at the TWA office.

"I couldn't eat dinner that night and it was three in the morning before I could get to sleep and when I awoke I had no appetite for breakfast either. I was hungry, but I'm accustomed to hunger because of my commando training and also because, when I was young, there were times when there wasn't very much food at home.

"In the morning—this was the 29th of August—I had to do some shopping at a very chic shop on the Via Veneto. I bought some very big sunglasses, a leather shoulder bag and a large-brimmed hat which alone cost 15,000 lira. Wickedly expensive I know, but this was all part of the uniform—I had to look like someone who usually travelled first class on a plane.

"Back at the hotel I got dressed. There was a chance that all the luggage would be destroyed when we blew up the plane after landing, so I put as little as possible into my suitcase. I'm not very interested in clothes but it seemed a waste of money to have things burnt so I put my two dresses and robe into my handbag and I wore two pants suits, one on top of the other. The lower one, psychaedelic flowers, was borrowed and I wanted to return it; the top one was in very smart white cotton, sleeveless, and I wore sandals.

"Because Flight 840 was late we had to wait an extra half hour in the lounge. I spotted the young man who was the other member of the Che Guevara commando unit. I didn't know him and had only seen his picture. Apart from a secret sign of recognition we took no notice of each other. This extra wait was an anxious time and two other things upset me before we got on the plane. I noticed an American lady with four young children who seemed very happy and excited about their trip. I then realised, with a shock, that something dreadful could happen to them if anything went wrong. I love children and I wanted to go and tell the lady not to travel on this flight. But when I thought of some of our Palestinian children, who have had nothing in life, I felt a bit stronger and braver.

"The second incident was in the bus going out to the plane. A man came and sat next to me and asked me where I was from, and I let him believe I was from Bolivia. Then he told me that he was a Greek returning to Athens after spending 15 years in Chicago and that his widowed mother, very happy at his homecoming, would be waiting to welcome him at the airport. This was another shock, the realisation that perhaps his mother would never see him and I felt it particularly because we Palestinians know what it is to be away from one's country and I too had a widowed mother waiting for me at home. He went on talking but I didn't hear the rest of what he said.

"My friend and I were in the first class section because that section is nearer the cockpit. But there were only five first class passengers in all so that the three cabin crew fussed over us a great deal, which was exactly what we did not want. Not long after take-off, the two of us seated ourselves in the front row nearest the cabin door. We both refused drinks before lunch—I don't drink anyway—and then we both refused lunch, because we didn't want to have the lunch trays across our laps hemming us in. But when the stewardess exclaimed at this, and so as not to be conspicuous, I ordered coffee and my friend a beer. To make his refusal of lunch more credible he also said he was feeling ill and when the hostess brought him a pill she told him that he smoked too much: perhaps he does, but then so do I.

"We didn't get rid of the cabin crew that easily. Instead of lunch they brought us a huge trolley laden with fruits and cakes and, to our dismay, parked it in front of us to help oursleves, completely blocking the way from our seats to the cabin door. We had been ordered to take over the plane 30 minutes to an hour after take-off; he had time in hand but were approaching deadline since the Rome-Athens flight only takes 90 minutes. We didn't want to ask the hostess to remove the trolley because that could have appeared suspicious. Finally, after what seemed an age, she took it away and another passenger who had been using the lounge seat right next to the cabin door also moved away. The way was clear and we could get into the cabin without having to frighten anyone—that's the one thing we wanted to avoid: frightened people can do foolish things.

"I asked for a blanket and the hostess tucked it in around me. My friend gave me a strange look, wondering whether I was becoming afraid. To reassure him I took out my toilet case and combed my hair. Then I looked at my watch and showed him five fingers signalling that in five minutes we would go into action—I was in charge of the operation, of course. Underneath the blanket—and this is why I wanted it—I took a pistol out of my shoulder bag and tucked it into the top of my pants and then I took out a grenade and took off the safety patch, which is shaped like a pin.

"Just as everything was ready, one of the hostesses with a tray in her hands came out of the cabin door; it opened outwards and she held it to with her elbow. We took this chance. My friend, holding his pistol and grenade, brushed across the front of the hostess and through the door. When the hostess saw the weapons she screamed, "Oh no," and threw her tray down—that was the only violence we had in the plane during the whole journey.

"As we went towards the cockpit my friend called out, "Don't move. Now you have to listen to the orders of the new captain." While he was speaking he heard the captain saying into his radio, "Two armed men have come into the cabin. This is a hyjacking."

"My part in the actual take-over was to stand facing down the plane to control the passengers with my pistol and grenade. But when I stood up with the grenade in my hand and reached for my pistol, I felt the pistol slipping down my leg inside my trousers. You see, I hadn't eaten for a day and the waist-band of my trousers was loose. It was such an anti-climax that I laughed. Instead of brandishing a pistol there was I bending over with my back to the passengers and fumbling for my weapon up the leg of my trousers, of two trousers actually. The captain swivelled round in his seat to see the new captain but all he could see of "him" was the top of a large, white lady's hat.

"Having retrieved the wretched pistol I put it into my pocket, never to take it out again—too scaring and too much like Hollywood.

"You can't imagine the look of total astonishment on the face of the captain when I went into the cockpit and announced, "I'm the new captain." Poor man, what did he see?—me, in my sleeveless white suit and floppy white hat, dark glasses and sandals. "I'm the new captain," I said, "Take this as a souvenir—it is the safety pin from this grenade" and held it under his nose. "It's a free hand grenade now. If you don't listen to my orders, I'll use it and the plane and everyone in it will be blown up." "What do you want?" the pilot asked. "Proceed directly to Lydda airport." "To Lydda," the co-pilot queried, "aren't we going to Athens." "You understand English," I said to him. "I'm speaking English so don't ask questions. Just do as you are told."

"We sat down in the two seats just behind the pilot. The grenade was in my left hand and it stayed there every minute until we landed. My friend put his away but he kept his pistol out.

"I asked the captain to give me his wireless headset and he was so flustered that he tried to put it on over my hat. "Excuse my hat," I said and pushed it back. I had had a ribbon specially sown on so that I could hang it round my neck: I wanted very much to save that hat too. I tried to raise Rome airport but there was no answer. I then turned to the flight-engineer and asked, "How many fuel hours of flight do you have?" I knew the answer because I had read this off the fuel gauge but I wanted to show the crew that I knew the instrument panel. I was sure he would tell me a lie and he did: "Two hours," he said. "Liar. I know you have three and a half hours. It's there on the fuel gauge. Why did you lie to me? The next time I ask you anything and you lie to me, I'll break your neck." "Why are you so angry," the captain asked. "Because I don't like liars," I replied. I wasn't really angry. I wanted to scare them a little so that they would take orders. The flight engineer said not one word for the rest of the flight.

The time was now about 15:20 hours

"The dials and switches and lights in a plane's cockpit may seem bewildering but we had been thoroughly trained and I really did know what the dials meant. I also had a thorough knowledge of almost everything else in a Boeing 707. (I can't talk about our training methods because they are still an operational secret.)

"Having put the crew in its place the next thing I did was to speak to the passengers on the intercom. Our message was this:

"Ladies and gentlemen,

"Your attention please. Kindly fasten your seatbelts.

"This is your new captain speaking.

"The Che Guevara Commando Unit of the Popular Front for the Liberation of Palestine which has taken over command of this TWA flight demands that all passengers on board would adhere to the following instructions:

"1—Remain seated and keep calm.

"2—For your own safety, place your hands behind your head.

"3—Make no move which would endanger the lives of other passengers on the plane.

"4—We will consider all your demands within the safe limits of our plan.

"Ladies and gentlemen,

"Among you is a passenger responsible for the death and misery of a number of Palestinian men, women and children, on behalf of whom we are carrying out this operation to bring this assassin before a revolutionary Palestinian court. The rest of you will be honourable guests of the heroic Palestinian people in a hospitable, friendly country. Everyone of you regardless of religion or nationality is guaranteed freedom to go wherever he pleases as soon as the plane is safely landed.

"Ladies and gentlemen,

"Our destination is a friendly country, and friendly people will receive you.

"Thank you for your cooperation,

"We wish you a happy journey."

"The person we were after was General Rabin (the former Israeli Chief of Staff) whom we knew had been booked on that flight. But he seemed to have changed plans at the last minute. I suppose prominent Israelis find it safer to travel on airlines other than El Al nowadays. Then I broadcast our message to the world:

"The Popular Front for the Liberation of Palestine informs you that its Che Guevara Commando Unit is now in complete control of the Boeing plane belonging to Trans World Airlines (TWA), flight no. 840, on its way from Rome to Lydda airport in the Occupied Palestinian Arab territory.

"Captain Shadia Abu-Shazali who has taken over command of this plane and her colleagues request all those concerned to use the following call sign in their communication with the aircraft:

"POPULAR FRONT—FREE ARAB PALESTINE

and let it be clear that unless the above mentioned call sign is used in communicating with the plane, we will not care to respond,

Thank you."

"Shadia Abu-Ghazali was my code name. The original Shadia was a girl resistance fighter in Al-Fateh who was killed in October of 1968 at the age of 21.

"After this I handed over our new route map to the captain. We did not follow the usual air traffic lane which passes over Athens and Nicosia. Instead we went straight down the entire coast of Greece, then south-east over Heraklion in Crete and eastward to Lydda. Not a very interesting flight because it was almost all over the sea at 33,000 feet.

"When the captain went on to the new course I noticed that he kept on turning to port so as to go south-westward. He may have been trying to take us to the American Wheelus airbase near Tripoli in Libya. But I was watching the compass and ordered him back on course. After that I told him exactly when to turn and onto what bearing number on the compass: we had all this worked out.

"After 15 minutes my friend reminded me that the passengers still had their hands above their heads. I looked down the aisle and so they did—a funny sight. I apologised for inconveniencing them and asked the hostess to serve them with whatever they wanted to eat and drink, champagne if they wanted it. Otherwise, throughout the flight we had no contact with the passengers or cabin crew.

"We tried to get on friendly terms with the three crew members but had no luck. We asked them if they wanted anything to eat or drink but they refused. We offered them our cigarettes but they refused those too. They didn't ask me a single question about us. From time to time the captain would turn round, look at me and shake his head unbelievingly. It made me smile but I can understand his bewilderment. The only human contact was when the co-pilot, like a child in school, asked if he could go to the toilet and I gave him permission.

"The pilot kept glancing at the grenade in my left hand, so finally to reassure him, I put my arm across his back and tapped him on the left shoulder with the grenade: "Listen, I'm accustomed to this thing. Don't be afraid." A little later I scratched my head with the grenade to show him just how familiar with it I was, but I doubt whether he was reassured.

15.15 hours. Compass bearing 140°

"There were long, uneventful periods during this eventful flight that were punctuated only by the messages I broadcast to the countries we flew past or over—Italy, Greece, the U.A.R., Lebanon and Syria. These messages explained what we had done and appealed for support "for the just struggle of the Palestinian people," and ended with the words, "Down with U.S. Imperialism and Zionism. We will win." The co-pilot looked at me every time I mentioned America. I also spoke, spontaneously, to the passengers over the intercom to explain our struggle: "We have hijacked this plane because we want to cut the roots that feed Israel. Don't come again to Israel because there is resistance on land and en route: tell this to your friends. We want to go back to our country and we can live with the Jews because we lived with them before." We tried to explain things to the crew but they were an unreceptive audience.

16.10 hours. Compass bearing 112°

"The exchange of messages I had with Cairo airport, in Arabic, were amusing. They were flabbergasted when a woman's voice told them what had happened and where we were going. I first had to tell them that I wouldn't respond till they used our own call sign. Then, the breathless response came from Cairo something like this: "You Popular you Front you Free you Arab you Palestine! Why-are-you-going-to-Israel?" And I replied, "Yes, we are going to Israel, to liberate it!"

Soon after this things became serious as we began our descent to Lydda. Of course, we had no intention of landing there, that possibility was the one thing that worried us. But we wanted to fly over our enemy's city just to show him we could do it. "Descend to one-two-zero," I told the pilot and the co-pilot chipped in, "You mean twelve thousand feet;" "You know what I mean." So we began the descent and out of the haze the coast of Palestine gradually grew clearer. "What shall we do when we get to 12,000?" the pilot asked. "Let's have a round twice," I replied and made a swinging gesture with my left hand and the pilot's eyes, as always, followed the grenade: "We want to have a picnic over our land," I said.

"Needless to say, my exchanges with Lydda airport were not friendly. The controller was very excited and shouted at me angrily the whole time. Having switched to the Lydda wavelength, I first read a message in Arabic for our people in Occupied Palestine. I tried to speak to the airport tower in Arabic but they wouldn't reply. "TWA 840?" they kept calling, so I responded, "Shut up! This is Popular Front Free Arab Palestine. We will not respond unless you use this call sign. We are coming down. We are landing. Give us space." I said this just to frighten them, because I don't think the Israelis wanted us to land anymore than we wanted to land there. My words seemed to have had the desired effect because Lydda tower shouted back, "Don't come down, don't come down, or else we'll send Mirages to shoot you down." And I told them: "Here is Free Arab Palestine. What can you do about it? I don't care for my life. This is our land. We want to die over our land. But you will be responsible for the lives of the crew and passengers." (While all this was going on at about 20,000 feet, my friend held the intercom microphone near my mouth so that the passengers could hear the exchange, which couldn't have been very comforting for them).

"There were more threats of Mirages from the ground and when I glanced ahead, lo and behold, there they were, two of them, just in front and a little to the right and left of us. We were still descending, but the captain said to me, "We can't descend anymore. It's too dangerous with these Mirages in front." This evidently, was how the Israelis were trying to prevent us from landing. The co-pilot then asked to speak to Lydda. He explained to them: "We have to follow her orders and descend or else the aircraft will be blown up. Clear the air. And, don't keep calling TWA 840. This is Popular Front." Perhaps because of his words, the Mirages moved out a little, though they still stayed with us and we descended to 12,000. We then did three big turns over Lydda and Tel Aviv. I was terribly curious to see Israel and I tried to see as much as I could out of the small cockpit windows. We were seven minutes in all over Tel Aviv: enough to make our point. My final message to Lydda, just to keep them worrying, was: "Bye bye for now, but we are coming back."

17.12 hours. Compass bearing 350°

"I gave the pilot a compass reading for a course due north and he suggested that we climb because we were using up too much petrol at 12,000 feet. I told him to go up to 25,000.

"In a very few minutes Haifa was before us—the hump of Mount Carmel, the harbour below it and over to the right the oiltanks and the cement factory with its long plume of white smoke. "This is my city," I told the crew, "Take a good look at it. This is where I was born." From maps I had a rough idea of the area in which our house stood and I think I identified the area but the city slipped away beneath us much too quickly. I felt like asking the pilot to make a turn over my home town so that I could have a better look at it but we were running low on fuel and every minute counted now.

"Just that fleeting glimpse, and a few dim childhood memories, are all that link me directly, personally, with my home in Palestine. I was born in April 1944, so I was just under four when my mother with us eight children left Haifa some time in March 1948. I remember a staircase, and one day there was a man with blood all over his face lying under the stairs. My mother says he died there, one of the victims of the battle for Haifa between the Arabs and the Jews that was going on all round our house. My father was away from home, with the Arab fighters, but when he came home a week before we left and found that my mother had packed up things to leave he ordered her to unpack everything because we were not going to leave, then or ever. But my mother was afraid and my father left again. The Greek Orthodox Bishop of Haifa was then evacuating thousands of children from Haifa; he took 8,000 children to the countryside for safety, I believe. My mother had eight children of her own and no man in the house. The street fighting increased, most of the other women and children had left, the Jews were advancing because they had arms and we did not, and they came in loud speaker trucks and ordered us to leave. Many, many times in the following years we asked our mother why she left and she would tell us that she was forced to. Certainly there was a lot of fighting in the nearby streets and she had relatives in Lebanon where she was born. She was afraid for her eight children and followed the example of the Greek Orthodox Bishop.

"The first taxi she sent for was hit and set on fire and I remember there was shooting very close to us as we got into the second taxi. We left in a confused hurry with little more than what we stood in. At the last minute, counting her brood of children in the car, my mother found that one was missing, myself. I was hiding under the stairs. I remember not wanting to leave home but my mother teases me saying that what I didn't want to leave was a box of sugared dates my father had brought to us. My mother left with a big bunch of keys because she had carefully locked up everything in the house. Like so many other Palestinians, my mother and father thought we would return in a fortnight and so they didn't even draw any money out of the bank for a longer stay. They believed that the armies of the Arab states would come and liberate Palestine for us. That was their mistake. Now we know we have to liberate our country ourselves. My generation has learnt its lesson.

"That is how my family became "refugees." But no Palestinian is really a "refugee." We are displaced persons or evictees. For if we were refugees and had found refuge, we would not want to go back to what we left. Because we didn't leave of our own free will, but were pushed out according to a deliberate Zionist plan, we want to go back, but haven't been allowed to. This determination to return makes us Palestinians unique among all the "refugees" of the world. There is no other people with our experience and our feeling.

"As the plane crossed the snout of Ras Nakura, that is the frontier between Israel and Lebanon, the co-pilot, looking rather worried, asked, "Are we going to Beirut?" "That is none of your business," I told him. "We don't have much fuel left, you know," he replied. "I know that, and I also know swimming in case anything happens."

"I, too, was worried about our fuel situation but I was also tremendously excited as we flew over the beautiful blue bay that lies beyond Ras Nakura. On the point opposite the Ras is Tyre which is where we have lived since leaving Palestine. Our apartment is almost on the beach looking south and I thought I could just about pick it out. Little did my mother know that one of her daughters was flying high above her head. I visited her on my last evening in Lebanon and even told her I would be home for dinner. I knew she would be anxious but I had to keep things secret. I had also left the usual farewell letter in case something happened. I could see the waves breaking on the beach where I had learnt swimming. That was how we passed our holidays—in the sea, where swimming is free. Tyre had no cinemas then and we had no money to go to them even if there had been any. Away to the right, at the head of this splendid bay is what looks like a town but is really a camp for Palestinian "refugees," 9,000 in all. For twenty years such camps have been the new homeland of our people, a floating world on its own.

"When we arrived at Tyre we were a family of destitutes and destitutes we remained for ten years. In Haifa my father was not a rich man but we were reasonably comfortable: he was a textile merchant and he also owned a small cafe and rented out a couple of shops. He lost all this, of course; but what was really bad was that, like many others, he got nothing of the money he had in the bank, even though it was a British bank. There was so much confusion when the Jews captured Palestine that for several months we had no word of my father and had given him up for dead: he ended up in Egypt. This was not an unusual occurrence, I know of many families who were scattered like this into the neighbouring Arab countries. My father was a sick man when we saw him again, with blood pressure and a bad heart. But what he was really sick from was the loss of his home and his work. Again, this was not unusual, I know of several other men of my father's age whose health was broken because their careers were broken. Perhaps he should have struggled on. Many Palestinians have made a success of their new lives—but when we do so, that too is held against us; "refugees" just can't win.

"For long spells my father couldn't work and he was bedridden for the last five years of his life: he died in 1966. Fortunately my mother is originally from Tyre so for the first year we lived with one of my uncles. Then we moved into a two-roomed house in which we lived for the next 16 years, and by that time there were 14 in the family. Crowded wasn't the word for it, but, still, we were luckier than the others living in tents in the camp. During the winter storms my friends wouldn't come to school because their tents had been blown down, and the small brother of one of my friends was washed away by a flash flood through the camp.

"The only regular cash coming in was a monthly payment to us of 100 Lebanese pounds by my mother's uncle (that is worth £ 12 or $30 now and was probably worth £ 20 or $60 then) which doesn't go far with 14 people. Happily we Palestinians still have strong family feelings.

"Also we had to register as "refugees" with the U.N. and from the U.N. Relief and Works Agency (UNRWA) we received rations. But UNRWA itself says it can't afford anything more than a bare subsistance diet of 1500 calories a day. So, as I have said, we learnt what it is to be hungry. Hunger one can learn to bear, but what was unbearable was the humiliation of having to collect the rations and having to stand in line with our cans and our sacks to receive our food as "bakshish." We had become beggars, just beggars, with our begging bowls in our hands, except that the alms came from the U.N. and not from individuals. In the photos UNRWA has of ration distribution you will see few adults in the queues. They can't bear to go, so they send the children, as was the case with us. When my sisters began working as school teachers in 1957, UNRWA cut our rations, which was a blow, but we felt happier for being less dependent.

"The best thing UNRWA has done for the Palestinians is to provide them with education. I liked school very much; I think we all did, because it was the only place where we could show that we were still human beings and not just a number on a ration roll. I first went to an Anglican school in Tyre and then to an American missionary school in the neighbouring town of Sidon on an UNRWA scholarship.

"I won another scholarship to the American University of Beirut where I planned to become a pharmacist, which is a good profession for a girl in this part of the world. But with my family in Tyre I had to be a boarder at A.U.B., the scholarship was not sufficient to cover all the costs and my family couldn't give me any help. So I could only stay a year at the University, and having to leave was the biggest disappointment I've faced so far.

"I took a job as a teacher of English in Kuwait and did this for six years. I don't particularly like teaching but I had to start earning in order to help the family. One of my brothers got his degree in engineering and is working in Abu Dhabi in the Arab Gulf, and another brother, who graduated in business administration, is in a bank, also in Abu Dhabi. In order to find work we Palestinians have had to scatter ourselves even further afield over the Middle East. The equivalent in Europe would be for a family in Madrid to have a daughter working in Paris and sons in Vienna. With all our contributions the family is comfortable once again. We can now afford to send one of my younger sisters to the University but, how ironical it is!—she's more interested in becoming a fedai, a Palestinian resistance fighter. One of my brothers and I are full-time fedayyin.

"Many of our Lebanese friends ask my mother, "Do you really want to go back to Haifa after all these years?" And my mother answers,

"Yes, I'd go tomorrow. It's true we have had a hard time and now things have become easy: we have a pleasant apartment, enough to eat, funds for the children's education and extras like T.V. What is mor~ I'm a Lebanese from Tyre. So I'm not a stranger, but I'm not at home. Lebanon is my country but it is not my place; my place is Haifa."

"And my friends ask me, who left Palestine as a small child, whether I want to return to a country I barely knew. And my answer is, "Yes," because I too have learnt that while I am never a stranger in any Arab country, I can never feel at home. What is more I have a right to return to the country I was born in, but I'm not allowed to. On my birth certificate my mother and father's nationality is given as "Palestinian." That is what the British said we were—a nation. A nation can't disappear into thin air. We have been dispersed, but we haven't disappeared.

"Now we are lost in this world, and people like us, without a country, feel that when we can't get what we want or do what we want it is because we are not in our own country—and most of the time this is true. This is why my brothers and sisters used to pester our parents with the cry, "Let's go back home." But we couldn't. It took 16 years of waiting before my grandmother, my father's mother, who still lives in Haifa, was allowed to cross through the Mandlebaum Gate into Arab Jerusalem to see my mother for just 48 hours.

"I learnt that I was something called a "refugee" when I was six or seven years old; I was quarrelling with a neighbour's child and she said to me, "You are a refugee so you shouldn't shout at me." How could I escape being aware of the Palestine problem? My parents talked of their former life in Haifa, my friends lived in the visibly unnatural conditions of the camp, we stood in those humiliating queues waiting for our rations—and we learnt about Palestine in school. By the time I was 16, I was, secretly, a member of the Arab Nationalist Movement, which believes in a liberated Palestine with a unified, socialist Arab world. My elder brothers and sisters had joined this party before me. I continued as a member of the A.N.M. when I was in Kuwait. We planned, we dreamed, we discussed. I visited the West Bank, what was left of Palestine, and travelled all over it to get to know my country.

17.25 hours. Compass bearing 070°

"It took June 1967, and the loss of all Palestine and the expulsion of another quarter of a million Palestinians to make me decide that I had to do something positive and active for the cause of liberation. This is the biggest defeat that the Israelis have brought on themselves by their military victories. They brought a whole new generation of Palestinians into the battle against them and we believe only in the armed struggle. In this world nobody gives anything; people only take; the Zionists took our country from us; we must fight to get it back. I asked to be trained in armed struggle in fighting, and so I joined the Popular Front for the Liberation of Palestine, the Palestinian military wing of the A.N.M. Last summer I did the full commando training course with the P.F.L.P. and after that I was selected and trained for this mission.

17.28 hours. Compass bearing 118°

"The Israeli Mirages stayed with us until we crossed the Lebanese-Syrian frontier. I spoke to the new Damascus airport tower in Arabic and told them we were going to land there—I didn't ask permission. He replied that we could land on the right runway but I told him we were going to land on the nearer left runway because we were very short of fuel.

"On the intercom I told the cabin crew to evacuate the passengers by the emergency exits as soon as the plane landed because it was going to be blown up. I asked the captain to switch off the engines as soon as we touched down, otherwise we would taxi too near the airport building. "I can't do it," he said. "Then I can do it," I replied. I also told him to apply the brakes slowly, otherwise I might fall and the hand grenade would go off. In fact, he made a very good landing indeed.

17.35 hours. Touchdown at Damascus

"As soon as we stopped rolling, I looked into the passenger cabin and called out, "Evacuate immediately." At this moment the crew seemed alarmed and dashed past us into the plane. They were in their shirt sleeves and my friend called to them, "Take your jackets." But they didn't stop. I also called, "Thank you for your cooperation." "You're most welcome," came from the co-pilot. In two minutes the plane was empty. I only saw the last four or five persons diving through the emergency exits and I told them, "Slowly, go slowly." But they didn't know who I was and didn't listen.

"I went down the length of the plane to make sure it was empty. My friend then placed his bombs in the cockpit. He dashed out and stood with me near an emergency exit and I threw two grenades into the first class compartment. As soon as we threw them, we slid down the emergency chute. My friend landed on my head with a terrific bump and I felt as if my legs were broken. We picked ourselves up and ran for twenty yards and waited for the explosion. Nothing went off. It was awful agony to think that the job would only be half done. Then my friend rushed back to the plane to reset the explosions. Because he is very tall he was able to pull himself up through another chute. I ran after him towards the plane because I couldn't bear to see him blown up. After a long minute in the plane, he slid out again and we ran back once more. Still no explosion. Only two minutes later was there a big bang and the nose of the plane crumpled. My friend fired many shots into the wing of the plane to set the fuel tanks on fire but there was so little in them that they didn't ignite.

"So it was all over. 'Thank God,' I said to myself, even though I don't believe,—who is there to pray to? I felt very relaxed and very relieved and glad that no one had been hurt.

"We started walking towards the airport building when a bus came along and picked up the passengers and us. We remained in the bus for a half an hour while the Syrians closed the airport building. I noticed my Greek friend and told him, "My friend and I did this." He burst into tears, and to comfort him I told him I would ask the Syrian authroities to cable his mother so she needn't worry unnecessarily. We offered the passengers cigarettes and my friend gave the children sweets which they took cheerfully.

"Since we had to wait, I said a few more things to the passengers to explain why we had hijacked the plane: "You may think we are criminals, but we are not. We are freedom fighters. The United States has supported Israel with Phantom planes and napalm and we have to make our protest felt by your government. It is not your fault. We were driven out 20 years ago and in 1967 Israel took the rest of our country and drove us out again. We are fighting to regain our freedom, our country and our homes. Tell others not to come to Israel as tourists. We are not against Jews, but only against Zionists."

"After I had finished speaking, a lady, who said she was from California, asked me whether I had learnt my English 'in America or in England.' 'In my country,' I said. 'We are not as ignorant as the Zionists say we are.'

"I would have liked to have seen the pilot again to ask him whether we had done a good job on the flight, to talk to him about Palestine and to invite him to visit us in Jordan. But this wasn't allowed. I only saw one of the pursers who told me that one lady had been injured getting out. I asked him to give her our apologies.

"Six weeks later when I returned to Amman, I went to the TWA office there and asked them to get me my suitcase which was on the plane. He said he would see about it and I am still waiting for it to be returned to me.

"I got engaged several months ago to another resistance fighter, but who knows when we will be able to get married.

"One question remains: will I have to hijack another plane to see my home town again? I hope not."

*   *   *

It is obvious that the lives of Sirhan Sirhan and of Leila Khaled were profoundly altered by the fact that they belonged to a people who live in exile. If they had not been expellees they would have been able to have finished their education and their lives would have then been very different. Both of them were strongly motivated by anger over the grant of planes to Israel by the United States. Both the Sirhans and the Khaleds locked up their houses in Palestine and took the keys with them in the hope of speedy return—a return which they still await. What is more important is the generalised Palestinian experience of which these are only two examples: here we have solid, decent, middle class folk whose world was shattered by an act of monumental injustice. Unless justice is done to them, and to hundreds of thousands like them, the Palestinians will produce more young people like Sirhan Sirhan and Leila Khaled, who are typical of their entire generation.

[Leila Khaled was later to attempt the abortive hijacking of an El-Al Israeli aircraft en route from Amsterdam to New York. Her partner was killed and she was arrested when the plane made an emergency landing at London's Heathrow Airport. She was later released, along with six other arrested Palestinian hijackers, in exchange for hostages taken from the successful three of the simultaneous four hijackings, and a BOAC plane commandeered a few days later.]

Epilogue

Are there any lessons to be drawn from the tragic intersection of the lives of Sirhan Bechara Sirhan, the poor young Palestinian, and of Robert Francis Kennedy, the rich and famous American?

If there were none, the event would be doubly tragic.

The Beirut newspaper, *Al Bayrak,* on June 6th, 1968, wrote: "The United States has begun to suffer, on its own soil, the effects of its foreign policy. The United States can no longer play with the destiny of the Palestinian homeland and in favour of the Jews without thus causing repercussions, wrong as they may be, at the hands of one of the people of this Palestinian homeland. The world has become very small, and the distance between Jerusalem and Los Angeles is now very short. The incident at Los Angeles calls for sorrow, because Robert Kennedy is perhaps the American politician least responsible for the Palestinian problem, and because the Arab people cannot accept the reasons given for his assassination. But the world has developed to such an extent that the United States or any other world power, can no longer set fire to any part of the world without also getting its fingers burned."

In other words, such is the deep commitment of oppressed people to their liberation that, their collective weakness or strength notwithstanding, they will attempt to strike back at those they see as their direct or indirect oppressors.

And it is a fact of contemporary conflict that all societies are fundamentally vulnerable to conflict, their conventional military superiority notwithstanding. Thus although the Vietcong are thousands of miles from America and cannot hope to invade her, yet there are serious repercussions to America for her seemingly "distant" engagement in the lives of the seemingly "unimportant" Vietnamese people. Her economy and her public morale are substantially adversely affected as a consequence.

Similarly, with the rash of airplane highjackings, the Palestinian guerillas have pointed out the fundamental vulnerability of conventional power.

What this illustrates is a new politics, demanding that once again all nations, no matter how powerful, confront, in their calculations of foreign intervention, the real possibility of repercussions from even the smallest group of oppressed peoples. This, it seems, should reintroduce ethics, fairness, and justice where expediency (military or economic), biased racial attitudes, and lopsided lobby pressures have dominated international politics. It is this warped attitude that allowed the creation of the Palestinian-Israeli conflict in the first place.

Furthermore, America can no longer continue to be insensitive to the feelings of peoples she is ignorant of. If the American press had had the slightest concern for the feelings of Palestinian Americans, it would not, in its almost gloating celebration of Israel successes in the six-day war, have treated the Arabs as if they were sub-human. If for no other reason, at least because there are other people in the world other than the white American, the Westerner, and the Jew. And these people do hurt. And when they hurt, they can be driven to the kind of rage, albeit irrational, that led Sirhan to assassinate Robert F. Kennedy.

Thus although it might have helped Democratic nominee for the U.S. Senate, Richard Ottinger, to gain fellow Jewish votes by referring to the Palestinian guerillas as "savage Arabs," as he did on ABC-TV on Saturday, August 12, 1970, there are enough Arab people to feel insulted. Actually, any person of decency would find such insensitive and primitive rhetoric offensive.

One cannot help but wonder how Ottinger, the directors of ABC-TV, and their New York viewers would have reacted if the expression were "savage Jews." No self respecting Jew would accept such an insult. With the impact of mass communications today, however, it is not sufficient to be sensitive to and respectful of only those we can use, or those we know, but we must show the same fundamental deference to all humanity, including those we still tend to call "them." And among those are the Palestinians.

Perhaps some thought should be given to the place of fairness, ethics, and good taste in American politics. Perhaps a vote is not exactly worth all it might take to get it. Perhaps the end does not always justify the means—and if this can be said of Sirhan's assault on his victim, Robert Francis Kennedy, it can also be said of the assault of the Zionist and pro-Zionist forces on the homeland and the psyche of their victim, Sirhan Bechara Sirhan.

Furthermore, the American public can no longer afford to continue in its bewildered blissful ignorance of what is going on in the rest of the world. More especially can it not afford to be deliberately kept in ignorance, or misinformed, as it is on the Middle East. If the average American makes no effort to know, then he is likely to be awakened from his euphoric daydreams by other such tragedies.

In 1948 Robert Kennedy wrote, "If the American people know the true facts I am certain a more honest and forthright policy would be substituted for the benefit of all." In 1968 Sirhan Sirhan said, "There is a spirit of fair play in the United States. Once they know the truth they would be on our side, not necessarily on our side, but on the side of justice. Were American people to understand the other side, the whole Middle East situation would be different."

Perhaps if the American media had been more sensitive, the American Middle East policy more equitable, and the American people less ignorant of the sensibilities of the rest of the world, Robert Francis Kennedy might yet have been alive today.

aid of highly complicated machinery. I have said to myself that that is wrong. My machinery must be of the elementary type which I can put into the homes of the millions." His slogan was "a miniature mill in every home."

"So," an interviewer summed up in November, 1934, "you are opposed to machinery only because and when it concentrates production and distribution in the hands of the few?"

"You are right," Gandhi replied. "I hate privilege and monopoly. Whatever cannot be shared with the masses is taboo to me. That is all."

It is interesting that today in India, where much of Gandhi's teaching is ignored, his economics, once considered retrograde or naïve, are being accepted by a growing body of Westernized, modern-minded Indians, by the Socialists,

Gandhi was not anti-West or anti-industry; his Indian eye simply saw the economic problems of India and Asia more clearly than the blind Europeanized votaries of machines for machines' sake.

Challenged to boredom as to whether he objected to machinery, Gandhi exclaimed, "How can I when I know that even this body is a most delicate piece of machinery? The spinning wheel is a machine; a little toothpick is a machine. What I object to is the craze for machinery, not machinery as such. Today," he continued, "machinery merely helps a few to ride on the backs of the millions. The machine should not tend to atrophy the limbs of man. For

---

people whose gratitude they craved but rarely received. The British were masters in somebody else's house. Their very presence was a humiliation. Imperialism is government of other people by other people for other people. It is a perpetual insult, for it assumes that the outsider has the right to rule the insiders who cannot rule themselves. Even if the British had converted India into a land flowing with milk and honey—they did make some deserts flow with humble water—they would have been disliked. Subjection breeds a desire for liberation. Hence imperialism digs its own grave—and there can be no good colonizers.

With the beginning of the twentieth century the number of educated Indians increased. An Indian middle class had arisen; numerous Indians, grown rich in industry and commerce, wanted economic elbow room. Native lovers of power were thwarted by alien rule. Japan's victory over Russia in 1904-5 (the first time a colored Asiatic country had defeated white Europeans) stimulated Indian nationalist opposition to England.

One school of British politicians wished to meet Indian

came a resolution to combat the dread disease of color prejudice. Intransigence and personal suffering highlighted the principle at stake and emphasized the need of fighting for it. Instead of staying a year in South Africa on a law assignment, he remained from 1893 to 1914, twenty-one years, during which he not only increased his moral and intellectual stature many cubits but became a successful leader and lawyer. In the end he won a great victory for freedom.

That chilly night in the Maritzburg station waiting room, the twenty-four-year-old Indian lawyer began to think of himself as a David assailing the Goliath of racial discrimination. Why Gandhi? What was it that started him up from Maritzburg to world greatness? Did he want to be morally strong because he was physically weak? Was he less fettered and more ambitious because his career so far had borne no fruit? Did he sense untouched talents within and realize that they would emerge only if harnessed to social service? Was it luck, destiny, inheritance, the *Bhagavad-Gita*, or some other immeasurable circumstance? Perhaps elements of these plus pride, moral indignation, and a feeling of inadequacy combined to make him reach out toward leadership. The British agent at Porbandar and the white policeman at Maritzburg were symbols of his and his people's weakness, and he resented it. Whenever Gandhi felt distressed or disturbed he wanted to do something about it. In the presence of evil he had to act. Mere headshaking and handwringing never satisfied him. Passivity riled him. There was not a single passive fiber in his character, and all his resistance was active.

Subsequent viceroys blessed it. But the blood-and-iron autocrats did not help the kid-glove moderates.

Torn between their political sagacity and their power lust, the British, through the years, yielded as much of the appearance of power as circumstances required and as little of its substance as conditions permitted. Inevitably, the more concessions they made the more they were asked to make and the die-hards therefore opposed any. To characterize this intransigent mentality, the Hunter Report of 1920, an official British document, quoted General Drake-Brockman of Delhi to the effect that, "Force is the only thing an Asiatic has any respect for." It was a widespread notion in the British administration. So was the concept of Field Marshal Lord Roberts: "It is this consciousness of the inherent superiority of the European which has won for us India. However well educated and clever a native may be and however brave he may have proved himself, I believe that no rank which we can bestow on him would cause him to be considered an equal by the British officer."

The Indians knew all this and hated it. Sir Edwin Montagu characterized British rule in India as "far too wooden, far too iron, far too inelastic, and far too antediluvian to subserve its purposes in modern times," a composite vegetable-mineral political dinosaur, in other words, incapable of change yet kept alive by feedings at the hands of die-hards in London and blockheads in Delhi. In due course, consequently, Montagu's implied promise of Dominion status, made at the low ebb of Britain's fortunes of war, turned into a yellowing parchment, and when peace came, a disappointed India ran riot.

Gandhi too was disappointed. His mind was a battlefield

APPENDIX

from *The Boston Post,* Thursday, June 3, 1948.

BRITISH HATED BY BOTH SIDES
by Robert Kennedy

Robert Kennedy, Special Writer for Post, Struck by Antipathy Shown by Arabs and Jews

This is the first of a series of stories on the Palestine situation written for the Post by Robert Kennedy, Harvard senior and son of the former ambassador to Great Britain. Young Kennedy has been traveling through the Middle East and his first-hand observations, appearing exclusively in the Post, will be of considerable interest in view of the current crisis.

Certainly, if Arthur Balfour, Britain's foreign minister during the first World War, had realized the conflicting interpretations which were to be placed on his famous "declaration" calling for a homeland for the Jews, he probably would have drawn it with its meaning clearer and saved the world the bloodshed that its double promises have caused. In his attempt to conciliate both Jews and Arabs in a time of distress for the British empire, he conciliated neither.

No great thought was given it at the time, for Palestine was then a relatively unimportant country. There were then not the great numbers of homeless Jews that we have now and no one believed then that the permission granted for Jewish immigration would lead 30 years later to world turmoil on whether a national home should mean an autonomous national state.

First let us consider the view-point of the Arabs in regard to the national homeland promised to the Jews in the Balfour Declaration.

The Arabs by word and deed leave no question in anyone's mind how they feel. They argue that the Balfour Declaration supports their point that no national state was promised, pointing to the clause in the declaration that says the national home shall be set up subject to the civil rights of the people living in Palestine at this time. In recent years they have pointed to the United Nations charter and the article dealing with the self determination of nations. Let us adhere to that, the Arabs say, and let the people, that is the Arabs who are involved, decide the question by the democratic process. If this policy of partition was truly adhered to, they say, then why couldn't there be a partition within "the" partition set aside for the Arab minorities?

Toehold

Jemal Heusenni, the Arab leader, suggested to me, during my recent visit to Palestine, that we Americans, who had been so solicitous of the rights of the Jewish people, take the Jews into the United States and set up a national state for them in California. The Arab world, he claimed, had certainly taken in more than their share of the Jewish race and it has been this policy that has led to today's troubles. If the United States feels so philanthropic about this minority question, he asked, why not be really good fellows about the whole problem and give the colored people the State of Georgia.

If the people of the world, Jemal Heussenni added, are selecting Palestine because of the lengthy sojourn there by the Jewish people, then the Arabs say give us back Spain where we were for 800 years.

The Arabs are most concerned about the great increase in the Jews in Palestine: 80,000 in 1918 to 800,000 in 1948. The Arabs have always feared this encroachment and maintain that the Jews will never be satisfied with just their section of Palestine, but will gradually move to overpower the rest of the country and will eventually move into the enormously wealthy oil lands. They are determined that the Jews will never get the toehold that would be necessary for the fulfillment of that policy.

Always Will Attack

They are willing to let the Jews remain as peaceful citizens subject to the rule of the Arab majority just as the Arabs are doing in such great numbers in Egypt and the Levant states, but they are determined that a separate Jewish state will be attacked and attacked until it is finally cut out like an unhealthy abscess.

The Arabs believe that they contributed greatly to making the Allied victory possible in the First World War. At the Paris peace conference they felt that they received nothing comparable to what they were promised for their fight under Lawrence against the Turks. Rather, due to power politics, British and French domination replaced that of the Ottoman empire. The Arab leaders attribute their country's backwardness to these 400 uninterrupted years as subservients to the Ottoman empire.

The Jewish people on the other hand believe that if it were not for the wars and invasions that racked Palestine and which sent them scattered and persecuted throughout the world, Palestine would today be theirs. It would be theirs just as when Moses led them from Egypt into the Palestinian plains which they point out were unoccupied except for a few Bedouin tribes.

Set Up Laboratories

They wish no other country, and in 1870, when Uganda was offered to them as a homeland, they were unanimous in their refusal. The Balfour Declaration, when it was made, however, they felt was the answer to their prayers.

Under the supposition that, at the finish of the mandate, this was to be their national state, they went to work. They set up laboratories where world-famous scientists could study and analyze soils and crops. The combination of arduous labor and almost unlimited funds from the United States changed what was once arid desert into flourishing orange groves. Soils had to be washed of salt, day after day, year after year, before crops could even be planted. One can see this work going on in lesser or more advanced stages wherever there are Jewish settlements in Palestine. From a small village of a few thousand inhabitants, Tel Aviv has grown into a most impressive modern metropolis of over 200,000. They have truly done much with what all agree was very little.

The Jews point with pride to the fact that over 500,000 Arabs in the 12 years between 1932-1944, came into Palestine to take advantage of living conditions existing in no other Arab state. This is the only country in the Near and Middle East where an Arab middle class is in existence.

The Jews point out that they have always taken a passive part in the frequent revolutions that have racked the country, because of the understanding that they would be eventually be set free from British mandateship! They wished to do nothing to impair this expected action. During the Second World War they sent numerous volunteer Jewish brigades which fought commendably with the British in Italy. In addition to that many Palestinian Jews fought as volunteers with Allied troops throughout the world and still others were dropped by parachute into German-held territory as espionage agents. They were perhaps doing no more than their duty, but they did their duty well.

The Jews feel that promise after promise to them has been broken. They can quote freely, for example, from speech after speech of labor party leaders in the election campaign prior to the victory of the Labor

Party in England, to attest to the fact that one need not even refer back to the controversial Balfour Declaration to learn Britain's attitude and promises toward a Jewish state. The machinery for the setting up of an autonomous Jewish state was to be one of the first acts of the Labor government if it were put into power. The Jews, remembering this, have rather bitterly named the block bombed out in the Ben Yehudia disaster, Bevin Sq.

It is an unfortunate fact that because there are such well-founded arguments on either side, each grows more bitter toward the other. Confidence in their right increases in direct proportion to the hatred and mistrust for the other side for not acknowledging it.

Never Searched

When I landed at Lydda Airport I became immediately aware of it. I carried letters of introduction to both Arabs and Jews and at the airport where both sides intermingle, it was explained to me by first one and then the other that I was taking a great risk. The Jew said it was all right for me to carry Arab papers in Jewish territory for I wouldn't be molested, but when I entered Arab territory I had better be rid of all letters to Jews for I would immediately be searched and, if they found anything, would be quickly shot. The Arab said exactly the opposite and I found both to be half right, in that I was never searched by either side.

Another fact I became immediately aware of was a basic violent hatred of the British by both sides. I talked to a British army sergeant who had been in Palestine for two years, and he placed the blame with the Palestine Colonial Police. Later I found many to be in agreement. He called them the "underpaid uneducated dregs of society." They were evidently the most corrupt group of police in the world, firstly because they were so underpaid and, secondly, because when colonial police were sent to their posts the worst of the lot were invariably sent to Palestine.

The Arab bitterness and also fear toward the British had as its starting point the 1936-1938 revolution, which was crushed most ruthlessly by the British.

Increasing Bitterness

Leading Arabs in the higher commission speak in all sincerity of the Indian brought by the British into the country because of the great skill and knowledge that he possessed in being able to torture with fire while leaving no scar tissue. Many claim to have suffered by having their nails pulled out from their fingers and toes and others of having burning matches thrust beneath their nails. I found little evidence that these stories were true.

The Jewish attitude toward the British has been one of increasing bitterness. The Jews have looked upon the British civil administration, which some years ago took over from the army, as most unfriendly and uncooperative and which has therefore led to much mutual mistrust. Jews received virtually no financial help for building of schools and hospitals in Jewish settlements and the post-office which was set up to serve Tel Aviv wasn't suitable for a village of several thousand inhabitants. I was forced to wait well over an hour in line in order to purchase stamps.

When told if they wanted a port they would have to build it themselves, the result was the port of Tel Aviv, which was constructed entirely through Jewish capital and labor. Nevertheless, it is taxed as high as the Arab port of Jaffa, which was built and maintained by funds raised by taxing both Arabs and Jews. These arguments are infinitesimal compared with the larger issues that have swept both sides during the last year, but they are mentioned to show that the hate that exists now is not something newly born and has a substantial background.

from *The Boston Post,* Friday, June 4, 1948

JEWS HAVE FINE FIGHTING FORCE:

by Robert Kennedy

Make Up for Lack of Arms With Undying Spirit, Unparalleled Courage—Impress World

This is the second of a series of four articles on the Palestine situation written for the Post by Robert Kennedy, Harvard senior and son of the former ambassador to Great Britain. Young Kennedy has been traveling through the Middle East and his first-hand observations, appearing exclusively in the Post, will be of considerable interest in view of the current crisis.

The Jewish people in Palestine who believe in and have been working toward this national state have become an immensely proud and determined people. It is already a truly great modern example of the birth of a nation with the primary ingredients of dignity and self-respect.

Maica and her family to me are the personification of that determination. She is a young girl of the age of 23 and her husband and four brothers are members of the Haganah. She herself is with the intelligence corps and worked on the average of 15 hours a day, which evidently was not unusual. She had seen and felt much horror and told me the story of a case she had just handled.

A Jewish girl in her teens was picked up by some members of the Haganah on the road from Tel Aviv to Jerusalem and, as she was injured, she was taken to the Hebrew Hospital in Jerusalem. They believed that she had somehow been separated from a Jewish convoy which had just gone through and which had had a scrap with the Arabs.

She was particularly noticed because of the strange people who were her visitors and by the fact that she insisted on being moved to an English hospital. Maica was sent to question her. She was turned away gruffly by the girl after the girl admitted that she had in reality been in a British tank with a boy friend and wanted nothing to do with the Jews. The Jewish Agency offered to send the girl out on a farm in order to let her regain her health and give her a new start, but she just demanded her release which they were forced to give her. She continued consorting with the British police despite warnings from the Stern gang.

Brother Shoots Sister

One night the Stern gang followed the tactics of the underground in the last war. They shaved all the hair off the girl's head. Two days after Maica told me this story the sequel took place. The girl's brother returned for leave from duty with the Haganah up in Galilee, and, finding her in such a state, shot her.

Maica's youngest brother is only 13, but every night he takes up his post as a sentry with the Haganah at a small place outside of Jerusalem. His mother and father wait up every night until midnight for him and his older brother, 15, to return home. The other two brothers, both younger than Maica, gave full time duty with combat troops.

An understanding of the institutions it contains, and of the persons that run these institutions, is most important if one would make up one's mind as to the worth of this "de facto" Jewish state.

I visited and inspected a community farm through the kindness of a Jew who 40 years ago was in Boston making speeches for my grandfather, John F. Fitzgerald, when he was a candidate for Congress. A third of the agricultural population live in such community farms which were originally set up to help newly arrived refugees who had no money or prospects. They are in reality self-sustaining States within a State and all the people in common undergo arduous toil and labour and make great sacrifices in order that their children might become heir to a home. An example of this is that when a child is 1 year old he is placed in a common nursery, with the result that all but the sick and infirm are able to devote their talents to the common cause. They get paid nothing for they need no money. Everything is financed by a group of elected overseers who get their money by selling what the farms produce. In our country we shrink from such tactics but in that country their very lives depend upon them.

The whole thing is done on a volunteer basis and one may leave the farm with his proportionate share of the wealth at any time he chooses.

The one we visited was at Givat Brenner and, although no one paid attention to the firing going on in the plain below, one could see all around preparations being undertaken for the coming fight.

I talked to members of the underground organization Irgun. They were responsible for the King David Hotel disaster and told me proudly that they were responsible for blowing up the Cairo-Haifa train which had just taken place with the loss of 50 British soldiers.

Disillusioned

They believed that the time had long since passed for the Jewish people to expect anything but treachery and broken promises from the outside world. If they wanted an independent state they would have to fight for it, and before they could even do that, they had to rid the country of foreign troops. They believe unquestionably that if it weren't for their so-called terrorist activities the British would have remained on in their country. Bevin's recent speeches in the House of Commons, they argue, have been ample proof of that. The question, though, in other Jews (sic.) minds is whether this compensated for what they have lost in good will by such tactics.

I went to the training camp at Nathanyam north of Tel Aviv, where for three weeks and with very little equipment Jewish youths, trained mostly by former British officers, were attempting to learn the basic tenets of army life. We watched a first-week group attempt an obstacle course, and for many the flesh was weak, but it emphasized all the more what can be accomplished when the spirit is willing. We watched a graduation class make its final round and they gave the appearance that they might well be whipped into a fighting force before much time had passed.

The security forces and Haganah are far more experienced. After landing at Lydda Airport, I was immediately taken to be questioned and my credentials examined by the Haganah. After being released and going to my hotel in Tel Aviv, I went for a walk around this city of 200,000 inhabitants. I wasn't out for ten minutes before I was recognized as a foreigner and picked up by the Haganah, blindfolded and once again brought to headquarters for questioning.

All Volunteers

Recognized immediately, I was released again with profuse apologies "that one can't be too careful." They are careful and have the means at their disposal to act. It is a volunteer force supported completely by the people by contributions and taxes that they levy on themselves. All the members are volunteers, but social ostracism results for those who are able to and have not donated their services. I was in a night club and "MPS" found a young man without his Jewish agency "draft card" which he claimed to have left at home. The proprietor refused to have music played or food and drinks served until the young Jew left the premises.

Besides these indications of spirit and determination, there is another equally important consideration—the remembrance of the brutal inhuman treatment received by the Jews in the countries of Europe.

A group of Jews were being herded out of Hungary across the Danube into Austria when one turned to the soldiers guarding them and said, "What shall we do? Where shall we go? The Germans don't want us." The guard pointed to the river.

I talked to a Haganah soldier who fled from Prague as the Germans were taking over the city and he and his brother, who was killed, fought with the British throughout the war. He received news that his mother and two sisters whom he had left in Prague were killed by the Germans and that his home had been completely destroyed.

Conditions in Russia

I talked to a former major in the Russian army who had spent five years with a tank corps. Although the official Russian government policy is one of hands off and toleration, he believed the individuals who formulate the policy and the Russian people as a whole are more anti-Semitic than the Germans. When he returned to his village after the war, things became so intolerable that he was finally forced to leave and had made his way to Palestine, where he had been for less than a month.

He told of standing in line for an hour in his Russian village to procure some rationed goods. When he finally got to the head of the line he was told that the store had just run out of that commodity. It began to happen with increasing regularity. He and his fellow Jews were completely ostracized from any of the political or social affairs of the community.

The Jews who have been lucky enough to get to Palestine are hardy and tough. They are limited to two alternatives, for there is no country or group of countries that would ever consider taking 800,000 Jews. They can go into the Mediterranean Sea and get drowned or they can stay and fight and perhaps get killed. They will fight and they will fight with unparalleled courage. This is their greatest and last chance. The eyes of the world are upon them and there can be no turning back.

Their shortages in arms and numbers are more than compensated by an undying spirit that the Arabs, Iraqui (sic.), Syrians, Lebanese, Saudi Arabians, Egyptians and those from Trans-Jordan can never have. They are a young, tough, determined nation and will fight as such.

(To be continued tomorrow)

from *The Boston Post,* June 5, 1948 (Saturday)

BRITISH POSITION HIT IN PALESTINE

by Robert Kennedy

Kennedy Says They Seek to Crush Jewish Cause Because They Are Not in Accord With It

This is the third of a series of four articles on Palestine situation writtenfor the Post by Robert Kennedy, Harvard senior and son of the former ambassador to Great Britain. Young Kennedy has been traveling through the Middle East and his first-hand observations, appearing exclusively in the Post, will be of considerable interest in view of the current crisis.

I was in Palestine over Easter week and even then people knew there was absolutely no chance to preserve peace. They just wanted the British out, so that a decision could be reached either way. An early departure of the British has been far more important strategically to the Jews than to the Arabs.

The city of Jerusalem has more Jews than Arabs but the immediate surrounding territory is predominantly Arab. Through part of that hilly territory winds the narrow road that leads from Tel Aviv to Jerusalem. It is by this road that the Jewish population within Jerusalem must be supplied, but it is fantastically easy for the Arabs to ambush a convoy as it crawls along the difficult pass. On my trip from Tel Aviv to Jerusalem I saw grim realities of that fact and while in Jerusalem the failure and destruction of another Jewish convoy made meat non-existent and lengthened food queues for other items.

The Arabs living in the old city of Jerusalem have kept the age old habit of procuring their water from the individual cisterns that exist in almost every home. The Jews being more "educated" (an Arab told me that this was their trouble and knew the Jews were going to really pay for it) had a central water system installed with pipes bringing fresh hot and cold water. Unfortunately for them the resevoir is situated in the mountains and it and the whole pipe line are controlled by the Arabs. The British would not let them cut the water off until after May 15th but an Arab told me they would not even do it then. First they would poison it.

Orthodox Community

Within the old city of Jerusalem there exists a small community of orthodox Jews. They wanted no part of this fight but just wanted to be left alone with their wailing wall. Unfortunately for them the Arabs are unkindly disposed toward any kind of Jew and their annihilation would now undoubtedly have been a fact had it not been at the beginning of hostilities the Haganah moved several hundred well-equipped men into their quarter.

This inability to make any long range military manoeuvres because of the presence of the British has been a great and almost disasterous handicap to the Jews. If the brief but victorious military engagement on the Tel Aviv-Jerusalem road had not taken place, the Jewish cause would have suffered such a setback as to be virtually lost. If the Haganah had waited for May 15th and the withdrawal of British troops, there would be few alive in Jerusalem today. Strong units of that body had moved into the hills on either side of that strategic road and repelled Arab counterattacks long enough for several hundred truck-loads to make the 40-mile trip into the city, and then, only after threats from the British commander to use force against them, had withdrawn from their positions. As a Jew said to me at the time, "This is our battle of the Atlantic." The manoeuvres had to take place and took place despite the British.

Power Supply

The same basic difficulty that exists in relationship to the water exists with regard to electric and power supply. Fortunately, an immediate danger is not yet present, but the Arabs have had months of preparation for a manoeuvre they know their opponents must eventually make.

The Jewish ghetto in the old city of Jerusalem would not have been in such an untenable position if it could have been periodically relieved, or if, with a Jewish victory in that area, it could have been connected with the main Jewish section in the new city.

The Jews have small settlements or community farms such as Givat Brenner in completely hostile territory. They take pride in that, despite the greatest difficulties, they have not evacuated any of them. From the very tip of Galilee right down to the arid Negev these communities exist with such Jewish names a (sic.) Zan, Safad, Yehsem, Mishmar Haemak, Ben Sheba, Laza. All have their supply problems. But no great military operation can be undertaken into Arab territory to relieve the increasing Arab pressure.

Need True Facts

In addition to these handicaps that the Jews suffered through the presence of the British, there are many more far-reaching aspects of British administration which unfortunately concern or, rather, involve us in the United States.

Having been out of the United States for more than two months at this time of writing, I notice myself becoming more and more conscious of the great heritage and birthright to which we as United States citizens are heirs and which we have the duty to preserve. A force motivating my writing this paper is that I believe we have failed in this duty or are in great jeopardy of doing so. This failure is due chiefly to our inability to get the true facts of the policy in which we are partners in Palestine. The British government, in its attitude towards the Jewish population in Palestine, has given ample credence to the suspicion that they are firmly against the establishment of a Jewish state in Palestine.

When I was in Cairo shortly after the blowing up of the Jewish Agency I talked to a man who held a high position in the Arab League. He had just returned from Palestine where he had, among other things, interviewed and arranged transportation to Trans-Jordan for the Arab responsible for that Jewish disaster. This Arab told me that after the explosion, upon reaching the British post which separated the Jewish section from a small neutral zone set up in the middle of Jerusalem, he was questioned by the British officers in charge. He quite freely admitted what he had done and was given immediate passage with the remark, "Nice going."

British Markings

When I was in Tel-Aviv, every night there were mortar duels between that city and Jaffa. One day I went to inspect the damage and found, amongst the ruins, the fin of a mortal shell with complete British markings. I was told by the commissioner of the Haganah defending Tel Aviv that this was very common and that the day before a British captain went so far as to come over and inspect his marksmanship.

Just before I arrived in Palestine there was the notorious story of the foundry outside of Tel Aviv. It was situated in a highly contested area and the British accused the Jews of using it as a sniper post for the Jaffa-Jerusalem road. One day the British moved in, stripping the Jews of all arms and ordered them to clear out within 10 minutes. The British had scarcely departed when a group of armed Arabs moved in, killing or wounding all the occupants. The British government was most abject in its apologies.

There is, of course, no way to tell whether these stories are true, but the fact remains that they have been widely distributed and are widely believed.

I came in contact personally, however, with evidence that demonstrated clearly the British bitterness toward the Jews. I have ridden in Jewish armoured car convoys which the British have stopped to inspect for arms. As always, there were members of the Haganah aboard and they quickly broke down their small arms, passing the pieces among the occupants to conceal them so as to prevent confiscation. Satisfied that none existed, the convoy supposedly unarmed was allowed to pass into Arab territory. If the arms had been found and confiscated and Arabs had attacked, there would have been a remote chance of survival for any of the occupants. There have been many not as fortunate as we.

British Informants

When I was in Tel Aviv the Jews informed the British government that 600 Iraqui troops were going to cross into Palestine from Trans-Jordan by the Allenby Bridge on a certain date and requested the British to take appropriate action to prevent this passage. The troops crossed unmolested. It is impossible for the British to patrol the whole Palestinian border to prevent illegal crossings but such flagrant violations should certainly have led to some sort of action.

Mr. Marshall's informants must have been British, for an items (sic.) appeared in the Herald-Tribune of April 23 quoting Mr. Marshall as saying that, according to all information available to him, "no invasion by the British-trained army of King Abdullah was planned and that a spokesman for the Arab League had assured the United States that Arab forces were not invading Palestine."

Five weeks ago I saw several thousand non-Palestinian Arab troops in Palestine, including many of the famed British-trained and equipped Arab legionnaires of King Abdullah. There were also soldiers from Syria, Lebanon, Iraq, Trans-Jordan, and there (sic.) were all proudly pointed out to me by a spokesman of the Arab higher committee. He warned me against walking too extensively through Arab districts as most of the inhabitants there were now foreign troops. Every Arab to whom I talked spoke of thousands of soldiers massed in the "terrible triangle of Nabulus Tukarim Janin" and of hundreds that were pouring in daily.

Oversubscribed

When I was in Lebanon and asked a dean at the American University at Beyruth if many students were leaving for the fight in Palestine, he shrugged and said, "Not now—the quota has been oversubscribed." When journeying by car from Jerusalem to Amman I passed many truckloads of armed Arabs and even then Jericho was alive with Arab troops. There is no question that it was taken over by the Arabs for an armed camp long before May 15.

Our government first decided that justice was on the Jewish side in their desire for a homeland, and then it reversed its decision temporarily. Because of this action I believe that we have burdened ourselves with a great responsibility in our own eyes and in the eyes of the world. We fail to live up to that responsibility if we knowingly support the British government who behind the skirts of their official position attempt to crush a cause with which they are not in accord. If the American people know the true facts, I am certain a more honest and forthright policy would be substituted for the benefit of all.

(To Be Concluded Tomorrow)

from *The Boston Sunday Post,* June 6, 1948

COMMUNISM NOT TO GET FOOTHOLD
by Robert Kennedy

Jews Guard Against Red Agents in Guise of Refugees—Want No Part of Russian Tyrant

This is the fourth and last of a series of articles on the Palestine situation written for the Post by Robert Kennedy, Harvard senior and son of the former ambassador to Great Britain. Young Kennedy has been traveling through the Middle East and his first-hand observations, appearing exclusively in the Post, will be of considerable interest in view of the present crisis.

The die has long since been cast; the fight will take place. The Jews with their backs to the sea, fighting for their very homes, with 101 per cent morale, will accept no compromise. On the other hand, the Arabs say:

Religious Crusade

"We shall bring Moslem brigades from Pakistan, we shall lead a religious crusade for all loyal followers of Mohammed, we shall crush forever the invader. Whether it takes three months, three years, or 30, we will carry on the fight. Palestine will be Arab. We shall accept no compromise."

The United Nations is scoffed at by both sides and the United States will never be able to regain the position of ascendency she previously enjoyed with the Arab world. She lost the love of the Arabs when she supported partition. She lost their respect when she reversed that decision. She lost it irreparably. For days on end Arab commentators drummed into their people that finally the power of the Arab world had been realized. No longer would it take second place to the United States and Britain.

The so-called great powers had learned that the Arabs were not a people who could be pushed around and from now on the Arabs were the ones who were going to dictate the terms.

The Jews are bitter in disappointment. As one Jew said, "Britain let us down for 25 years but you bettered them in a week." The feeling stops at disappointment and there is none of the hatred that exists for the British. They can understand us not wishing to send troops and so become entangled in a war that does not immediately concern us, but they plead only for the right to make this fight themselves. They want arms and frankly admit if they cannot get them from us they will turn to the East. "What else can we do?" They are fighting for their very lives and must act accordingly.

Won't Accept Communism

That the people might accept communism or that communism could exist in Palestine is fantastically absurd. Communism thrives on static discontent as sin thrives on idleness. With the type of issues and people involved, that state of affairs is non-existent. I am as certain of that as of my name.

There is no question that Russia is sending agents into Palestine in the guise of refugees. But she is sending them into every country in the world, and that just happens to be the manner which she has judged best for Palestine.

When I was in Tel Aviv, a group of refugees was landed and amongst them the Jewish Agency's "FBI" immediately picked up one of these agents. He was loaded down with money and papers and all agreed that he must have been sent with the intention that he be captured to mislead the security forces into thinking that all the Russian agents would be as inept as this one and equally easy to capture. Lethargy would set in and it would be then that they would smuggle in their Mata Hari.

Demands Allegiance

Communism demands alleginace to the mother country, Russia, and it is impossible to believe that people would undergo such untold sufferings to replace one tyrant by another. Robert Emmet, the Irish patriot, on trial for his life before a British tribunal, stated the principle. When accused of attempting to bring French forces into Ireland to help wrest it from the British, he said why he, who loved and had been fighting for his homeland, deem it to his country's interests to replace a known tyrant by an unknown one. These people want a homeland of their own. That to them is the sole issue.

Vehemence and hatred between the Jews and Arabs increases daily. But in many cases Jews and Arabs work side by side in the fields and orange groves outside of Tel Aviv. Perhaps these Jews and Arabs are making a greater contribution to the future peace in Palestine than are those who carry guns on both sides.

The Arabs in command believe that eventually victory must be theirs. It is against all law and nature that this Jewish state should exist. They trace expectantly its long boundary and promise that if it does become a reality it will never have as neighbours anything but hostile countries, which will continue the fight militarily and economically until victory is achieved.

Stabilizing Factor

The Jews on the other hand believe that in a few more years, if a Jewish state is formed, it will be the only stabilizing factor remaining in the near and middle east. The Arab world is made up of many disgruntled factions which would have been at each other's throats long ago if it had not been for the common war against Zionism. The United States and Great Britain before too long a time might well be looking to a Jewish state to preserve a toehold in that part of the world.

Both sides still hate the British far more deeply than they hate one another. There was a British high commissioner who, when attending the opera, used to have his car parked directly in front of the main door, a place usually reserved for discharging passengers. An even more unpopular practice was the regulation that at the end of the opera everyone had to remain in their seats until the British high commissioner was out of the opera house and in his car.

But the British have left—and now the issue is to be resolved in a bitter war between Jews and Arabs. I do not think the freedom-loving nations of the world can stand by and see "the sweet water of the River Jordan stained red with the blood of Jews and Arabs." The United States through the United Nations must take the lead in bringing about peace in the Holy Land.

The End

COMMENTARY

The articles by Robert Kennedy on the situation in Palestine in 1948 are an anthology of the standard propaganda myths about Zionism and the Jewish State.

The most oft repeated myth in the Kennedy articles is the charge that the British hindered the establishment of Israel, thus refusing to make good on a promise that Palestine should be a Jewish state. Kennedy said, inter alia, that Britain prevented Jewish immigration to Palestine and that British troops obstructed Jewish paramilitary activities during the battle for Palestine. The truth of the matter is that Britain promised the Jews a National Home in Palestine in the 1917 Balfour Declaration, not that Palestine should be the Jewish State. Under the British Mandate the Jewish population increased from 60,000 in 1918 (not 80,000 as Kennedy believed) to some 600,000 in 1947–48, more than 80 per cent due to immigration. Moreover, between 1936 and 1939 the British suppressed an armed Palestinian popular rebellion in order that the gates of Palestine would be kept open to Jewish immigration. In April and May 1948, British forces withdrew from Palestine in stages, allowing Jewish forces to assume control as the British troops left—thus the Palestinian Arab towns of Haifa, Jaffa, Acre, Tiberias and hundreds of Palestinian villages fell to the Zionists before the proclamation of the State of Israel.

Kennedy asserts that at the beginning of the Mandate when the Zionists really began their work, they found an empty desert and that after the Zionists had made this desert bloom 500,000 Arabs immigrated to Palestine. That Palestine was a desert was a fantastic assertion. Sir Moses Montefiore, an early and distinguished Zionist, was among the 19th century travellers to Palestine who remarked on the fruitfulness of the country, saying that it was still "the land of milk and honey." Furthermore, the famous "Jaffa orange grown by Palestinian Arab farmers appeared in European markets in the 19th century, long before the Zionists took to citrus cultivation. Most of the groves now producing the "Israeli Jaffa oranges" were planted by Palestinian farmers, now refugees. In the Zionist literature sent to prospective immigrants, Palestine was indeed presented as "the land of milk and honey" and the "Jaffa orange."

Kennedy's immigration figures are no less fantastic. According to British official figures the total immigration to Palestine of "Arabs" and "Others" between 1920 and 1945 was 33,304, while legal Jewish immigration during that period was 367,845.

Robert Kennedy was obviously unaware of what was happening in Palestine while he was there. On April 1 the Jewish military offensive against Palestinain Arab towns and villages began. It was hardly a case of the Jews having their "backs to the sea," rather of the Palestinian Arabs being driven into the desert (about 300,000 at that time), or into the sea as was the fate of the Palestinians of Acre on May 14. Thus during the 50-year struggle for Palestine the hard fact is that only Palestinians, not Jews, have been "driven into the sea"—the exact opposite of the Zionist charge that the Arabs wish to "drive the Jews into the sea."

Young Kennedy was also mistaken in believing that one-third of the Jews in Palestine lived on Kibbutzim, as the figure is closer to 5 per cent. He said that Iraqi troops were entering Palestine in April, 1948, which they most definitely were not—they came in late May. And, he linked the fate of Jewish refugees in Europe to the political and territorial future of Palestine, a common argumentation by liberals who are reluctant to accept Jewish refugees in their own countries.

This Commentary on Robert Kennedy's Palestine dispatches is by Michael E. Jansen. The reasons why Kennedy and other Americans accept and repeat such inaccuracies are analysed in her "The United States and the Palestinian People," the Institute for Palestine Studies, Beirut.